BEYOND WEALTH

The Road Map to a Rich Life

ALEXANDER GREEN

John Wiley & Sons, Inc.

Published by John Wiley & Sons, Inc., Hoboken, New Jersey.
Published simultaneously in Canada.

For general information on our other products and services or for technical support, please contact our Customer Care Department within the United States at (800) 762-2974, outside the United States at (317) 572-3993 or fax (317) 572-4002.

Wiley also publishes its books in a variety of electronic formats. Some content that appears in print may not be available in electronic books. For more information about Wiley products, visit our web site at www.wiley.com.

Library of Congress Cataloging-in-Publication Data:

Green, Alexander, 1958-
    Beyond wealth : the road map to a rich life / Alexander Green.
      p. cm.
    Includes bibliographical references and index.
      ISBN 978-1-118-02761-5 (hardback); 978-1-118-07832-7 (ebk);
    978-1-118-07833-4 (ebk); 978-1-118-07834-1 (ebk)
      1. Success in business.   2. Success.   3. Wealth—Psychological aspects.   4. Conduct of life.   5. Self-actualization (Psychology)   I. Title.
    HF5386.G73 2011
    650.1—dc22

                                                                2011002025

Printed in the United States of America
V10003112_080918

To Karen

When the Buddha began to wander around India shortly after his enlightenment, he encountered several men who recognized him as an extraordinary being.

They asked him, "Are you a god?"

"No," he said.

"Are you a saint?"

"No."

"Are you a prophet?"

"No," he said again.

Perplexed, they asked, "well, what are you then?"

The Buddha replied, "I am awake."

—The Pali Canon (29 BCE)

To be awake is to be alive. I have never yet met a man who was quite awake. How could I have looked him in the face?

—Henry David Thoreau, *Walden* (1854)

CONTENTS

Foreword   ix
Introduction   xiii

PART ONE: DOLLARS AND SENSE   1

Are the Rich Smarter than You?   5

Are You Losing Your Soul?   10

Impatient Optimism . . . and Radical Generosity   14

You Can't Google This   18

The Only Thing that Really Matters   22

The Principle Thing   25

The One Thing that Changes Everything   28

The Trouble with Happiness   31

The Key to Personal Freedom   35

Change Your Perspective, Change Your Life   38

How Your World Will At Last Be Built   42

The Most Important Job on Earth   46

One of Life's Great Miracles   51

The Power of Negative Visualization   55

How to Reclaim Your Life   58

Why It's One of the Seven Deadly Sins   62

The Ruling Passion of the Noblest Minds   65

PART TWO: WEALTH BEYOND MEASURE   69

Are You Uncurious?   71

The Road Not Taken   74

They Make Us All Richer   77

Are You Ready for the Grand Tour?   81

The Quintessence of Life   85

What Women Really Want   89

An Incandescent Drop of American Fire   92

The Most Civilized Thing in the World   95

How to Eat Like a Zen Master   99

The Sublimest Activity of the Human Mind   103

Drunken Monkey Ice Cream . . . and the Wisdom of
    Thornton Wilder   107

The Lost Art of Conversation   110

What Success Really Means   113

What Are Your Sins of Omission?   116

The Beauty of Slowing Down   120

When Entertainment Becomes Art   123

Do You Have a Secret?   128

Are You Amusing Yourself to Death?   133

In Praise of Idleness   137

The Tyranny of the New   140

Why You Should Know "The Indispensable Man"   143

A Revelation at 4,500 Feet   146

PART THREE: KNOWING AND BELIEVING   149

Tolstoy's Forbidden Book   151

A Shameless Veneration of Heroes   154

A Path to Personal Freedom   158

Your Greatest Risk   162

Are You Part of "The Great Conversation"?   166

A 2,600-Year-Old Manual for Living   170

If You Knew What Jim Brown Knows   176

The Noblest Expression of the Human Spirit   179

The Art of Living Consciously   183

How to Let Your Life Speak   188

A Legacy of Inspiration   192

The Only Thing New in the World   195

The University on Your Shelf   198

We Are All Greeks Now   202

The Wisdom of Hillel   205

Meditations of the Philosopher-King   208

PART FOUR: MATTERS OF LIFE AND DEATH   211

Discovering a New Sense of the Sacred   214

The Highest of Arts   218

Emerson: The Quintessential American   221

The Life You Can Save   224

Coming of Age in the Milky Way   229

The Literature of Truth   234

Your Connection to Everything   238

The Difference between Knowing and Believing   241

The Lessons of Haiti   244

Your Trip to "The Undiscovered Country"   247

The Beginning of Wisdom   252

Of Lost Souls and Lucky Stiffs   255

How to Pull the Universe Out of a Hat   258

It Makes Everything Meaningful   262

The Truth about Myths   265

Your Place In "The Great Story"   269

Seven Principles of Spirituality   277

Afterword   285
Appendix   287
Further Reading   289
Acknowledgments   295
About the Author   297
Index   299

FOREWORD

As the head of a $45 million financial publishing company, I lead a very "bottom-line" kind of life. I spend a good deal of time thinking about how our team can generate more products, more revenue, more profits, and more satisfied customers.

Yet, like many of us who are employed full time, I strive for balance between work and play, responsibility and enjoyment. Too often, for instance, I've forfeited a beautiful Saturday morning outside for work projects that could have been delegated or postponed. That may give you a clue why I consider the book in your hands essential reading.

Since you've picked it up, it's safe to assume you already know there's more to a genuine sense of wealth than just working, saving, and investing. For one thing, we have to define what "being rich" actually means to us. Then, no matter how much financial success we enjoy, we have to learn how to spend not just our money but also our two most precious commodities: our time and attention.

During my 20-plus years as publisher for The Oxford Club, I've had the good fortune to work closely with some of the most astute investing "gurus" in the business. Certainly, the author of this book is one of the best. Alexander Green is a "wealth master," a trusted guide for hundreds of thousands of regular readers.

More than 10 years ago, in his desire to help others reach financial independence, Alex left a major investment bank to join the Oxford Club as our Investment Director. Soon after, the Club's Communiqué track record was named one of the best in the nation, and still is by the leading industry-tracking group.

Thanks to Alex and his clearly defined investment principles and recommendations, I've made better personal financial decisions than ever before. And, as he leads the world's largest private investment club, countless others have benefited from his work, too. Perhaps the most rewarding part of my job as his publisher is to read the testimonials that hit my inbox each day. This comment about The Oxford Club was recently posted on the respected financial web site *MarketWatch*:

> The key player is undoubtedly Editor Alexander Green, who has developed a dramatically successful track record, expressed through several portfolios, since arriving in 2001.
>
> —Peter Brimelow, author of *The Wall Street Gurus* and an editor of the independent *Hulbert Financial Digest*

About three years ago, however, Alex proposed a new kind of advisory for our members, one that discusses wealth not in material but spiritual terms. At first, I thought it might be too risky. So did my colleagues. The subject matter would be deeper and more controversial than our normal financial communications. It might offend our most conservative membership. It would take us beyond the "core competence" of our normal business. Worse, it would cost money to produce with no expected financial return.

But Alex knew there is a questing, philosophical side of me—and our readers—that would be intrigued. I liked the idea of exposing a great talent like Alex to a broader audience. Once he showed me a few drafts of what he had in mind, I couldn't say no. I subdued my bottom-line rationalizations and recognized that this kind of "wealth guidance" could be priceless.

And so, after much going round on the name, we launched the first issue of *Spiritual Wealth* in February 2008. It was one of the best moves I've made and an instant hit with readers, generating more positive feedback and gushing testimonials than anything we publish.

Through *Spiritual Wealth*, Alex deftly manages to present his readers with fresh insights on how to lead a mindful, compassionate, and intelligent life— being ever respectful of different religious and political beliefs. With each concisely written essay, he titillates us with a nugget of truth or lesson from history that we can apply to our lives, here and now.

After a year of broadcasting *Spiritual Wealth* online to our readers, John Wiley & Sons published the first 65 essays in an anthology, *The Secret of Shelter Island: Money and What Matters*. The book was an immediate success, climbing the best-seller lists within days of publication.

Alex has now taken the next 65 essays and turned them—along with some of his other thoughts—into the book you now hold in your hands. If your experience is typical, you won't just enjoy it, you'll tell your family and friends about it and give it often as a gift.

Alex stands out in the financial publishing world because his writings are smart and accessible to readers. His views are sharp, uplifting, and often amusing. More importantly, his investment advice works.

But his thoughts on how to live a fuller life are just as valuable, perhaps more so. In *Beyond Wealth*, Alex engages us further, both intellectually and soulfully, fostering our inner wisdom so we can see things more clearly and make better choices in our lives.

Alex is a master craftsman of the written word. Through each short essay, we are provoked to give attention to the things in our lives that matter most.

You will notice in these essays that he virtually never tells you what to do—or even what to think. Yet the sheer persuasiveness of his voice compels you to acknowledge his point of view and follow his pathway to a richer life.

If you are like me, whenever you come across something that makes you feel energized, uplifted, reborn, set straight, or enlightened, you want to share it. It could be a new song or piece of art that exhilarates you or touches a deep chord. It could be reading a short story that opens your eyes to something new or meeting someone that you want to have in your life. When these magical moments happen, we want to share them. That is how I feel about *Beyond Wealth*. I already know you're going to love it.

Julia Guth
Executive Director
The Oxford Club

INTRODUCTION

"Beyond Wealth?" a friend asked with a strange look when she heard the title of my new book. "Why *beyond* wealth? I'd be happy to settle for wealth."

No she wouldn't.

You can't wear your stock portfolio, ride on your bank account, or eat gold and silver coins. Money is never an end, only a means to an end.

Even if you have plenty of money and the things it can buy, your life won't mean much if you don't have decent health, someone to love, close friendships and personal interests, and something to get you out of bed in the morning.

I don't mean to downplay the importance of money in today's world. Over the past 25 years, I've worked as an investment adviser, research analyst, and financial writer. I feel strongly that everyone should strive for some measure of financial freedom, whether you define that as being independently wealthy or just getting out from under your credit card debt.

You can't reach your potential or live life to the fullest if you spend your days swimming in concerns about money.

Money is independence. It liberates you from want, from work that is drudgery, from relationships that confine you. No one is truly free who is a slave to his job, his creditors, his circumstances, or his overhead.

Money determines the kind of house you live in, the neighborhood your kids grow up in. If you're sick, it can mean the difference between a good doctor and an amazing doctor. If you need an attorney, it's the difference between using an ambulance chaser and getting the best legal representation money can buy.

Wealth is the great equalizer. It doesn't matter if you're a man or woman, black or white, young or old, tall or short, handsome or homely, educated or not. If you have money, you have power—in the best sense.

Wealth is freedom, security, and peace of mind. It allows you to do and be what you want, to support worthy causes and help those closest to you. It enables you to follow your dreams, to spend your life the way *you* choose.

Money gives you dignity. It gives you choices. That's why every man and woman has the right—perhaps even the obligation—to achieve some level of financial independence.

If the most pressing concern in your life right now is money (or the lack of it), let me direct you to my first book, *The Gone Fishin' Portfolio*. A *New York Times* best seller, it reveals one of the shortest, simplest, most direct routes to financial freedom.

However, this book is not about success, but rather, *significance*. In these pages, I don't talk about earning and saving more or generating a higher return on your investments. Nor do I have any brilliant ideas about how you should spend what you've got. (You have your own ideas on that subject, I'm sure.) Rather, this collection of essays is about something else: living a richer life.

You might reasonably wonder how I could tell *you* anything about that. After all, I probably don't know you personally. Your passion may be NBA basketball or interior decorating or rebuilding vintage automobiles. You'll find nothing here on those subjects. And even if I were to hit one or two of your interests, who am I to define *the good life*?

The answer is that human beings have had a few thousand years to ruminate on the subject. And the best ideas are not new. That doesn't mean, however, that most of us are familiar with them.

In school, you will learn plenty about differential equations, the life of a cell, or how to find France on a map. But as to what constitutes the best life, you're pretty much on your own.

That generally means learning things the hard way. Too many of us wind up chasing the false rabbits of success—money, fame, status, and possessions—and then feel curiously empty when we achieve them, if we do.

Too often, the world is governed by false values. Rather than following our own path, we look around and start doing pretty much what everyone else is doing. You can easily get the impression that you should strive to know important people, gain power over others, acquire expensive things, or be highly thought of by your neighbors. But these are just the tinsel of life, glittering but worthless.

Socrates famously said that the unexamined life is not worth living. Yet many of us never really stop to consider what matters most, what it is we are really living for. This subject is so personal, in fact, that it can be a bit awkward to talk about, even with those we know best. Yet the subject can't help but captivate us.

These essays are some of my thoughts about what constitutes a rich life. And while my personal biases are on full display, many of the best ideas here I am merely passing along. However, I did consult some of the greatest minds of all time, including Aristotle, Plato, Epictetus, Marcus Aurelius, Jesus, Buddha, Thomas Jefferson, Tolstoy, Gandhi, Einstein, even Richard Feynman and Stephen Hawking.

We are all ignorant of many things. The world is too big and complicated for it to be otherwise. But none of us should be ignorant of *how to live*. It makes sense to understand something about what the wisest men and women down through history have thought about love, work, honor, trust, freedom, death, fear, truth, beauty, and other important subjects.

I touch on all of these—and many more—in the pages ahead, as well as a few personal interests, including wine, jazz, travel, chocolate, literature, art, and . . . um . . . hummingbirds.

More than anything else, my goal is to convey the sheer delight of discovering things, of seeing, listening, reading, and experiencing great ideas.

Perhaps the book of Proverbs says it best: *With all thy getting, get understanding.* That's an excellent first step to a richer life.

PART ONE

DOLLARS AND SENSE

In the early spring of 2009, Jay, a good friend and art dealer, called and said he needed to meet with me privately and immediately. His tone was serious.

He asked if we could talk over dinner at a local steakhouse that evening. I agreed.

I couldn't imagine what was troubling him or how it involved me. When I walked into the restaurant a few hours later, he was already at the bar and waved me over.

We made the usual small talk, but he was edgy and stiff, not his usual relaxed self. I asked what was wrong, but he insisted that we wait and discuss it over dinner. When we finally settled down and ordered our meal, he took a long pull on his vodka tonic, leaned forward, and said he needed my advice.

His financial fortunes had recently taken a dramatic turn for the worse. With the economy in a deep recession, his art business was on life support. He had essentially no income. To make matters worse, he had seen his investment portfolio decimated by the recent financial crisis. As he was hoping to retire soon, this really troubled him.

Jay had been a good friend for over a decade. I knew he was a conservative guy who invested exclusively in diversified stock and bond funds. But even tried-and-true approaches provided little protection in the meltdown of 2008. And 2009 wasn't kicking off any better.

"Alex," he said, looking pale, "I've worked hard, saved, and compounded my investments all my life. Now everything is circling the drain. I'm 65 years old and for the last 25, I've considered myself financially independent. I've always invested smart and added to my portfolio regularly. I've never touched principal, not a dime. Now I'm afraid I don't have enough to retire. Never in a million years did I imagine I'd be in this position."

I nodded.

"I'm not asking for investment advice," he said. "Because even if you told me this was a great time to buy stocks, I wouldn't move a penny into the market now. I can't afford the risk of buying anything. But I'm not going to sell everything near the bottom either. I don't know what to do."

He tipped back his vodka tonic again. He looked pretty desperate.

"I brought my statements with me," he added. "I just want you to take a look at what I own and tell me what you think."

I agreed and he reached down and pulled them out from under the table. Looking over his holdings, I saw a lot of solid, blue-chip names. He was right. He hadn't invested unwisely. He had just gotten caught up in the financial maelstrom like millions of other investors.

As I leafed through the pages, Jay kept shaking his head and muttering that he didn't know what he was going to do.

I asked him a few questions about his investment income, his monthly overhead, and how much he thought he needed to live comfortably when he retired. Then I asked him what he thought—conservatively—his portfolio would earn over the next 10 years.

I thought his answer was too conservative, but I didn't object. "And how long do you think you'll live?" I asked.

"I'm in good health," he said. "I might live another 30 years."

I pulled out a financial calculator and showed him how much he could draw down his portfolio every month for the next 30 years, even if it never recovered and he earned only the modest return he projected. I pointed out that he would gradually spend the capital itself—something he had never done—but that his portfolio would last 30 years, as long as he withdrew only "this much" every month. (Incidentally, this is called a systematic withdrawal calculation, something everyone approaching retirement should do.)

The numbers amazed him. Like many lifelong savers, he is a frugal guy. He wasn't currently spending as much as he could withdraw every month. And he expected to spend even less in the years ahead (a good thing since inflation steadily erodes your purchasing power).

He brightened up immediately. The financial meltdown had stung him, but he realized it wasn't the end of the world. He wouldn't have to spend his golden years counting nickels or living in a Sub-Zero carton. The change in his demeanor was instantaneous. His whole disposition did a one-eighty. He even grabbed the check with a flourish.

Over the next week, Jay called me three times to thank me. He hadn't been sleeping well before and had been snappish with his wife. He had felt the weight of the world on his shoulders. Now it was lifted.

"Thanks to you, old buddy," he kept saying. "Thanks to you."

This outpouring of gratitude confounded me. After all, what had I done? I didn't take over the management of his portfolio. I hadn't suggested he make changes. In fact, I didn't recommend he take action of any kind.

Then it dawned on me. He was grateful for something else. I had helped him change his perspective—and that made all the difference.

What does this have to do with these essays? Everything, really. My goal here is to subtly shift your perspective by sharing ideas that helped me change my own. It might be a new finding of science or the rediscovery of an ancient philosophy. It might be a conversation with a historian or a money manager or an experience with a stranger that altered my point of view. In each case, the subject is something that, however slightly, altered my own worldview.

This may seem unusual coming from an investment analyst who writes a financial letter. After all, I make my living showing readers how to invest, how to reach their financial goals. But I have spent a lot of years reading and thinking about things that can't be measured in dollars and cents. Here are a few of them.

ARE THE RICH SMARTER THAN YOU?

Growing up, when I got into an argument with my mother, she would sometimes resort to the nuclear option, her tried-and-true conversation stopper.

Putting her hands on her hips and using the worst faux Southern accent imaginable, she'd say, "Well if you're so damn smart, why aren't you *rich*?"

I never knew how to respond to this. Of course, I was twelve at the time, and the deadbeats on my paper route kept margins low. Still, it ingrained in me the notion that the rich must have a little something extra going on upstairs; otherwise, we'd all be rolling in it. Right?

There is, in fact, some evidence to support this. According to a recent report from the U.S. Census Bureau, there is a strong positive correlation between education and income. Over an adult's working life, high school graduates should expect, on average, to earn $1.2 million; those with a bachelor's degree, $2.1 million; those with a master's degree, $2.5 million; those with doctoral degrees, $3.4 million; and those with professional degrees, $4.4 million.

But here's the rub. Studies show that those who earn the most aren't necessarily the richest. To determine real wealth, you need to look at a balance sheet—assets minus liabilities—not an income statement. Just ask Thomas J. Stanley. The bestselling author of *The Millionaire Next Door* (Andrews McMeel, 2004), *The Millionaire Mind* (Andrews McMeel, 2000), and *Stop Acting Rich . . . and Start Living Like a Real Millionaire* (John Wiley & Sons, 2009), Dr. Stanley is the country's foremost authority on the habits and characteristics of America's wealthy. And many of his findings are counterintuitive.

For example, we generally envision millionaires as Lexus-driving, Rolex-wearing, mansion-owning, Tiffany-shopping members of exclusive country clubs. And, indeed, Stanley's research reveals that the "glittering rich"—those with a net worth of $10 million or more—often meet this description.

But most millionaires—individuals with a net worth of $1 million or more—live an entirely different lifestyle. Stanley found that the vast majority:

- Live in a house that cost less than $400,000.
- Do not own a second home.
- Have never owned a boat.
- Are more likely to wear a Timex than a Rolex.
- Do not collect wine and generally pay less than $15 for a bottle.
- Are more likely to drive a Toyota than a Beemer.
- Have never paid more than $400 for a suit.
- Spend very little on prestige brands and luxury items.

This is certainly not the traditional image of millionaires. And it makes you wonder, who the heck is buying all those Mercedes convertibles, Louis Vuitton purses, and $60 bottles of Grey Goose? The answer, according to Dr. Stanley, is "aspirationals," people who act rich and want to be rich, but really aren't rich. (The Texas term, I believe, is "All Hat, No Cattle.")

Many are good people, well educated and perhaps earning a six-figure income. But they aren't balance-sheet rich because it's almost impossible for most workers—even those who are well paid—to hyperspend on consumer goods *and* save a lot of money. (And saving is the key prerequisite for investing.)

In his new book, *Stop Acting Rich . . . and Start Living Like a Real Millionaire,* Dr. Stanley recalls an appearance on *Oprah* when a member of the audience asked *the question,* one he's heard hundreds of times before:

> "What good does it do to have all this money if you don't spend it?" She was angry, indignant even. "These people couldn't possibly be happy."

Like so many others, this woman genuinely believed that the more you spend, the better life is. Bear in mind, we're not talking about people who live below the poverty line. (Clearly, *their* lives would be better if they were able to spend more.) We're talking about middle-class consumers and up, those who often live beyond their means and then find themselves under enormous pressure, especially in a weak economy.

Some were overly optimistic. Others didn't realize that they are up against an army of the best and most creative marketers in the world, whose job it is to convince you that "you are what you buy," that you need to outspend—to outdisplay—others. The unspoken message behind the constant barrage of TV and billboard ads featuring all those impossibly good-looking men and women is that you are special, you are deserving, and you need to look and act successful *now.*

According to Dr. Stanley:

> The pseudo-affluent are insecure about how they rank among the Joneses and the Smiths. Often their self-esteem rests on quick-sand. In their minds, it is closely tied to how long they can continue to purchase the trappings of wealth. They strongly believe all economically successful people display their success through prestige products. The flip side of this has them believing that people who do not own prestige brands are not successful.

Yet "everyday" millionaires see things differently. Most of them achieved their wealth not by hitting the lottery or gaining an inheritance, but by patiently and persistently maximizing their income, minimizing their outgo, and religiously saving and investing the difference.

They aren't big spenders. According to Stanley's surveys, their most popular activities include:

- Socializing with children/grandchildren (95 percent)
- Planning investments (94 percent)
- Entertaining close friends (87 percent)
- Visiting museums (83 percent)
- Raising funds for charities (75 percent)
- Attending sporting events (69 percent)
- Participating in civic activities (69 percent)
- Studying art (63 percent)
- Participating in trade/professional association activities (56 percent)
- Gardening (55 percent)
- Attending religious services (52 percent)
- Jogging (48 percent)
- Attending lectures (44 percent)

The cost associated with these activities is minimal. Most millionaires understand that real pleasure and satisfaction don't come from the car you drive or the watch you wear, but time spent in activities with family, friends, and associates.

They aren't misers, either, especially when it comes to educating their children and grandchildren or donating to worthy causes. Although they are disciplined savers, the affluent are among the most generous Americans in charitable giving.

They "give" in another important way, too. According to the IRS, the top 1 percent of America's income earners pays 37 percent of the entire federal income tax bill. The top 5 percent pays 57 percent. The top 10 percent pay 68 percent. (The bottom 50 percent pay less than 4 percent.) It's a far cry from the populist complaint that the rich "don't pay their fair share."

Just how prevalent are American millionaires? According to the Spectrum Group, there were 6.7 million U.S. households with a net worth of at least $1 million at the end of 2008. Very few of them won a Grammy, played in the NBA, or started a computer company in their garage. Clearly, thrift and modesty—however unfashionable—are still alive in some parts of the country.

So while millions of consumers chase a blinkered image of success—busting their humps for stuff that ends up in landfills, yard sales, and thrift shops—disciplined savers and investors are enjoying the freedom, satisfaction, and peace of mind that comes from living beneath their means. These folks are turned on not by consumerism but by personal achievement, industry awards, and recognition. They know that success is not about flaunting your wealth. It's about a sense of accomplishment . . . and the independence that comes with it. They are able to do what they want, where they want, with whom they want.

They may not be smarter than you, but they do know something priceless: It is how we spend ourselves—not our money—that makes us rich.

ARE YOU LOSING YOUR SOUL?

I recently bumped into an old acquaintance I hadn't seen in years. "Are you still managing money?" he asked.

"No, I write investment advice now," I said.

"Well, it must not be panning out too well," he said with a wink, "or you wouldn't still be working!"

I've heard variations of this line over the years. And while it's always offered in jest, it hints at a particular mind-set: Why would anyone continue to work if he didn't have to?

Yet I'd be bored to death without a job and even more of a pain in the neck to everyone around me, I'm sure. (Warren Buffett and Bill Gates—two gentlemen who have a few dollars—apparently feel the same way.) Yet, according to over 40 Gallup studies, three quarters of us are disengaged from our jobs. The most recent U.S. Job Retention Survey found that more than 60 percent of employees are currently searching for new employment opportunities.

It's odd that we spend most of our waking hours at work—in occupations often chosen by our younger selves—and yet seldom ask ourselves how we got there or what our occupations really mean.

When we meet someone new, for instance, the question we most frequently ask, after discerning where they're from and whether we have any common acquaintances, is what he or she does. Our work, to a great extent, defines us.

10

It wasn't always this way. Three hundred years ago, Voltaire argued that work exists to save us from three great evils: boredom, poverty, and vice. But, as a society, we have since put our belief in two great ideas: romantic love and meaningful work.

Historically, our faith in these grew up together. We started to think that we should marry for love at roughly the same time we started to think that we should work not only for money but for self-fulfillment.

These are two beautiful ideals, but rarely does either go long without hitting a rough patch. And the pain can be immense. When we are without work, as 29 million Americans are today, we lose more than income; we are cut off from an identity. We can't explain any more what we do, and hence who we are.

It's always a shame to see a person's talents wasted. And that's just as true for those who are employed but disengaged. Ideally, your work should allow you to take the best of what's in you and express it to the world. It should give your life dignity and meaning, whether you're writing software, fixing teeth, or just raising happy, productive kids.

No matter how you spend your days, you have a clear choice. You can think of your work entirely in terms of responsibilities and obligations, or you can view it as a contest, a challenge, an opportunity. Because if you don't enjoy what you're doing, there's little chance your work will please or impress anyone else.

I have a sneaking suspicion that a lot of folks who are unhappy at work tend to equate a "good job" entirely with money, benefits, and security, rather than whether it allows them to express their talents.

Big mistake. Yet even those who recognize the dead-end nature of their current position are often reluctant to change. Why? Reasons vary, but some are so caught up in the pursuit of status, display, and material possessions that they've put themselves in a bind.

Choosing meaningful employment often means accepting at least a temporary pay cut. But that isn't always possible if you have a big mortgage, hefty car payments, or a lifestyle that keeps you 60 days from insolvency. Ironically, giving up the dream of "having it all" is often the first step in the right direction.

The other reason so many remain stuck in unsuitable work—whether they admit it to themselves or not—is fear. Fear whispers that, even if you reduce your overhead, you won't be able to make it work financially. Fear betrays you, insisting that you're being unrealistic; that you don't have the heart, the talent, or the discipline to see it through; that doing work you love is reserved for someone else.

It's not true. One of the best prizes that life offers is the chance to work hard at something worth doing. Think enthusiastically about how you spend your days and you'll put a touch of glory in your life.

This is true for retirees, too. A life of meaning generally comes from finding a way to either increase the pleasure or decrease the suffering of your fellow man, whether you're compensated for it or not. If you're still in the workforce and—due to circumstances—tied to a job that is less than fulfilling, there are still ways to use your talents in meaningful ways.

A few years ago, for instance, the AARP asked some attorneys if they would offer basic services to needy retirees at $30 an hour. They said no. But then AARP's program manager had a brilliant idea: He asked the lawyers if they would offer their services to needy retirees for free. Overwhelmingly, they said yes.

How could zero money be more attractive than $30 an hour? The original offer seemed insulting to some, a request for legal services at below-market wages. But when the request was reframed as volunteer work—and therefore meaningful—most were happy to oblige.

In *Zen and the Art of Making a Living* (Lightning Press, 1992), Laurence G. Boldt writes:

> Without self-expression, life lacks spontaneity and joy. Without service to others, it lacks meaning and purpose . . . Conceiving of ourselves as artists in whatever work we do gives us a metaphor for a life of integrity, service, enjoyment, and excellence . . . I know of no better nutshell statement of the path to finding one's true

calling in life than the simple formula given by Aristotle: Where your talents and the needs of the world cross, there lies your vocation. These two, your talents and the needs of the world, are the great wake-up calls to your true vocation in life. To ignore either is, in some sense, to lose your soul.

You'll find that the happiest, most engaged individuals are those who are deeply involved in their workplace or community (or both), even if their time is unpaid.

Work is the natural outlet for our energy and enthusiasm. What could be more enjoyable than to love what you do and feel that it matters?

After all, the highest reward for your work is not what you get, but what you become.

IMPATIENT OPTIMISM . . . AND RADICAL GENEROSITY

Is being rich a good thing? According to a long line of philosophers, politicians. and religious leaders, the answer is a resounding no. Karl Marx argued that the rich exploit the working class. Teddy Roosevelt railed against "malefactors of great wealth." The book of Isaiah condemns the rich who "crush my people" and "grind the face of the poor."

Yet American attitudes toward wealth remain largely unchanged, especially among young people. The Pew Research Center recently polled a large sample of 26- to 40-year-olds and 18- to 25-year-olds, asking them, "What are your generation's most important goals in life?" Sixty-two percent of 26- to 40-year-olds said their highest goal is "to get rich." Eighty-one percent of 18- to 25-year-olds answered the same way.

Some will say this simply reflects our increasingly materialistic culture. But money is also freedom, the ability to make important choices. And great wealth often leads to something else: radical generosity:

- Steel magnate Andrew Carnegie established a foundation "to promote the advancement and diffusion of knowledge and understanding." It has funded public libraries and universities across Scotland and the United States.

- Henry Ford left the bulk of his fortune to the Ford Foundation. It grants more than $530 million annually for community and economic development, education, arts and culture, and human rights.
- The W. K. Kellogg Foundation, funded by the breakfast cereal pioneer, donates hundreds of millions annually to promote education and health care for the poor.
- David Packard, founder of Hewlett Packard, set up the David and Lucile Packard Foundation to build community hospitals across the nation.
- Intel founder Gordon Moore has given hundreds of millions to conservation groups and universities. (In 2007, his foundation donated $200 million to Caltech and the University of California for the construction of the world's largest optical telescope.)
- Standard Oil founder John Rockefeller gave birth to Rockefeller University and through his foundation established the first schools of public health, developed the vaccine for yellow fever, and funded agricultural development around the world.

The tradition of radical generosity continues today. Take Microsoft founder Bill Gates, for example. His parents were heartbroken when he dropped out of Harvard his sophomore year to pursue a business opportunity he was convinced would vanish by the time he graduated.

But he could not have been more right. Within just a few years, he licensed his computer operating system to IBM for $80,000 rather than selling it outright. He reckoned that other PC makers would soon copy IBM's open architecture and would need to license his system.

It was one of the great business decisions of all time. Collecting royalties from both PC makers and software developers worldwide, Gates made a fortune for early shareholders and quickly became the world's richest man, with a net worth of more than $50 billion. Lately, however, he has turned his attention elsewhere. . . .

In setting up the Bill and Melinda Gates Foundation, Gates wanted—like all philanthropists—to give away his fortune wisely. He explored several avenues. But Gates found his mission when he discovered that every month one million parents lose a child they will grieve forever to easily preventable diseases like measles, malaria, and diarrhea. Before long he was reading titles like *The Eradication of Infectious Diseases, Mosquitos, Malaria & Man,* and *Rats, Lice, and History.*

After an initial donation to combat the problem, Gates invited a group of doctors, scientists, and leaders in the field of immunology to his home one evening to learn more about what could be done. He was surprised to find that 30 million children a year weren't receiving vaccines. He challenged his guests to investigate what could be done and at what cost. His parting words of encouragement that night were "Don't be afraid to think big."

Today, the Bill and Melinda Gates Foundation grants generous gifts to a number of worthy causes here and abroad, including education, technology, agriculture, birth control and microfinance. But its primary focus is improving health care and reducing extreme poverty in the world's developing nations. One major goal is vaccination. Why? When you look at the benefits they provide, vaccines represent the most efficient and cost-effective tool medicine has. Administering them a few times during a child's first year dramatically improves mortality rates.

The $800 million the Gates Foundation currently spends each year to fight infectious diseases is roughly the same amount given by the U.S. Agency for International Development—and approaches the annual budget of the United Nations' World Health Organization, a group receiving donations from 193 nations.

In 2008, Gates gave up his day-to-day role at Microsoft to devote more time to his foundation. His generosity has already saved millions of lives. Yet he's just getting started. He calls himself "an impatient optimist."

Gates understands how incredibly fortunate he was to be born in a country that values freedom, education, and individual initiative. He also knows his success could never have occurred in a society without adequate health care, property rights, free-market incentives, and well-developed capital markets. Many are born into this world with no such advantages—indeed, with little chance of surviving their first year.

Gates has taken this problem and embraced it as his own.

Some will grouse that a poor man sacrifices more when he gives $10 than Gates and Buffett do when they donate $10 billion. And I won't argue the point. But these men are doing a lot more good and provide an inspiring example. They don't just know how to make it. They know how to give it away.

■ You Can't Google This

The other day I had lunch with a friend. But I can't say I enjoyed it.

Every five minutes, he pulled his BlackBerry out and glanced at his e-mail. Sometimes he would just scan it. Other times he would offer an apology and type out a message. When he finished, he would thrust the phone back in his pants pocket, unable to trust himself with the device in plain sight. Five minutes later, it was out again.

It reminded me of an Experimental Psych course I took in college. I trained a lab rat so that every time he pressed a bar in his cage, he received a food pellet. Then I required him to press the bar twice for a pellet. Then 3 times. Then 5 times. Then 10 times. Before long, the rat was a bar-pressing maniac, oblivious to everyone and everything around him.

Sound like anyone you know?

Don't get me wrong. The Internet is a godsend. Nobody knows this better than writers. Twenty years ago, I wrote research reports for an international brokerage firm. This generally required multiple phone calls to investment banks and trading houses where I coaxed, cajoled, wheedled (okay, begged) other analysts to send me what I needed. When the information arrived—usually days later—it required follow-up calls to update the data.

The Web has changed all that. Research that once required hours in the periodical room at the library or days sifting through reports is done in minutes. Information and ideas scattered or hidden around the globe can be gathered instantly. Being a financial writer today is like going back to school and finding that every exam is an open-book test.

Only a Luddite would argue that the speed, the efficiency, the convenience, and the cost savings of the Internet are not a blessing. Still, it comes at a price. Consider, for example:

- A 2008 international survey of 27,500 adults between the ages of 18 and 55 found that people are spending 30 percent of their leisure time online. And these figures don't include time spent on cell phones and other mobile devices.
- According to a new survey by the Henry J. Kaiser Family Foundation, kids are spending an average of more than seven-and-a-half hours a day using electronic media, which includes TV, the Internet, video games, and mobile devices. Kids are plugged into some kind of electronic device for more than 53 hours a week, more time than most adults spend at work.
- Children who are heavy media users tend to have lower grades than those who are light users. (Yet less than half of kids report that their parents set any rules or limits on usage.)
- Three quarters of all 12- to 17-year-olds now own cell phones, but not for talking much. Half of all teens send 50 or more texts a day. One in three sends more than 100 text messages a day, over 3,000 texts a month. Apparently, there is hardly a thought that doesn't require instant communication.
- Particularly scary is that 34 percent of cell-owning 16- to 17-year-olds admit that they sometimes text while driving. Half say they have been in a car while the driver was texting. (My advice? Keep your eyes on the oncoming lane and your hands in the 10-2 position.)

You might assume that our time spent texting and surfing the Net at least comes out of the hours we would otherwise spend watching TV. Nope. The Nielsen Company's research shows that as Internet use has gone up, TV viewing has either held steady or increased. In 2009, the time we spend in front of the tube—thanks in part to widespread adoption of the DVR—rose to a record

153 hours a month. (And this doesn't include television programs watched online.) We are a nation addicted to electronic media.

Optimists point out that at least people spending time online are reading. That's good. But studies show that most of the reading we do on the Internet is pretty shallow. We skim, we scroll, we hypertext from page to page.

Some argue that these links save time and facilitate learning. But the jury is still out. Psychologists say readers on the Internet are distracted and overstimulated by hypermedia. We give less attention to what we read and remember less of it.

The online environment promotes cursory reading, distracted thinking, and superficial learning. And the more we use it, the less patience we have for long, drawn-out, nuanced arguments—the kind of arguments, for instance, found in books.

Books—including e-books—require calm, focused, undistracted concentration that allows ideas to germinate and take hold.

Deep reading inspires new associations, insights, and the occasional epiphany. Thoughts expand, language grows, consciousness deepens.

This kind of reading enhances and refines our experience of the world. It strengthens your ability to think abstractly and enriches life outside the book. Deep reading requires the time and attention that cultivates an educated mind. Yet polls show that Americans now spend less than 20 minutes a day reading printed matter of any kind.

We're on the Net instead. Even when away from their computers and mobile devices—even on vacation—millions itch to check e-mail, Web surf, or do some Googling. They seek an Internet connection the way a man with his hair on fire seeks a pond. They want to feel connected.

For many, the digital revolution has put the computer—desktop, laptop, and handheld—in control. The silicon chip is Big Brother, not because electronic media won't let go of us, but because we can't let go of it.

I'm not much different than most. I work online. I use my browser to book flights and hotel rooms, pay my bills, schedule appointments, watch my stocks, and check the news. But I don't hesitate to disconnect. My cell phone is usually off. Except for business trips, my laptop stays home. My e-mail goes unchecked for days at a time, especially on weekends. My colleagues think I'm an anachronism, but it feels great.

Walking around the University of Virginia campus the other day, I enjoyed the crisp weather and the red, orange, and yellow leaves. But I wondered if the students noticed. Eyes down, thumbs on tiny keyboards, they shuffled toward some unseen horizon, oblivious to their surroundings.

I realize some people have jobs or unusual circumstances where they simply must stay connected 24/7. But for millions of others, that's not the case. We seem to have developed a terrific anxiety about wandering off the grid. We fear that if we stop e-mailing, surfing, texting, or posting, we will disappear.

The electronic-media obsessed forget that they have a choice. They can log off and pay attention to something—or someone—else. So spark a counterrevolution. Unplug the Tube. Turn off the iPhone. Get outside.

Psychological studies over the past twenty years reveal that spending time in a quiet rural setting, close to nature, creates greater attentiveness, stronger memory, and generally improved cognition.

Why? I don't know. Maybe it's because it's normal . . . or relaxing . . . or part of our DNA. But it feels great to reconnect with those around you and the Great Outdoors.

Here's a tip, though. You can't do it on Google.

THE ONLY THING THAT REALLY MATTERS

Why do some folks look back on their lives in old age and say they wouldn't change much—or anything? Is there a formula—some mix of love, work, habits, or attitudes—that offers the best chance of experiencing the good life?

Believe it or not, researchers at Harvard have been examining this question for 72 years, following 268 men who entered college in the late 1930s through war, career, sickness, health, marriage, parenthood, grandparenthood, and old age. Their discoveries about what constitutes a well-lived life might surprise you.

Just listen to Dr. George Vaillant. Since 1967, the Harvard Medical School professor has dedicated his career to following the men of Harvard's "Grant study," named after its patron, department-store magnate W. T. Grant.

Vaillant's specialty is the longitudinal method of research, the comprehensive study of a small number of people over a long period of time. His subjects were never a representative sample of society. They were all young men, Harvard students, from relatively privileged backgrounds.

Yet Vaillant's findings offer profound insights into the human condition. They have universal applications. And they illuminate the one single factor that correlates most highly with a positive life assessment in old age.

From the beginning, the Grant study was meant to be exhaustive. Harvard researchers assembled a team that included medical doctors, physiologists, psychologists, psychiatrists, social workers, anthropologists, and other specialists.

Over more than seven decades, participants were monitored, interviewed, and studied from every conceivable angle, including eating and drinking habits, exercise, mental and physical health, career changes, financial successes and setbacks, marital history, parenthood, grandparenthood, and old age. They were subjected to general aptitude tests and personality inventories, and were required to provide regular letters and documentation.

Many of the Grant study men achieved dramatic success. Some became captains of industry. One was a best-selling author. Four members ran for the U.S. Senate. One served in a presidential cabinet. And one—JFK (we now know)—was president. (His files are sealed until 2040.)

Some of the subjects were disappointments, too. Case number 47, for example, literally fell down drunk and died. (Not quite what the study had in mind). Most of the participants remain anonymous, although a few, like Ben Bradlee, the long-time editor of the *Washington Post,* have publicly identified themselves.

Over the past four decades, the lives of the Grant men were Vaillant's personal and professional obsession. In his book *Adaptation to Life* (Little, Brown, 1977), he writes, "Their lives were too human for science, too beautiful for numbers, too sad for diagnosis and too immortal for bound journals." Yet more than seventy years of data and analysis enabled Vaillant to reach some broad conclusions.

He found seven major factors that predict healthy aging, both physically and psychologically: education, stable marriage, healthy weight, some exercise, not smoking, not abusing alcohol, and "employing mature adaptations." (Vaillant believes social skills and coping methods are crucial in determining overall life satisfaction.)

However, his most important finding was revealed in an interview in 2008 when he was asked, "What have you learned from the Grant Study men?" Vaillant's response: "That the only thing that really matters in life are your relationships to other people."

The Grant study confirms that a successful life is not about the grim determination to get or have more. Nor is it about low cholesterol levels or intellectual brilliance or career accomplishments. It's about human connections: parents, siblings, spouses, children, friends, neighbors, and mentors.

Without them, life quickly loses its flavor, whatever material successes we enjoy. Lasting satisfaction is rare outside of meaningful, human relationships. Look back at your life and you'll almost certainly find that the most significant moments were births, deaths, weddings, and celebrations.

Your most profound moments? When you touched others . . . or they touched you. In times of suffering—loss, sickness, death—it is not prescriptions, formulas, or advice we seek, but the healing presence of another. When we forget this—when we think only of ourselves—we choke the source of our development.

Real meaning comes from taking care of those you love, letting them know how you feel. Fortunately, we have countless opportunities to give a bit of ourselves each day through a thoughtful act, a word of appreciation, or a sense of understanding.

As Dr. Vaillant concludes, true success "is more about us than me."

THE PRINCIPLE THING

When I speak at investment conferences and seminars, the attendees usually want to know what lies just ahead for the economy and the stock market. I hate to disappoint them. But I tell them anyway: "I don't know—and neither does anyone else."

Fortunately, this isn't important. Investment success is not about following the right predictions. It's about following the right principles.

This is true in virtually every aspect of life. Imagine a tunnel, bridge, or skyscraper erected without using proven designs, building materials, or construction methods. The results would be calamitous.

A composer is free to create beautiful music, but only within the boundaries of harmony, melody, and rhythm. (Few can bear to listen to a so-called "atonal masterpiece.")

If you are a golfer, you have to use the proper stance and grip. You have to keep your head still, your left arm straight, and your right elbow tucked in. You won't become a champion by reinventing the golf swing. Players were whacking balls around St. Andrews before Columbus discovered America.

In sum, principles are the collective wisdom of our species. They tell us what is valuable. They warn us what is not. Principles of law safeguard society and protect our rights. Health principles guide us on nutrition, exercise, and the prevention of disease. Scientific principles further technology and explain the natural world. Spiritual principles guide our lives. Or should.

There will always be arguments about doctrine, of course. But there is little disagreement on core principles: honesty, compassion, forgiveness, tolerance, perseverance, justice, humility, charity, and gratitude.

These principles aren't binding. They're liberating. They imbue life with meaning. And, make no mistake, human beings are meaning-seeking creatures. Without a reason to live, people easily fall into depression or despair. In some sense, we are all spiritual seekers.

You may revere the Ten Commandments, the Sermon on the Mount, the Four Noble Truths, the Five Pillars, or some other timeless set of ethical principles.

"Anything else you worship," argued David Foster Wallace at a commencement address at Kenyon College in 2005, "will almost certainly eat you alive. If you worship money and things—if they are where you tap real meaning in life—then you will never have enough. . . . Worship your own body and beauty and sexual allure and you will always feel ugly, and when time and age start showing, you will die a million deaths before they plant you. . . . Worship power—you will feel weak and afraid, and you will need ever more power over others to keep the fear at bay. . . . Worship your intellect, being seen as smart—you will end up feeling stupid, a fraud, always on the verge of being found out."

On some level, most of us understand this. The message is embodied in our myths, proverbs, and aphorisms, our classic films, our great novels. Yet society and culture, and even our unconscious, tug us the other way.

Madison Avenue surrounds you—in the streets, on the airwaves, in your home—showing you what you could have; how you could look; how you will feel when you finally acquire the latest, greatest, and most fabulous bauble yet. (And did I mention it's new and improved?)

The modern economy doesn't just meet our wants. It continually creates new ones. This isn't all bad, of course. I'm not unhappy that business has brought us iPads, Miracle bras, and 60-inch plasma TVs.

It's just that a life based on craving—on the worship of self—is no more satisfying in the end than a bowl of jellybeans. Fortunately, the great spiritual principles are there, like Polaris, guiding you toward true north, reminding you that it's really not all about you, suggesting that the most important thing you can do today may not be to obtain or even achieve something, but to show those around you that you care in a dozen little unsexy ways. It may not be glamorous. But it's the truth.

Ralph Waldo Emerson understood this. He ends his famous essay "Self Reliance" with these words: "Nothing can bring you peace but yourself. Nothing can bring you peace but the triumph of principles."

THE ONE THING THAT CHANGES EVERYTHING

Whether you realize it or not, one indispensable quality affects every relationship in your life. It holds together all your associations. It determines whether you realize your dreams, both personal and professional. It virtually defines you to others. Without it, true success is impossible.

Stephen M. R. Covey is even more emphatic. He writes:

> There is one thing that is common to every individual, relationship, team, family, organization, nation, economy, and civilization throughout the world—one thing which, if removed, will destroy the most powerful government, the most thriving economy, the most influential leadership, the greatest friendship, the strongest character, the deepest love.
>
> On the other hand, if developed and leveraged, that one thing has the potential to create unparalleled success and prosperity in every dimension of life. Yet, it is the least understood, most neglected, and most underestimated possibility of our time.
>
> That one thing is trust.

Simply put, trust is confidence in an individual or organization. It is other people feeling good about relying on you. And its value can hardly be overstated. Trustworthiness is the universally accepted test of good character.

When you trust someone, you have confidence in his or her honesty and abilities. You can delegate things easily and effectively. You can relax. You have peace of mind. But when you doubt someone's integrity, question his accomplishments, or worry about his agenda, confidence is replaced by suspicion and anxiety.

Take a moment and picture someone you trust implicitly. It could be a spouse, a parent, a sibling, a friend, or a business associate. How does this relationship make you feel? How easily do you communicate? How quickly do things get done?

Now imagine someone you distrust. How does this relationship feel? How easily do you communicate? Do you enjoy this relationship, or is it complicated, cumbersome, and draining?

The difference between a high-trust and low-trust relationship is night and day. In a high-trust relationship, you can say the wrong thing and your listener still understands you. In a low-trust relationship, you can choose your words carefully, be very precise, and you may still be misunderstood.

Sadly, trust is at an ebb in our society. A Harris poll reveals that only 27 percent of Americans trust the government, only 22 percent trust the media, only 12 percent trust big companies, and only 8 percent trust political parties.

Personal trust is waning, too. Many people nowadays look back on contracts or commitments as something to negotiate. Half of all marriages end in divorce. Many (perhaps most) of them founder on a lack of trust.

Each of us naturally gravitates away from individuals we can't believe or rely on and toward those we can. Low trust is the very definition of a bad relationship. And once you forfeit someone's confidence, it's awfully hard to win it back.

This is particularly true in business. We all survive by selling a product, service, or skill. Yet every sale has five basic obstacles: no need, no money, no hurry, no desire, no trust.

If trust is lacking, forget the other four. You're done. The moment someone suspects your motives, everything you do becomes tainted.

That's why successful companies make a priority of building and maintaining confidence. John Whitney, Professor Emeritus of

Management at Columbia Business School, estimates that mistrust doubles the cost of doing business. You may have the best product, great service, competitive pricing, mountains of supporting facts and figures, and testimonials galore. But if you don't command and deserve trust, you will not enjoy long-term success.

It is never enough to simply invite trust. It must be earned.

In personal relationships, that means handling responsibility, proving your credibility, allowing yourself to be relied upon again and again. It's not just about integrity. It's about looking out for the other person's interests as well as your own.

Employers build trust with employees by assigning them important responsibilities, giving them the freedom to make mistakes, and setting an example. Real leadership is about getting results in ways that inspire confidence.

In a world that changes as quickly as ours, trust is a critical factor. It is the vital currency.

Business consultant Tom Peters calls trust "the issue of the decade." Trust makes work easier and more productive. It makes relationships stable and predictable. It creates a sense of community.

That's why it's crucial that we not violate it. Trust can take years to build but only a moment to destroy. And you may not get an opportunity to restore it.

For each of us—and for every organization—trust is something to be built up, protected, valued, cherished, and carefully preserved. It is the one thing that changes everything.

THE TROUBLE WITH HAPPINESS

Our nation has a happiness fetish. Each year, publishers print thousands of books on the subject. Talk show hosts offer advice from psychologists and therapists. Magazine covers promise "The Short-Cut to Total Joy" or "The Seven Secrets of Wedded Bliss."

You might reasonably wonder why the market is so large. A Pew Research Center poll reports that almost 85 percent of Americans say they are happy or very happy.

Yet millions want to be happier still. And they feel they could be, if only they pursued it a little more ardently.

Except . . . that won't work. Happiness is a by-product. It is achieved indirectly, by producing something beautiful or useful or by making someone else happy. The search for happiness is one of the chief sources of unhappiness.

Take a look around. Much of the economic misery we see today is due to the unbridled pursuit of bigger houses, fancier cars, and more exorbitant trips. The lure of consumer culture and an obsession with more is precisely what keeps so many from contentment.

The Stoics argued that happiness results not from pursuing affluence and status but rather virtue and wisdom. Pythagoras, the sixth-century BC philosopher and mathematician, asked that his followers take time, before going to sleep each night, to pose three questions: What have I done? Where have I failed myself? What responsibility have I not fulfilled?

If we fixate instead on gratifying all our desires, we may become superficial, acquisitive, deluded, or foolish. The headlong rush for happiness can also blind us to serious problems or numb us to the pain of others. After all, every life is lived between the poles of joy and sadness. Laughter and love are part of it. But so are pain and suffering. To deny the tragic aspects of the world is to suppress a large part of what it means to be human.

Playwright Tennessee Williams understood this. Asked in an interview to define happiness, he replied, "Insensitivity, I guess."

Great artists often try to awaken us—or stir our conscience—by reminding us of the more doleful aspects of life. In response to the 16th Street Church bombing in 1963, an attack by the Ku Klux Klan in Birmingham that killed four girls, saxophonist John Coltrane wrote "Alabama," an instrumental work that expresses anguish and sorrow more eloquently than words.

Poetry, too, can inspire us with its sorrowful realizations. Seventeenth-century British poet Robert Herrick famously wrote, "Gather ye rosebuds while ye may / Old Time is still a-flying; / And this same flower that smiles today / Tomorrow will be dying."

Shakespeare captured the same sentiment in *Cymbeline:* "Golden lads and girls all must / As chimney-sweepers, come to dust."

History shows that men and women of genius are often melancholic. Consider writers like Ernest Hemingway and Virginia Woolf. Composers like Rossini and Mahler. Statesmen like Lincoln and Churchill. Artists like Michelangelo and Gauguin. Philosophers like Schopenhauer and Kierkegaard.

In 1890, Vincent Van Gogh, overcome by feelings of worthlessness, walked out into the southern French countryside and shot himself in the gut with a pistol. Just 37, he died from the wound two days later. Yet in the previous two years—and despite his bleakness—he completed more than 200 paintings, many of them masterpieces.

Handel, after years spent at the top of the musical world, fell into terrible poverty, ill health, and deep depression. Yet from the depths of profound despair, he completed his greatest work, "Messiah."

Beethoven raged against advancing deafness and his own finitude, yet created immortal works during this period, including his Fifth symphony; his only opera, *Fidelio;* his late string quartets; and the Ninth symphony, with its triumphant "Ode to Joy."

Not all innovators are melancholy, of course, and not all melancholy souls are innovative. And I don't mean to romanticize clinical depression, an often-debilitating illness. But there can be no joy without sorrow, no daybreak without the night. Periods of unhappiness are natural and even valuable. How are we to measure our best moments except against those that are not?

Contentment often saps our motivation. Dissatisfaction is the great spur to progress. Imagine the innovations we would lack today if we were satisfied with quill pens, horse-drawn carriages, or the "evil spirits" theory of disease.

Today, millions equate happiness with money. But studies show that once people are lifted out of poverty, their happiness is not dependent on income but rather love and meaningful work. Reported levels of well-being are also dependent, in part, on genetics, health, circumstances, and coping skills.

Happiness results when our aspirations are being fulfilled and we are optimistic about the future, when we are developing our capabilities or helping others develop theirs. In short, we are happiest when happiness itself is not the goal.

Contemporary philosopher Robert Nozick writes:

> We want experiences, fitting ones, of profound connection with others, of deep understanding of natural phenomena, of love, of being profoundly moved by music or tragedy, or doing something new and innovative, experiences very different from the bounce and rosiness of the happy moments.

Of all the prescriptions for happiness, perhaps the least helpful one is the now-fashionable idea that you can defeat the blues by "paying attention to yourself." Hardly. The happiest individuals are invariably those whose ordinary, everyday mode of living is being busy and unconcerned with self.

That doesn't mean sacrificing your interests for someone else's. Rather, it means asking not just "what would it take to make me happy?" but also "What limits should I set on this pursuit?" "How should I weigh my own happiness against that of others?" And "What else matters aside from happiness?"

We all want to be happy. But life is also about education, work, courage, honor, empathy, and resilience in the face of hardship. Real contentment comes from a feeling that your life is worthwhile, that it is dissolved into something meaningful and great. That leads to gratitude.

And gratitude, it turns out, is an indispensable part of happiness.

The Key to Personal Freedom

Due to rising unemployment and the sharp contraction in the economy, personal bankruptcies are hitting record levels, up more than 50 percent from a year ago.

There is another factor here, too, of course. Millions overreached. In some ways, this is understandable. It's natural to want to improve our circumstances, enjoy the best life has to offer, and "go for the gusto." Without moderation, however, our wants have no natural limits.

True, some of us have fewer desires than others. Yet conservative spenders don't necessarily lack ambition, imagination, or even money. More often than not, they have spent years cultivating an attitude of restraint.

Freedom, after all, is not the absence of responsibility. It is the absence of restraints imposed by others. To be truly free, however, we must generally impose severe restraints on ourselves. That often means delaying gratification . . . or settling for less . . . or simply doing without.

This is bitter medicine to the thousands of consumers who hang on to their material desires like caterpillars to a cabbage leaf. Especially when the media glamorizes the materialistic lifestyle, their neighbors—who may be two payments from the edge—are living high, and advertisers bombard them daily with subtle— and not-so-subtle—messages meant to stir their cravings.

There is a reliable defense, however. And it begins with your frame of mind. If you or someone in your family suffers from the "urge to splurge," here are four steps to help reclaim your personal freedom and, perhaps, your credit rating:

1. Recognize that we are wired to feel dissatisfied with our circumstances. It's in your genes. An early human who was content with what he had—who spent his days lazing on the African savannah admiring the clouds and thinking "Ahh, life is good"—was far less likely to survive and reproduce than his neighbor who spent every waking hour trying to gain some advantage.

2. Understand the psychology of desire. We all tend to "miswant"—to want things we don't really need and won't appreciate once we acquire them. Recollect how your last major purchase failed to do it for you and you're less likely to believe that this time will be any different.

3. Stop regarding life as an ongoing competition for social status. Opt out of the game—even if everyone else seems to be playing it—and you can't be controlled or disappointed by the opinions of others. Do work you enjoy, even if it's lower paying. Spend your time and money collecting great memories rather than more stuff.

4. Instead of focusing on what you want, try appreciating what you already have. Nothing cures your craving for the next bauble like the thought of losing your partner, your children, your health, or the things you already own.

In *On Desire: Why We Want What We Want* (Oxford University Press, 2005), William B. Irvine argues that what many of us lack is

a sense that we are lucky to be living whatever life we happen to be living—that despite our circumstances, no key ingredient of happiness is missing. With this sense comes a diminished level of anxiety; we no longer need to obsess over the things—a new car, a bigger house, a firmer abdomen—that we mistakenly believe will bring lasting happiness if only we can obtain them. Most importantly, if we master desire, to the extent possible to do so, we will no longer daydream about living the life someone else is living; instead, we will embrace our own life and live it to the fullest.

Sounds simple enough. Yet we face a powerful headwind. Modern culture and our own heritage have programmed us to want ceaselessly, spend liberally, and compete for resources in order to keep up with the Joneses. Millions today suffer from so-called "status anxiety."

This prison, however, is entirely self-imposed. The key is right between our ears. We can make the conscious choice to turn our backs on the consumptive lifestyle and live simply, happily, and with dignity.

Some may call this idealistic. But then what is freedom if not an ideal?

CHANGE YOUR PERSPECTIVE, CHANGE YOUR LIFE

I recently received a note from a reader who yearns for an era long gone.

"There is so much corruption, so much greed, inhumanity, and despoiling of the planet," she wrote. "How I wish I could have lived in Europe a thousand years ago and enjoyed the beautiful medieval churches, the pageantry, the romance, the innocence and the spiritual passion. Life has never been more tragic and depressing than it is today."

She cannot be serious.

As someone who underwent a slightly uncomfortable but completely pain-free root canal last week, I'm not inclined to believe that things were necessarily better back in the "good old days." Yet her view is not uncommon, especially among those who marinate in TV news, where every act of war, natural disaster, or mass murder is delivered to your home each day—and cycled repeatedly—in living, high-definition color.

All things considered, life is pretty good today. A thousand years ago, by contrast, our ancestors lived a life of brutality, ignorance, and delusions, one that was—in Thomas Hobbes's famous phrase— "nasty, brutish, and short." It was an era of treachery, depravity, and barbarism. And if you happened to have been born into it, there wasn't a thing you could do about it.

Consider, for example, that during the Middle Ages:

- The vast majority of people were peasants who labored hard for a subsistence living.
- There was no social safety net, and hunger was often terrible. During famines, people devoured bark, roots, grass, even clay.
- Political freedoms were nonexistent. Despots, confronted by opposition, struck back with fury. Enemies of the king were routinely hanged, or drawn and quartered.
- Abduction for ransom was an acceptable means of livelihood for skilled but landless knights.
- It was an era of shocking everyday violence. Murders were twice as frequent as death by accident. (And English coroners' records show that only one of every hundred murderers was ever brought to justice.)
- Outlaws were seldom pursued. Anyone intrepid enough to travel between towns alone was on their own. Thieves, kidnappers, and killers simply hid in the forest and waited. In *A World Lit Only by Fire* (Little, Brown, 1993), historian William Manchester writes that, "honest travelers carried well-honed daggers, knowing they might have to kill and hoping they would have the stomach for it."
- Villagers were insular, staying close to home and marrying their neighbors. Local dialects were often incomprehensible to those living only a few miles away.
- The vast majority of men and women were illiterate and believed in magic, sorcery, and all manner of myths, routinely killing those whose superstitions were different from and, therefore, an affront to, their own.
- Witch-hunting was a popular sport. When a witch—often someone with a mental illness—was discovered, he or she was generally put to the stake.

- Sanitation was primitive; plumbing was unknown. Excrement, urine, and offal were simply flung out windows. This created rat and flea infestations. These, in turn, bred deadly pandemics.
- The Black Death is estimated to have killed up to 60 percent of Europe's population in the mid-1300s. At night, carts creaked through town streets, with gravediggers crying out, "Bring out your dead!"
- The Church—often doubling as the government—taxed workers without their consent, made war on its enemies, and offered to erase transgressions by selling indulgences.
- The threat of capital punishment was often used in religious conversions—and medieval threats were seldom idle.
- Death was also the prescribed penalty for hundreds of other offenses, particularly those against property.
- Courts required little evidence and were frequently merciless. A slanderer might have his tongue ripped out. A thief could have his hand cut off. (And the Middle Ages was not a good time be an adulterer.)
- Females were often married when they reached the age of 12. They seldom chose their mates. Parents usually arranged their children's marriages by their seventh birthday.
- The toll at childbirth was appalling. A young girl's life expectancy was 24 years.
- Men rarely reached their late 40s. If they did, their hair was as white and their backs as bent as an octogenarian's today.
- People marked time by the sun, the stars, and the changing of the seasons. There was no such thing as a clock or—apart from the Easter tables at the local church—anything resembling a calendar.
- To the average person, the Earth was flat, the population beset by demons, and the lands beyond the horizon a total mystery.

Today, we have a great bias, a widely accepted belief in the steady nature of progress. Yet for most of human history there was none. There are, for example, enormous differences between everyday life in 1810 and 2010. But between 810 and 1010 there were virtually none. We don't call it the Dark Ages for nothing.

Yet for most of human history and prehistory, life was even more brutal. You've seen those nature specials that show how predators routinely cull the old, the sick, and the weak from the herd? Our ancient ancestors all met this description at some point. Most of them lived short lives and suffered agonizing deaths.

Paleontologists have discovered, for instance, that the dens of saber-tooth tigers are sometimes full of human skulls, indicating we were relatively easy prey for 700-pound feral cats.

We all know today's world is far from perfect. Yet there is great satisfaction to be found doing some small part to make it better. And a bit of context might help you recognize that your life today is almost certainly better than it was for 99 percent of your ancestors.

If you want to improve your life, you might start by changing your perspective.

How Your World Will At Last Be Built

Every spring, millions of young men and women graduate from high school or college. As a friend or family member, you may be wondering what to give this year. Fortunately, I know just the gift your graduate wants.

Cash. (Yes, the same thing he or she wanted last year.)

However, it never hurts to throw in a lagniappe, something small but meaningful. Ideally, a graduation gift should encourage the graduate's dreams, with one eye on the past and the other on the future. That's why I like to tuck the envelope inside a copy of James Allen's timeless classic, *As a Man Thinketh*.

Born in Britain in 1864, Allen was a slight boy who suffered from poor health. In 1879, his father—out of work and facing insolvency—sailed to America, hoping to set up home and send for his family. Soon after arriving, however, he was robbed and murdered.

At age 15, Allen was forced to work as a factory knitter and later as a private secretary to support his family. He found the work mindless and unfulfilling but took solace in the evening among his books, often reading the Bible, Shakespeare, Tolstoy, and Whitman into the early hours. In 1903, he decided to devote himself full time to writing and that same year published his best-known book, *As a Man Thinketh*.

It's a slim volume, one that can be read in less time than it takes to snooze through the average commencement address. But it packs a powerful wallop. The essential premise is that, even if you're unaware of it, your underlying beliefs shape your character, your health, your circumstances, and, ultimately, your destiny. Your thoughts create your reality. You literally are what you think.

For this reason, you should be at least as meticulous about the ideas you feed your mind as the food you feed your body, since your life will largely become what your thoughts make it.

This is not to say that your mind alone can heal a serious illness, fix your finances, or change the world. Allen was no purveyor of New Age mumbo-jumbo. He was, above all else, a pragmatist and an advocate of hard work and effort. Yet he understood that every great undertaking begins with a particular state of mind.

Or, as he put it:

- Men are anxious to improve their circumstances, but are unwilling to improve themselves; they therefore remain bound.
- Let a man radically alter his thoughts, and he will be astonished at the rapid transformation it will effect in the material conditions of his life. Men imagine that thought can be kept secret, but it cannot; it rapidly crystallizes into habit, and habit solidifies into circumstance.
- All that a man achieves and all that he fails to achieve is the direct result of his own thoughts . . . a man can only rise, conquer, and achieve by lifting his thoughts. He can only remain weak, abject, and miserable by refusing to lift up his thoughts.
- As the plant springs from, and could not be without, the seed, so every act of man springs from the hidden seeds of thought, and could not have appeared without them.
- A man's mind may be likened to a garden, which may be intelligently cultivated or allowed to run wild; but whether cultivated or neglected, it must, and will bring forth.

■ Whatever your present environment may be, you will fall, remain, or rise with your thoughts, your Vision, your Ideal. You will become as small as your controlling desire; as great as your dominant aspiration.

Allen believed that circumstances don't make you. They reveal you. And while you cannot always command the situation, you can always command yourself.

Allen was hardly the first to recognize this. More than 2,300 years old, *The Dhammapada* begins with these words:

Mind is the forerunner of all actions.
All deeds are led by mind, created by mind.
If one speaks or acts with a corrupt mind,
  suffering follows,
As the wheel follows the hoof of an ox pulling a cart.

Mind is the forerunner of all actions.
All deeds are led by mind, created by mind.
If one speaks or acts with a serene mind,
  happiness follows,
As surely as one's shadow.

Allen—frail throughout his life—died of consumption at 47. His nineteen books have sold millions of copies—all of them are still in print—but most were published posthumously. Allen was never a wealthy man, at least in the traditional sense. Yet he believed deeply in his mission. His words have inspired men and women the world over. He was an enormous influence on followers like Dale Carnegie, Napoleon Hill, and Norman Vincent Peale.

More than anything else, *As a Man Thinketh* is a meditation. But it is also a revelation. Allen demonstrates how your life is enhanced and ultimately perfected by inward development. It's a good message for graduates just setting out to tackle the world—and not a bad reminder for the rest of us, either.

Others have preached a similar message, of course. But few have put it in more poetic language than Allen:

> He who cherishes a beautiful vision, a lofty ideal in his heart, will one day realize it. Columbus cherished a vision of another world, and he discovered it. Copernicus fostered the vision of a multiplicity of worlds and a wider universe, and he revealed it; Buddha beheld the vision of a spiritual world of stainless beauty and perfect peace, and he entered it.
>
> Cherish your visions; cherish your ideals; cherish the music that stirs in your heart, the beauty that forms in your mind, the loveliness that drapes your purest thoughts, for out of them will grow all delightful conditions, all heavenly environment; of these, if you but remain true to them, your world will at last be built.

The Most Important Job on Earth

My friends John and Nancy seem to have it all—great health, a beautiful family, a lovely home, plenty of money.

The problem? Their teenage kids are driving them completely nuts. My wife, Karen, and I recently spent a weekend with them at their home in upstate New York.

"It's so exasperating," complained Nancy. "They don't study. They stay out until all hours. We never know where they are or whom they're with. Of course, it's uncool for them to answer a phone call from their parents when they're out, but they won't even text us back. It's infuriating."

"Who is supplying them with the cell phones, the cars, and the money?" I asked.

"Well, who do you think?" she said, irritated just thinking about it.

I let it go at that. This conversation wasn't improving the evening and, besides, it was none of my business. But I couldn't help thinking how different things were growing up at my house.

I was one of four boys, fairly close in age. Like all boys, we acted up. Regularly. But if things started getting out of hand, my dad would threaten to "lower the boom." (I'm not sure any of us really knew what that meant, exactly. But from the look in his eye and the tone of his voice, it was clear that any "boom lowering" would not accrue to our advantage.)

That was when we were young, of course. But by the time you reach your teenage years, your relationship with your parents is pretty well established. And the way my brothers and I were raised, it would have been unthinkable to treat our mom or dad like a doormat.

Yet I have several friends who tell me they are experiencing pretty much the same thing as John and Nancy. They complain about their kids' poor grades and bad manners, their lack of respect and motivation, their general feeling of entitlement.

What I don't hear many of them saying is what role they as parents are playing in this state of affairs. Some of them might benefit from thinking a little less about fixing their kids and a little more about fixing the way they parent.

This is a touchy subject, I know. Everyone who has had a parent or a child—every living soul, in other words—is an expert on the subject. But could any job be more important?

As parents, it's our responsibility to educate our kids about the consequences of their behavior. This requires frequent communication (and sometimes punishment). Yet, according to a recent study, the average parent spends three and a half minutes per week in meaningful conversation with his or her children. No wonder so many kids are a mess.

What should parents communicate? For starters, guidance, understanding, and opinions about what is right and wrong. They need to stress the importance of education and hard work. Most of all, parents need to communicate that their love is unconditional, but their approval is not. Kids need to understand that eventually we all sit down to a banquet of consequences.

And it's a tough world out there. In 1940, for example, public school teachers claimed that the top seven disciplinary problems were talking out of turn, chewing gum, making noise, running in the halls, cutting in line, dress code infractions. and littering. Today, it is drug abuse, alcohol abuse, pregnancy, suicide, rape, robbery, and assault.

We can speculate on the reasons for this—violent and sexually charged television shows, movies, and video games; millions of homes without fathers; or other factors—but there is no denying the general coarsening of the culture.

Things really are tougher for parents now. But that only means good parenting is more important than ever. Yes, the schools will teach them reading, science, history, and math (or should). But it is up to us to teach our kids about important things like work, health, money, relationships, and integrity.

Part of this, of course, is setting an example. Your kids may not hear much of what you say. But they are watching what you do like a hawk. And while there are different approaches to parenting, in my view there are certain core values all kids should be taught:

- Respect your elders.
- Two ears, one mouth: Listen twice as much as you talk.
- When you give your word, keep it. Always.
- Look people in the eye when you talk to them.
- Stand up for yourself.
- Smile—it doesn't cost anything.
- If you don't have the time to do it right, how will you find the time to do it over?
- Spend less than what you earn. Save and invest the difference.
- Always say "please" and "thank you," "yes sir," and "no ma'am."
- Understand that the workplace is a hierarchy, not a democracy.
- If you borrow something, return it in better condition than you got it.
- Learn to think for yourself.
- If you don't know something, look it up.
- Cigarettes don't make you look cool. They make you look dumb.
- Drugs deliver short-term highs and lifelong lows.
- Sex is great, but unwanted pregnancies and sexually transmitted diseases are not.
- When you need help, ask for it. When others need help, give it.

- Doing the right thing always has its reward.
- If you mess up, apologize.
- Anything worth having is worth working for.
- Do what you love and the money will follow. (Not enough to make you rich necessarily, but enough to live an authentic life.)
- You don't need someone to complete you. Complete yourself.
- Successful people make a habit of doing the things unsuccessful people don't want to do.
- Hold the door for people—men and women alike.
- Accept responsibility for yourself.
- If you face a difficult decision, ask, "How will this make me feel about myself?"
- And never forget: Illegitimi non carborundum. (That's mock Latin for "Don't let the bastards grind you down.")

This is just a partial list, of course. Eighteen years is about how long it takes to learn what we need to know to become responsible adults. After all, most of us don't start by making good decisions until we've screwed up making so many bad ones.

In the end, parents only have so much ability to guide their children's behavior. Scientists still don't know how much we're shaped by nature versus our environment—and probably never will. But preparing our kids for adulthood is an awesome responsibility, the most important job on earth. So it behooves us—and the rest of society—to do it well.

Family is the cornerstone of society, the ultimate economic and spiritual unit of every civilization. Twenty-five hundred years ago, Confucius said, "The father who does not teach his son his duties is equally guilty with the son who neglects them." (This is just as true of mothers, especially today when so many kids are growing up without fathers around.)

Parenthood is and will always be a sacred task. When our kids are grown, they will have to deal with the consequences of their choices. No parent wants to live with regrets about what he or she "should have told them."

For most of us, our families are what we care about most. If I felt I had failed as a father, no success in any other area could make up for it. Yet each family is unique and no one will ever know the full reality of your situation.

Still, imperfect as we are, there is great satisfaction imprinting the best of ourselves on our kids and doing whatever we can to give them a leg up in our competitive world, knowing that, however we fell short in one area or another, we did the best we could.

ONE OF LIFE'S GREAT MIRACLES

Today, I'd like to say a few words about an extraordinarily important group of people. Pastor John S. C. Abbott said they have "as powerful an influence over the welfare of future generations as all other earthly causes combined." Historian Will Durant called them nothing less than "the nucleus of civilization." A Jewish proverb tells us that God created them because He couldn't be everywhere.

I'm talking, of course, about mothers.

Consider yours. Without her, you wouldn't be sitting here. Yet biology is the least of it, really. We would not have survived— not any of us—had we not been deeply loved and cared for in the first years of life.

Your mother is almost certainly your first memory. Yet even before memories, her voice created your first sense of security, her touch your first experience of affection, her constant care and attention the impression that we live in an idyllic world of limitless compassion.

We don't, of course, but isn't it a beautiful way to start? Your mother was your earliest teacher, your strongest advocate, your first love. And as you grew, so did her sacrifices. When you got sick, she took care of you. When you got in trouble, she took up for you. When you had some place to go, she carted you.

As one of four boys, I grew up convinced that my mother was born to be a cook, maid, nurse, counselor, referee, and, of course, chauffeur. (Peter DeVries once described a mother as someone whose role is "to deliver children obstetrically once, and by car forever after.")

In a large household, a mother's work is never really done. Friends, however, would sometimes remind my Mom how fortunate she was to have five strong men around to help out. Yet I'll never forget the time a neighbor dropped by during the playoffs. "Hey," he said looking at the five of us draped across the furniture, "how come all you guys are in here watching the game and your Mom is out front mowing the lawn?"

"I dunno," I remember saying. "I think she likes it."

How's that for appreciation?

In our home, my mom ran everything, organized everything, remembered everything, and, it's embarrassing to recall, *did* almost everything that needed doing, too. To top it off, she made—and still makes—a vegetable soup that is nothing short of spectacular. I don't mean it's tasty. I mean it is ambrosia.

If you're skeptical that anything truly stunning can be done with something as pedestrian as vegetable soup, it only means you've never tasted hers. No one who has would contest the claim. (See the Appendix for the recipe.)

A mother's influence is impossible to overstate. In many ways, it is incalculable. Her love—the strongest, blindest, and most exquisite—is neither acquired nor deserved. Nor can it ever be fully acknowledged.

Former U.S. Poet Laureate Billy Collins captures this sentiment beautifully in one of his poems:

The Lanyard

The other day as I was ricocheting slowly
off the pale blue walls of this room,
bouncing from typewriter to piano,
from bookshelf to an envelope lying on the floor,
I found myself in the L section of the dictionary
where my eyes fell upon the word lanyard.

No cookie nibbled by a French novelist
could send one more suddenly into the past—
a past where I sat at a workbench at a camp
by a deep Adirondack lake
learning how to braid thin plastic strips
into a lanyard, a gift for my mother.

I had never seen anyone use a lanyard
or wear one, if that's what you did with them,
but that did not keep me from crossing
strand over strand again and again
until I had made a boxy
red and white lanyard for my mother.
She gave me life and milk from her breasts,
and I gave her a lanyard.
She nursed me in many a sickroom,
lifted teaspoons of medicine to my lips,
set cold face-cloths on my forehead,
and then led me out into the airy light
and taught me to walk and swim,
and I, in turn, presented her with a lanyard.
Here are thousands of meals, she said,
and here is clothing and a good education.
And here is your lanyard, I replied,
which I made with a little help from a counselor.

Here is a breathing body and a beating heart,
strong legs, bones and teeth,
and two clear eyes to read the world, she whispered,
and here, I said, is the lanyard I made at camp.
And here, I wish to say to her now,
is a smaller gift—not the archaic truth

that you can never repay your mother,
but the rueful admission that when she took
the two-tone lanyard from my hands,
I was as sure as a boy could be
that this useless, worthless thing I wove
out of boredom would be enough to make us even.

You have the opportunity to honor the person whose place no one else can take, the woman to whom you owe your very existence. Perhaps she deserves not a card, a phone call, or an occasional box of chocolates, but an expression of genuine gratitude.

If she is around, cherish her. If not, cherish her memory.

Before you were conceived, she wanted you. Before you were born, she loved you. When you arrived, she was willing to sacrifice everything for you. Is this not one of life's great miracles?

The Power of Negative Visualization

When Norman Vincent Peale wrote *The Power of Positive Thinking* 60 years ago, he received a stack of rejection slips from publishers. Dejected, he threw the manuscript into the trash, forbidding his wife to remove it. She didn't. The next day, however, she took the manuscript, still inside the wastebasket, to a publisher who accepted it. The book became a foundation stone of the human potential movement, selling more than 20 million copies in 47 languages.

Much of Peale's homespun advice sounds quaint or even amusing to us today. But the book did a good job of articulating a basic truth: To a great extent, you create your world with your thoughts. Most personal achievements begin with an abiding faith that we can and will accomplish them.

Even realizing your goals, however, will not lead to lasting satisfaction. That's because human wants are insatiable. Most of us are trapped on what psychologists call the hedonic treadmill. We work to achieve what we desire. Those things satisfy us for a while. But we soon adapt to them and dissatisfaction returns. So next time we set the bar a little higher.

Our lives can easily become a pastiche of unfulfilled desires. We yearn for a better-paying job, more recognition, greater social status, a newer car, a bigger house, a firmer abdomen, or a sexier spouse.

Dissatisfaction is not all bad, of course. Desire can motivate us to achieve good things in our lives, too. But a continual sense of lack creates anxiety. It undermines our satisfaction. Peace of mind eludes us.

Fortunately, the ancient Stoic philosophers knew a technique to override the adaptation process and recapture the contentment we seek. It's called negative visualization.

Negative visualization is spending time each day imaging that you have lost the things you value most. Vividly imagine, for example, that your job has just been terminated, that your house—with all your possessions—has burned to the ground, that your partner has left you, or that you have lost your sight, your hearing or the use of your limbs.

This sounds bleak, I know. But the Stoics were onto something here.

They understood that everything we enjoy in life is simply "on loan" to us from Fortune. Any of it—all of it—can be recalled without a moment's notice. Epictetus reminds us, for example, that our children have been given to us "for the present, not inseparably nor for ever." His advice: In the very act of kissing your child, silently reflect on the possibility that she could die tomorrow.

The Roman philosopher Seneca advises us to live each day as if it were our last, indeed as if this very moment were our last. He's not suggesting that you drop your responsibilities and squander the day in frivolous or hedonistic activities. He's encouraging you to change your state of mind.

Most of us are already living the dream we once had for ourselves. Along the way, however, we become jaded, bored, numb to the blessings that surround us. The Stoics' goal is to wake us up, to make us appreciate what we have today.

Some will argue that negative visualization is fine for those of us who are happy, healthy, and prosperous, but how about the troubled, the less fortunate? Negative visualization works for them, too. If you have lost your job, imagine losing your possessions. If you have lost your possessions, imagine losing the people you love. If you have lost the people you love, imagine losing your health. If you have lost your health, imagine losing your life.

There is hardly a person alive who could not be worse off. That makes it hard to imagine someone who wouldn't benefit from this technique. Adaptation diminishes our enjoyment of the world. Negative visualization brings it back. It also prepares us for life's inevitable setbacks. Survivors of tornados, earthquakes, hurricanes, and other natural disasters, for example, may suffer terribly. Yet afterwards they often tell us that they were just sleepwalking through life before. Now they are joyously, thankfully alive.

No one should need a catastrophe to feel this way. You can attain the same realization through negative visualization. Moreover, it can be practiced regularly, so its beneficial effects, unlike a catastrophe, can last indefinitely. Try it and you'll see. It's perfect for when you're standing in line or stuck in traffic, time that would be wasted anyway.

By contemplating the impermanence of everything in your world, you can invest all your activities with more intensity, higher significance, greater awareness.

Norman Vincent Peale got it half right. Positive visualization helps you get what you want. Negative visualization helps you want what you get.

HOW TO RECLAIM YOUR LIFE

For years my wife, Karen, and I toyed with the idea of moving our family from Florida to Virginia. Three years ago, we finally took the plunge and rented a home near Charlottesville.

Our strategy was straightforward. If we liked it, we'd stay. If we didn't, we'd return to Florida knowing we had at least given it a shot.

The move itself turned out to be an easy one. With the new home furnished right down to the bath towels and wine glasses, we packed up a few suitcases, flew to Virginia, and threw our things in the closets. Done.

We quickly fell in love with Charlottesville and our new neighbors. We also learned something we hadn't counted on. All that stuff back home in Florida—the drawers, closets, cabinets, and storage bins overflowing with stuff we'd accumulated—we don't miss it one bit. In fact, leaving it behind was, in many ways, liberating.

Maybe this shouldn't have surprised us. According to Peter Walsh, the organization expert for *Clean Sweep,* a series on TLC, we, as a nation, are overwhelmed with "stuff" and drowning in the clutter. In some cases, it becomes overwhelming. Many of us have lost the ability to deal rationally and realistically with what we own.

It shouldn't be that way, of course. Your home is a metaphor for your life. It represents who you are and what you value. Eighteenth-century architect William Morris argued that you should not have anything in your home that is not beautiful or functional.

Yet many of us flunk this basic test. It's not just that our homes are filled with more things than we could possibly use. Roughly 10 percent of American households have items in one of the more than 40,000 self-storage facilities in this country. This is a 75 percent increase over twelve years ago, even though the size of the average American house has increased by half.

Some consumers have even been tempted to move to bigger homes—or purchase a second one—to house all their stuff. These folks are really flying the white flag.

Your home should be the place where you live, breathe, love, relax, and create. How can you do these things easily or well if you feel hemmed in? No wonder people often describe their clutter in terms of suffocation, as in "I can hardly breathe in the garage" or "I'm buried under the mess in my office."

There are severe health ramifications, too. Studies show that those who live with severe clutter are more likely to experience:

- Depression and anxiety-related illnesses
- Asthma, allergies, and other respiratory problems (thanks to mold, dust, and mildew)
- Headaches
- Sleeplessness
- Moodiness
- Low self-esteem
- Strained relationships
- Fatigue and low motivation

Aside from health issues, there are other good reasons to address this problem:

1. Clutter makes you forget your priorities. We all have important photographs, keepsakes, and memorabilia. If something is truly valuable, it deserves a place of honor and respect in your home. But ask yourself if you really have

the time—or interest—in savoring all those old magazines or the minutiae from your past buried in boxes in the attic or the garage?

2. Clutter jeopardizes your relationships. It causes tension among family members. It creates arguments about personal habits and disorganization. Some even confess that they rarely have visitors over because they are mortified by the clutter.

3. Clutter costs you money. We often hang on to unnecessary things because we "paid good money for them." But if you can't use them, give them to someone who can— or to charity. Remember, too, that unused possessions are often expensive to store, insure, transport, and maintain. (In worst cases, they create a fire hazard.)

4. Clutter steals your space. What good is your guest bedroom or home office if you can't use them or have to wade through? Clutter-free spaces create greater clarity, better moods, and positive energy.

5. Clutter monopolizes your time. You may think you don't have time to deal with all the junk you've accumulated. But what is it costing you in terms of lost items (including unpaid bills), stress, embarrassment, and aggravation?

6. Clutter prevents you from living in the now. If we become fixated on stuff from the past or things "we might need some day," we lose the only time we have to be alive: the present moment.

7. Clutter erodes your spiritual self. Your possessions should be tools to help you achieve your dreams, not hurdles that impede your progress. As Walsh writes in *It's All Too Much* (Free Press, 2006), "One of the main reasons I am so adamant about removing clutter is that I see how the space it occupies in people's lives seriously hinders their personal growth and development. It crushes them spiritually."

What's the solution? Reclaim your life by making some hard choices.

According to Walsh, organizational discipline is secondary. Getting on the right path begins with imagining your ideal life, the atmosphere you want to create in your home, and the relationship you want to have with those you live with.

Some of us have been surrounded by clutter for so long we don't see it. (Even if we can't see over it.) Others are apparently fine with it. Einstein, reputedly, was one of them.

However, most of us are not Einsteins. And we should be smart enough to realize that no one is going to resolve the mess but us—or, ultimately, our heirs. (And do you really want someone you love to inherit that headache?)

Clutter doesn't just block your space. It distorts your vision. It prevents you from living the life you've envisioned. It can stress you out and alienate you from your partner, your family, and your dreams.

So dig yourself out. And if you feel like you really can't deal with it, if the clutter is just too overwhelming, well . . . there is another house opening up down the street in Charlottesville.

Why It's One of the Seven Deadly Sins

I come from a long line of Braxtons.

My father's name is Braxton. His mother was Agnes Braxton.

My youngest brother is Carter Braxton. My older brother is Hugh Braxton. His elder son is Hugh Braxton III.

It's not unusual for a family name to be widely distributed. But for generations it has been a point of pride in our clan that we are direct descendants of Carter Braxton, one of the signers of the Declaration of Independence.

Aside from this single fact, however, I'd never known much about my illustrious forebear. That changed two weeks ago when I visited Monticello with friends and picked up a copy of *Signing Their Lives Away* (Quirk Books, 2009), a collection of biographical essays about the signers by Denise Kiernan and Joseph D'Agnese.

It was an eye-opener.

The Declaration, of course, is our nation's birth certificate, our most celebrated document, a model and inspiration for freedom movements and struggling peoples around the world and throughout history.

Taking my cue from John Trumbull's famous painting, I'd always imagined my ancestor, surrounded by leaders of the American Revolution, striding forward to sign his name—with an emphatic flourish—to that famous document at that historic moment.

Except that's not what happened. The document was circulated and signed at different times. According to Kiernan and D'Agnese, "Carter Braxton was the most reluctant of all Virginia's signers. Some say he was the most reluctant of the whole lot."

Perhaps that explains why his name is the last two words at the bottom of the parchment. (If you're buying your dream home or marrying the love of your life, put your John Hancock on the legal documents. If you're signing foreclosure papers or a receipt for certified mail, just offer your Carter Braxton.)

Still, as every schoolchild knows, the signers gave their assent to the proposition that all men are created equal, risking their necks and everything they owned. Carter Braxton was no exception. A wealthy landowner, he had much to lose, including plantations worked by hundreds of slaves.

This itself is nothing extraordinary. Most of the signers were aristocrats, and many of the Founding Fathers—including the author of the Declaration himself—were slave owners. Most had serious misgivings about it.

Thomas Jefferson wrote, "There is nothing I would not sacrifice to a practicable plan of abolishing every vestige of this moral and political depravity."

Benjamin Franklin called slavery "an atrocious debasement of human nature."

George Washington said, "There is not a man living who wishes more sincerely than I do to see a plan adopted for the abolition of slavery."

Carter Braxton wrote, "I am told there is a great trade carried on from Rhode Island to Guinea for Negroes and I should be very glad to enter into partnership with some gentleman for a voyage or two and have [the slaves] sent here where I believe they will sell as well as anywhere."

He further offered that, "The Gold Coast slaves are esteemed the most valuable and sell best. The prices of Negroes keep up amazingly. They have sold from 30 to 35 sterling a head clear of duty all summer."

Apparently, Carter Braxton believed that all men are created equal. But some are worth more at the point of sale.

"Despicable as they are," write Kiernan and D'Agnese, "Braxton's surviving letters help historians shed light on the unsavory world of slave trading."

Historical research further reveals that as late as July 1, 1776, Braxton opposed American independence. He wasn't just reluctant to break with Britain. Turns out he was uncomfortable with the very idea of democracy. Yet he intensely disliked the Crown picking his pocket.

This intelligence makes a letter from the "Descendants of the Signers of the Declaration of Independence" ring a bit hollow:

> The fifty-six Signers of the Declaration of Independence were inspired by as high a patriotic purpose as humanity has ever known. . . . It is, therefore, extremely fitting, that the direct lineal descendants of the men who inscribed their names upon the first page of the history of the United States of America should form an association."

Yes, well . . . whatever. Pride isn't one of the deadly sins for nothing. And some family trees could use some trimming.

Personally, I'd rather take my inspiration from Abraham Lincoln, who said, "I don't know who my grandfather was; I am much more concerned to know what his grandson will be."

Incidentally, Carter Braxton was nothing if not prolific. He had 18 children. If each of them had 2 children who survived to adulthood, and each in turn had 2 children of their own, and so on down the line, there are more than 146,000 direct descendants of Carter Braxton alive today. Hardly an exclusive club, whatever the benefits of membership.

Of course, it's fun to have distinguished friends or relatives or ancestors. But the glory belongs to them, not to us. Perhaps our responsibility is not to recite their accomplishments, but to work at becoming worthy ancestors ourselves.

As short story writer Dana Burnet once said, "I'd rather have an inch of dog than miles of pedigree."

THE RULING PASSION OF THE NOBLEST MINDS

Americans don't talk much about honor every day.

I'm not referring to awards bestowed for exceptional merit, but honor itself. At its simplest, honor is the good opinion of others, the natural consequence of character, integrity and fair dealing. Yet the word sounds faintly musty to some. Or, worse, judgmental. Author James Bowman even argues that we live today in what he calls a "post-honor society."

Let's hope not.

Wealth, fame, and reputation are things that must be won. Honor, by comparison, must not be lost. More than 2,000 years ago, the Roman poet Juvenal declared there is no iniquity greater than preferring life to honor and losing all that makes life worth living. His contemporary, Publilius Syrus, agreed, asking "What is left when honor is lost?"

Yet over the past fifty years or so, our culture has changed. Some people feel justified in doing their own thing, even if it means being unpleasant or disrespectful. They imagine it warns others they can't be trifled with. More often, it is simply boorish behavior. Rudeness is the weak man's imitation of strength.

An NBA star, for example, pushes a man through a plate-glass window and proudly proclaims that he is "not a role model." (No argument here.) Corrupt and dishonorable politicians believe they can rehabilitate their careers with a tearful confession and a public apology. And scoundrel-supreme Bernie Madoff lived high on the hog while bilking his clients out of their life savings, even stealing $15.2 million from the charitable foundation of holocaust survivor Elie Weisel. You can't get much lower than that.

Columnist George Will once observed that parents used to raise their children to adopt the values of the culture, but today they struggle to prevent them from adopting them. That's unfortunate, especially since the country was founded by men and women who sought not wealth and celebrity above all else, but something very different.

In letters to one another, the Founding Fathers often wrote, "act well your part." This was shorthand. Classically educated, they were referencing Alexander Pope's famous lines, "Honor and shame from no condition rise; Act well your part, there all the honor lies."

These weren't just words. They were ideals. Alexander Hamilton, who fought a fatal duel with Aaron Burr in 1804, described honor as "the ruling passion of the noblest minds." John Adams called the desire for distinction the "great leading passion of the soul." In many ways, this thirst defined them. In the Declaration of Independence, they famously pledged not just their lives and fortunes but their sacred honor. Personal integrity wasn't just essential. It was hallowed.

This is not an exclusively American quality, of course. The same sentiment echoes down through history. Nineteenth-century German statesman Otto von Bismarck said, "Gentlemen, my honor lies in no-one's hand but my own, and it is not something that others can lavish on me; my honor, which I carry in my heart, suffices me entirely, and no-one is judge of it and able to decide whether I have it."

Honor means standing up for the right principles both personally and as a nation. Soldiers are sometimes called upon to risk "the ultimate sacrifice." Yet pacifism and misplaced idealism have eroded the value of honor in some quarters. You hear this clearly in the absolutist slogan "War is never the answer."

Not so, unfortunately. Mohandas Gandhi and Martin Luther King were successful in their nonviolent campaigns for justice precisely because they dealt with humane, democratic governments. Against a more ruthless adversary, nonaction in the face of evil can be cowardice . . . or suicide. You can be sure that Hitler, Stalin, and Mao loved pacifists. (Especially with lemon and butter.) Bin Laden was emboldened to strike the United States on 9/11 precisely because our response to his previous attacks on American targets overseas was tepid.

Who we are still depends a great deal on what we are prepared to stand up for—and our willingness to actually stand up for it. We should never cease to honor such sacrifices.

Aside from patriotic honor, there is the everyday matter of personal honor. Do we treat others fairly? Do we carry ourselves with dignity? Do we speak respectfully of those people and institutions that deserve respect? Do we act with courage and personal integrity?

At FreedomFest in Las Vegas two years ago, psychologist Nathaniel Branden gave a talk on self-esteem. Self-esteem, he said, is not about looking in the mirror and saying, "I'm so special, aren't I wonderful?" Nor, he argued, is self-esteem something that is a gift of nature. It has to be cultivated. It has to be earned.

To illustrate the point, he told a story about his friend and fellow author Charles Murray. On a trip to California to visit Branden, Murray—an avid wine collector—was shown a rare and exorbitantly priced Cabernet at a local wine shop. He looked at it admiringly but told the owner the cost was prohibitive.

When he arrived back at Branden's home, however, he discovered that the storeowner had mistakenly sold him the expensive wine at the price of the modest bottle he had selected. So he rode back to town to return it. The store owner was both relieved and astonished. He had quickly recognized his mistake, but since Murray was an out-of-towner and had paid in cash, he felt certain he would never see him again.

Back at Branden's home, Murray conveyed his own disbelief. "I don't understand his surprise," he said. "If I had kept that bottle of wine, I wouldn't have liked the way that made me feel about myself."

Finishing the story, Branden paused and looked out at the audience. "That," he said emphatically, "is self-esteem."

Perhaps. But I prefer to think of it as honor.

PART TWO

———————

WEALTH BEYOND MEASURE

What does it mean to be truly wealthy?

Polls show that most Americans equate wealth with a high income. (And for some reason $250,000 seems to be the level that demarks "rich" these days.) This view is understandable. Greater income creates opportunities to have or experience more. Yet earned income is often a poor indicator of wealth. Apple CEO Steve Jobs, Citigroup CEO Vikram Pandit, Google CEO Eric Schmidt, Yahoo! CEO Jerry Yang, and Oracle CEO Larry Ellison are among the world's richest men. Yet they all receive annual salaries of $1.

A moment's reflection will demonstrate that wealth is better determined by a balance sheet than an income statement. It is generally a high net worth, not a high salary, that creates financial independence.

However, it is certainly possible to live a rich life without a lot of money or financial security. I know. I lived one for many years after college. Those days were supremely happy, even though I earned a modest living, had almost no savings, drove a beat-up Volkswagen (the stereo was worth more than the vehicle), and shared a home with friends since none of us had enough to live on our own. Of course, deprivation is easier to endure when you are young. And this is even truer if you have never tasted affluence.

No one can be happy for long in poverty, but it takes more than money to create a rich life. As I mentioned earlier, decent health, a few close friends, and someone to love—at a bare minimum—are necessary to make most of us feel as though we are living *the good life*.

Yet there is another essential ingredient to a rich life: *a wealth of interests*. The more you look outside yourself and your immediate concerns, the more you will find to love in this world. Your life becomes more interesting. I have just a passing interest in baseball, for example. But I could listen to columnist George Will wax enthusiastic about the national pastime all day. His passion is infectious.

I admire great pieces of art but I am no expert. That is why I so enjoy the books and documentaries of Sister Wendy Beckett, a British nun and art expert. I used to spend a few minutes each evening studying the pictures in her art books, noticing and drinking in everything I could before reading her commentary. Without exception, she made me notice things I simply hadn't seen before. I liked that.

What follow are a handful of essays on a few of my own interests. On some of these topics, like reading and music, I tend to have a fairly high level of knowledge. In other areas, like poetry and wine, I'm just a dabbler. And one (my anti-interest)—the idiot box—makes me despair.

You may or may not share these interests. And that's fine. My goal here is just to express a few personal enthusiasms, and perhaps inspire you to pursue your own.

ARE YOU UNCURIOUS?

You may know hundreds of people. Yet how many would you describe as *fascinating?*

I've often wondered about these men and women. What gives them that indefinable quality, that magnetism, that makes them so enjoyable to be around? Some will say it's education, talent, money, humor or celebrity. But I think it's something within the reach of us all: curiosity.

Curious people are interested in the world and everything in it. They seek out new friends and novel experiences. They pay attention to what's going on around them and why.

Take Denny Zeitlin, for example. Zeitlin is a world-class jazz pianist and recording artist. He is also a practicing psychiatrist; a professor of psychology at the University of California, San Francisco; and, in my view, a fascinating individual.

I can say this with confidence even though I've never met him personally. I merely stumbled onto his website recently and was captivated by his essays and short videos on everything from wine collecting and bone fishing to mountain biking and travel. His quiet enthusiasm on all these subjects—not to mention jazz—is intoxicating.

(Feel free to browse around www.dennyzeitlin.com. And be sure to take a few minutes to watch both his wine cellar tour and his "Salt Water Adventures.")

Zeitlin is a man in love with life. His attitude is infectious. (And so is his music, incidentally.) He is filled with curiosity and a lust for learning.

We all start out that way, of course. But, too often, children are given rules and obligations that squelch their natural inquisitiveness. They are told to know their place, to avoid controversial topics, to stay away from strangers, and not to challenge their parents, teachers, or pastors.

"Curiosity killed the cat," we tell them.

Astronomer Carl Sagan once lamented that when a child asks a perfectly good question like "Why is the sun round?," it's not unusual for an adult to give a dismissive response like, "What do you expect it to be, *square?*"

(Of course, most adults are unaware that intense gravity pulls material toward the sun's center, forming a sphere. But there's never any shame in answering a question with, "I don't know. Let's find out.")

By the time they reach adulthood, many folks are already jaded or closed-minded. They tend to speak with, read, and praise only those people who share their own point of view.

When a personal view is challenged, of course, the instinct is to defend it (even if it might be wrong). In the process, however, we may miss the opportunity to learn something.

Other times, it is the desire for certainty that suppresses our natural curiosity. After all, why bother looking into a matter further when you've already got it all figured out?

Dr. Todd Kashdan, a clinical psychologist and professor of psychology at George Mason University, says lack of curiosity is a breeding ground for stereotyping and discrimination, ignorance, rigid conformity, inflated confidence, and dogmatism.

Uncurious people tend to see the world in black and white. People are good or bad. Choices are right or wrong. (And, indeed, sometimes they are.) Yet alternatives are not always that stark. Life comes in infinite shades of gray. And nothing demonstrates a low tolerance for ambiguity like a lack of curiosity.

High curiosity, however, opens us up to multiple perspectives. It is regularly tied to greater analytic ability, problem-solving skills, and overall intelligence.

Curiosity drove many of the world's finest scientists and explorers. Our greatest discoveries often come when we question authority, the status quo, or our own beliefs.

Curiosity is also what leads many of us—often late in life—to take up the guitar . . . or fly-fishing . . . or ballroom dancing . . . or visiting all 50 states.

And it is something that can be practiced. Often, it's just a matter of greater awareness. When you're making your schedule, what are you planning that you haven't tried before? When you're having a conversation, what opinions are you hearing that you haven't heard before? When you're traveling, what are you seeing that you haven't seen before?

Curiosity is essentially an attitude toward living. It shows we are interested in adding to our knowledge, our skills, our areas of competence. We are willing to break out of our routines and experiment with our lives.

When you're curious, you're energized. You're learning. Your focus goes beyond yourself and your own petty concerns. You're making discoveries, finding opportunities, adding to your quality of life.

Best of all, these pursuits don't just make your life more fascinating. They make *you* more interesting, too.

■ THE ROAD NOT TAKEN

In the first half of our nation's history, most Americans earned a living in tough, physical jobs like farming, mining, animal husbandry, forestry, or construction. But, today, we live in a white-collar world. Most of us do little physical labor. If we don't make a concerted effort to exercise, we get none.

Yet according to Dr. Barry Franklin, head of the Cardiac Rehabilitation Program at the William Beaumont Hospital in Royal Oak, Michigan, "Starting at the age of 20, we lose about 1 percent of our aerobic fitness each year. A walking program can improve that fitness from 10 to 20 percent in three months. That's the same as 10 to 20 years of rejuvenation."

Medical research shows that regular exercise helps fight off colds and flu, reduces the risk of chronic diseases, and slows the aging process. According to the American College of Sports Medicine, a brisk 30- to 45-minute walk five times a week lowers the risk of stroke 27 percent, reduces the incidence of high blood pressure by 40 percent, can reduce mortality and the risk of breast cancer by approximately 50 percent, lowers the risk of colon cancer by over 60 percent, reduces the incidence of diabetes by approximately 50 percent, reduces the risk of developing Alzheimer's by 40 percent, and can decrease depression as effectively as Prozac or behavioral therapy.

Inactivity poses as great a health risk as smoking—and contributes to heart disease, hypertension, arthritis, and osteoporosis. Even lean men and women who are inactive are at higher risk of death and disease. Yet the Centers for Disease Control and Prevention says 36 percent of U.S. adults don't engage in any leisure-time physical activity. That's unfortunate, especially since—no matter where you live—all you need are clear skies and a pair of comfortable shoes.

The benefits aren't just physical. Walking has always had a close association with poets, philosophers, and spiritual leaders:

- Ancient Japanese and Chinese philosophers meandered around lakes and mountains, preserving their thoughts in gemlike poetry.
- Jesus of Nazareth was an itinerant preacher who walked 40 days and nights through the wilderness of Judea.
- The lyrical ballads of the English romantic poets were composed on long strolls through the countryside.
- Thomas Jefferson wrote to his favorite nephew Peter Carr: "You must take at least two hours a day to exercise; for health must not be sacrificed to learning. . . . Walking is very important. Never think of taking a book with you. The object of walking is to relax the mind. You should therefore not permit yourself even to think while you walk, but divert yourself by the objects surrounding you."
- William Wordsworth is estimated to have walked 170,000 miles in his life and sparked a cottage industry of walking tours in England and Europe.
- Leaders of the American Renaissance—Walt Whitman, Henry David Thoreau, and Ralph Waldo Emerson—recommended long daily tramps. Thoreau wrote that he had "a genius, so to speak, for sauntering."
- In a letter to his niece Jette, existentialist Søren Kierkegaard wrote, "Do not lose your desire to walk; every day I walk myself into a state of well-being and walk away from every illness; I have walked myself into my best thoughts, and I know of no thought so burdensome that one cannot walk away from it."
- Wallace Stevens composed his poetry on daily walks between his home and his office in downtown Hartford. In his poem

"Of the Surface of Things," he wrote, "In my room, the world is beyond my understanding. But when I walk, I see that it consists of three or four hills and a cloud."

Walking is elemental, as basic a human activity as eating, breathing, and sleeping. It distinguishes us from the other primates, indeed from every other species on earth. More than 80,000 years ago, our great ancestors walked out of Africa and colonized the world.

For most of our history, walking wasn't a choice. It was a given. Walking was our primary means of locomotion. But, today, you have to choose to walk. We ride to work. Office buildings and apartments have elevators. Department stores offer escalators. Airports use moving sidewalks. An afternoon of golf is spent riding in a cart. Even a ramble around your neighborhood can be done on a Segway.

Why not just put one foot in front of the other? You don't have to live in the country. It's great to take a walk in the woods, but I love to roam city streets, too, especially in places like New York, London, or Rome, where you can't go half a block without making some new discovery.

A long stroll slows you down, puts things in perspective, brings you back to the present moment. In *Wanderlust: A History of Walking* (Viking, 2000), author Rebecca Solnit writes that, "Walking, ideally, is a state in which the mind, the body, and the world are aligned, as though they were three characters finally in conversation together, three notes suddenly making a chord."

Yet in our hectic, goal-oriented culture, taking a leisurely walk isn't always easy. You have to plan for it. And perhaps you should. Walking is good exercise, but it is also a recreation, an aesthetic experience, an exploration, an investigation, a ritual, a meditation. It fosters health and *joie de vivre*.

Cardiologist Paul Dudley White once said, "A vigorous five-mile walk will do more good for an unhappy but otherwise healthy adult than all the medicine and psychology in the world."

A good walk is anything but pedestrian. It lengthens your life. It clears, refreshes, provokes, and repairs the mind. So lace up those shoes and get outside. The most ancient exercise is still the best.

They Make Us All Richer

Last week, some friends and I were in Vienna and visited the Belvedere, a magnificent Baroque palace that is now an art museum.

My publisher, Julia Guth, is a fan of Austrian painter Gustav Klimt, a turn-of-the-twentieth-century artist who was once marginalized but is now considered a modern master. As some of his best-known work was on exhibit there, we decided to have a look.

The highlight was Klimt's most loved piece, "The Kiss," a remarkable 72-inch by 72-inch painting that depicts a couple, in various shades of gold and symbols, locked in an embrace and sharing a kiss against a bronze background. The painting, which now adorns everything from coffee cups to calendars, is one of the most recognizable icons of modern art.

I enjoyed the piece, but something else struck me. As our group stood admiring it, a young woman in the room turned and suddenly recognized the painting. Her mouth fell open and she stepped slowly forward, her right hand curling up to her heart. She stood in front of the painting for several minutes, wide-eyed and speechless. When we left the museum half an hour later, she was still anchored there.

What is it about art that shocks, amuses, provokes, or enchants us? Like language, art emerges spontaneously and universally across cultures, from the Paleolithic cave paintings of Lascaux to the experimental art of today.

Art is a quintessentially human activity. It separates us from the rest of the animal kingdom. Sure, we have intelligence, but other animals do, too, even crows. We have complex language, but so do dolphins and whales. Even our use of tools is not unique. More than 40 years ago, Jane Goodall discovered chimpanzees in East Africa extracting termites from their mounds with blades of grass. They were effectively "fishing" for dinner.

Only *Homo sapiens* has an aesthetic sense, a need for expression in words, music, painting, or sculpture, although no one really understands why.

Art objects are among the most opulent, extravagant, and glittering creations of the human mind. They expand our understanding of the world. They intensify experience and give us a sense of the sublime.

Art can be dangerous, too. Plato feared that immoral art would steer people away from the virtuous and the good. In his *Republic,* he recommends that the state censor the arts for the protection of the citizens. (Not one of his better ideas.)

A museum is a cathedral of contemplation, a place to discover riches of imagination and insight. "Art teaches nothing," said Henry Miller, "except the significance of life." Proust said, "Thanks to art, instead of seeing one world, our own, we see it multiplied, and as many original artists as there are, so many worlds are at our disposal."

Art surprises you, makes you see things in new ways. A particular work can stretch your perceptions and expand your mental capacities. It can purge emotions, clear your mind, edify and enlarge the soul.

Art means different things to different people, of course. I don't agree with those who insist you need to appreciate a certain artwork for the right reasons. There may be wrong reasons for disliking a piece of art, but there can't be a wrong reason for liking one. You might easily enjoy a particular landscape painting not because it exemplifies some school or movement, but because of its loveliness or realism. Or maybe it just reminds you of home. Interpretations are bound to vary.

We often see in pictures what we would like to see in our lives. We all enjoy beauty in nature and harmony in our relationships. Yet we can also admire pictures of war or tragedy or evil. These, too, are facets of life.

Some things can't be adequately verbalized. Art gives full expression to love, compassion, humor, delight in life, tenderness, self-sacrifice, and intimations of mortality, as well as confusion, alienation, terror, or sadness.

Artists with extraordinary skill probe the content of life and articulate strong emotions. They create a feeling of recognition and communion with others. It is more than just the sheer wonder of seeing something beautiful or new. A great artist stimulates our imagination. The action takes place in the theater of the human mind.

However, the *raison d'être* of art is to communicate not emotion but understanding. Indeed, art shares something important with science. Both are truth-seeking activities that attempt to probe the nature of reality and tell us about ourselves and our world. Success in each field depends on the creative originality of a few rare individuals who take imaginative leaps into the unknown. Is it possible to have a full understanding of life without some acquaintance with both?

Art expresses individuality—and not just the artist's. What you hang on the walls of your home or office reveals your interests, your passions. To a lesser extent, this is also true of clothing, jewelry, and makeup. Why does it create an awkward moment when two women show up at a dinner party wearing the same evening dress? Because the event is an opportunity for personal expression. Clothes can represent our taste and individuality, but that isn't easy when someone else is wearing the same thing.

Art isn't always practical. It is meant for aesthetic enjoyment, often expressed as art "for its own sake." And while only a few fortunate souls are able to create objects of enduring beauty, most of us have some corner of our souls that yearns for it.

What is it that enables some men and women to create truly great works of art? Most artists want to receive market value for their work, but few are motivated by money. In *Human Accomplishment* (HarperCollins, 2003), Charles Murray puts forward the idea that the greatest art was historically created against a backdrop of "transcendental goods"—a belief that real beauty exists, there is objective truth, and the good is a value independent of human culture.

He notes that when the great Gothic cathedrals of Europe were built, many of the gargoyles and other ornaments were carved high on cathedral walls and behind cornices. Why would stonemasons hide their work in places where they could not be easily seen? Because they believed they were carving for the eye of God.

This notion clearly inspired many of history's greatest artists. Leonardo da Vinci painted to the greater glory of God. Michelangelo's devotion is well displayed on the ceiling of the Sistine Chapel. French author Andre Gide once said, "Art is a collaboration between God and the artist, and the less the artist does the better."

A true masterwork doesn't relate to just its time or our time but all time. It's this level of virtuosity that makes you stop and say, "I can't believe another human being did that."

Most of us enjoy being bowled over. In *The Art Instinct* (Bloomsbury Press, 2008), Denis Dutton writes, "Standing before a masterpiece you are in the presence of a power that exceeds anything you can imagine for yourself, something greater than you ever can or will be. The rapture masterpieces offer is literally ecstatic—taking you out of yourself."

That feeling clearly affected the woman I saw standing before "The Kiss" last week. Her encounter was a life-enhancing moment, perhaps even a spiritual one.

How fortunate artists are to possess these talents, to create objects of beauty and meaning, to have the power to move us, to make us feel what that young woman felt. They make all our lives richer.

ARE YOU READY FOR THE GRAND TOUR?

Last November, my wife, Karen, and I toured the Mediterranean with a group of friends, landing one day at the Great Pyramids at Giza.

It's not those marvels of the ancient world that I remember most vividly, however, or the majesty of the Sphinx, or the sweep of the desert beyond. It's the camel abduction.

On the way to the pyramids, our guide told us to keep a wary eye on the local peddlers. "Having someone take a photo of you in front of the pyramids should cost a dollar," he said. "A short camel ride is about three dollars."

Minutes later, as I was gazing up at the imposing Pyramid of Khufu, an older gentleman invited me to take a jaunt on his camel, a mangy beast who was, unfortunately, standing just upwind. As I looked on with mild interest, he whistled for the animal to kneel down.

The next thing I knew he was firmly escorting me onto the saddle and whistling for the camel to rise. Our group laughed and cheered as the camel driver led me off toward a rocky outcrop 80 or so yards away.

As soon as we were out of sight, however, the driver brought the camel to a halt and I was quickly surrounded by 8 or 10 Arab men shouting angrily at me in broken English to pay them each $20 for the ride—now!

I said no and told the camel driver to take me back. He turned away as if he couldn't hear me.

The group of men pressed in tighter, feigning greater anger, as if I had somehow stiffed them all for the ride, which had so far lasted about 45 seconds. "Pay us now!" they shouted again, their hands stretched upward.

We were at an impasse. I wasn't about to pull out my wallet in front of this pack of hyenas. And I was too high up and boxed in to jump down. The men continued shouting and waving their arms. I shook my head and sat on my wallet like Jack Benny, wondering how this was going to play out.

About then, a fellow tourist wandered by, recognized what was going on, and barked at the men to back off. "He said he would pay you," he insisted. "Let him go!"

At this, the Arab men melted away and the camel driver turned and led me back.

I'm sure this incident would have infuriated some, but I was more amused than rattled. I had never sensed any real danger. The men didn't threaten violence or brandish any weapons. This was sheer intimidation, a tawdry little shakedown, a reminder that Egypt is not Des Moines.

Back home, I discovered that friends and colleagues were only vaguely interested in the ruins of ancient Greece, the history of Jerusalem, or the serene beauty of the Amalfi coast. "Tell us again about the camel abduction," they said.

Apparently, it was the highlight of the trip.

Not all travel is a success. With expectations high, things can go awry, especially in a foreign land. But even the occasional bad incident makes a good story. (And, perversely, the worst trips make the best ones.)

Most of my travel abroad, however, has not only been great fun but the best part of my education. This idea was once widely accepted.

In his "Essay Concerning Human Understanding," John Locke argued that we absorb knowledge from our immediate environment.

If you spend too much time in one place, you can "use up" its educational value. In order to grow, you must change locales.

In Victorian England, for example, travel abroad was more than just a mark of privilege. A "change of scenery" was a mandatory part of an upper-class education. The Grand Tour was the capstone of scholarship.

It was a rite of passage that marked a superior understanding of the world. Young aristocratic gentlemen (and later young ladies) set out from the white cliffs of Dover for the Continent with their personal tutors in tow to gain knowledge from the worlds of classical antiquity and the Renaissance, to understand the cultures and ideas that underpin Western Civilization.

Of course, the urge to travel—to open our minds and move beyond the familiar—is as old as mankind itself. It drove our ancestors out of Africa and around the globe. It motivated the ancient Romans to visit Verona's amphitheater and Athens's Acropolis. Philo of Byzantium was already listing his Seven Wonders of the Ancient World in the third century BC. The spirit of adventure, the quest for understanding, and, of course, the dream of great riches pulled Marco Polo to the East and men like Columbus and de Soto to the West.

Travel broadens the mind, increases tolerance, and connects you with fellow human beings. The more we understand others, the better we understand ourselves.

There are good people and unusual sights everywhere you go. Venture widely enough and you'll enjoy exotic foods, extraordinary architecture, and jaw-dropping landscapes.

Exploring the world is like attending a classroom without walls. It enriches and changes you. The only requirements are patience, curiosity, and a bit of money. (A traveler's tip: Pack half the clothes you think you'll need and twice the cash.)

Travel abroad fills in the gaps in our knowledge, dispels our preconceptions, and offers endless surprises. Those who forego the opportunity really don't know what they're missing.

It's sad to go through life thinking foreigners are just strangers who dress oddly, eat bizarre foods, speak in incomprehensible tongues, and drive on the wrong side of the road. As Mark Twain observed, "Travel is fatal to prejudice, bigotry and narrow-mindedness." A voyage abroad teaches acceptance and humility. When you travel, you are the stranger. You are the foreigner.

Your kids and grandkids should discover this, too, beginning with travel closer to home. Years ago, I became mildly nauseated by all the toys and games my son and daughter were receiving on their birthdays and at Christmas. A trip—even if it's only to the local fair or the town next door—is a far better gift. For kids, every outing is an adventure. Why not spend your time and money collecting memories instead of more stuff?

It doesn't need to be some place exotic, especially when they're young. Just make for the horizon and see what's out there. Traveling without knowing where you are going, without having any particular destination in mind, is one of life's great pleasures.

Of course, there are plenty of resources to get your mind working on places you've never considered. One of my favorites is *Journeys of a Lifetime: 500 of the World's Greatest Trips,* a lavish volume put together by National Geographic. Another handy guide is the best seller *1,000 Places to See Before You Die* by Patricia Schultz. It's a fine way to investigate destinations both on and off the beaten track. I've gotten in the habit of taking it with me on business trips to make sure I don't miss the local sights and events. (If you're on a tight budget or unable to travel overseas, there's even a version dedicated solely to the United States and Canada.)

In short, travel broadens our perspective and sharpens our view of the world. Rather than imagining how things may be, we see them as they truly are. Your mind becomes more tolerant, your heart more magnanimous, your opinions better informed. And once your perspective is enlarged, it never shrinks back to its original state.

Some people make a pledge to visit all 50 states, or all seven continents, or fulfill some other checklist. And that's fine. Your ultimate goal, however, is not a place but a new way of seeing things.

THE QUINTESSENCE
OF LIFE

Sunday, I attended a recital at the Frick Collection in New York.

Classical pianist Rustem Hayroudinoff, a good friend and Chandos recording artist, dazzled the audience with a program of preludes and fugues by Chopin, Shostakovich, Franck, and Rachmaninoff. The audience was clearly moved by the power of his performance, jumping to their feet and cheering enthusiastically at the end, many shaking their heads in disbelief. Over dinner afterwards, I told Rustem I'd never heard him sound better.

The next day, however, I received an e-mail from a friend who insisted the music left him befuddled. Classical music is only mildly interesting, he wrote. It has "no theme, just rambling in an unpredictable way."

He couldn't be more mistaken. Yet there are countless others who share his view and have little or no taste for great music. Just look at industry figures. Classical music makes up less than 3 percent of industry sales. Radio and television programming are off sharply in recent years. Ticket sales are down. At least 17 orchestras have closed in the past 20 years.

But it is too early to sing a requiem. The American Symphony Orchestra League observes that there are approximately 1,800 orchestras in the United States giving roughly 36,000 concerts a year, 30 percent more than in 1994. Many cities have built or are building state-of-the-art performing arts centers. (I particularly enjoy performances at the Meyerson in Dallas.) Internet deep-catalog shops like arkivmusic.com offer virtually any CD in print. And classical music now makes up 12 percent of sales on iTunes, four times its share of the CD market.

Today, we have a breadth and ease of access to classical music far greater than what our parents had, let alone earlier generations. (Bear in mind, music was not recorded until about 100 years ago or even accurately notated until a few hundred years before that.)

Yet many remain uninterested. Why? Some will lay the blame on the disappearance of music education from public schools. Others will point to the increasing vulgarization of popular taste. But millions are still drawn to this music. The immortal works of history's greatest composers are among humanity's crowning achievements, transcending geographical boundaries, language barriers, and differences of politics and religion.

Music is intelligible but untranslatable, the most abstract and sublime of all the arts. Schopenhauer felt music expresses "the quintessence of life," passion, love, and longing. English essayist and scholar Walter Pater declared that all art aspires to the condition of music. Without music, Nietzsche concluded, life would be a mistake.

Music is the universal language of emotion, bypassing the intellect and tackling the heart directly. Making music is one of the fundamental activities of mankind, as characteristically human as language or drawing. It has existed everywhere in all cultures. (Even Paleolithic cave paintings depict people singing and playing music.)

Music goes further than pictures, deeper than words. It can move us, lift our spirits, change our mood, get us dancing. Our auditory systems, our nervous systems, are exquisitely tuned for music. Even listeners who can't read musical notation and who have never attempted to learn an instrument are deeply affected by it. Yet classical music confounds many. Raised on the verse-chorus-verse simplicity of pop music, they aren't sure what to think—or feel.

Fortunately, appreciating classical music is a skill that can be cultivated. By learning something about composition, for example, we can more thoroughly understand and enjoy great music. All it requires is your attention, some imagination, and a bit of abstract thinking.

Some, of course, will insist they have no time for this music. They are so busy getting and spending—so caught up in the pursuit of conventional success—that fine art and great music are completely absent in their lives. That's unfortunate because greater material wealth doesn't necessarily make life more worth living. And classical music can provide a welcome escape from the stress and frustrations of everyday life.

The free market and today's recording technologies allow us to own and enjoy, at minimal cost, the finest works of history's best composers. And we should. Scientists tell us this music affects our brain chemistry. There is a power and magic here that shames self-absorption and makes personal preoccupations look petty. Much of the music of Haydn, Mozart, and Vivaldi, for example, can dispel irritation, banish a mood of depression, and deepen your appreciation of life.

Recognizing this doesn't make you a music snob, incidentally. I grew up listening to rock and pop music. I still enjoy them.

But I disagree with the notion that popular music is on par with classical, that it's all just a matter of personal preference. Embedded in that mind-set is hostility to the idea that discriminating judgments can be made in art, that hierarchies of value exist, or, indeed, that there is such a thing as objective truth.

I'll never forget the time I told my college music professor that I didn't think the music of Robert Schumann was all that great. He peered over his glasses a few seconds and then replied, "That says more about you, Mr. Green, than it does about Schumann."

By the time I pulled the arrow out of my forehead, I had reached an epiphany of sorts. Popular music is like a hamburger and fries. (And sometimes a burger and fries are just what you want.) The great masterworks, however, are linguine and white clam sauce with parsley, black pepper, crushed oregano, and finely minced garlic, with a smattering of Parmesan cheese.

You may not have developed a taste for it. But that doesn't mean it's not objectively better.

Encounters with the great musical minds allow us to experience transcendent beauty. They also allow us to live lives that are less circumscribed, less trivial, more imbued with meaning.

As the poet Joseph Addison wrote, fine music is "the greatest good that mortals know, and all of heav'n we have below."

WHAT WOMEN REALLY WANT

Sigmund Freud is considered one of the great thinkers of the early twentieth century. He discovered the unconscious mind, treated mental disorders, interpreted dreams, pioneered psychoanalysis, and did important neurological research into cerebral palsy.

Yet late in life he still confessed, "The great question that has never been answered, and which I have not yet been able to answer, despite my 30 years of research into the feminine soul, is 'What does a woman want?'"

Hapless men have speculated on this subject for millennia. Occasionally, we think we've stumbled on the answer. Women want love, affection, honesty, beauty, commitment, kindness, security, empathy, and appreciation. At least, most of them do. Yet this is still the wrong answer. What women truly want—watch them nod in agreement—is chocolate.

Ninety-nine percent of women polled say they enjoy it. (The other 1 percent, apparently, can't be trusted.) Men don't exactly turn up their noses at the stuff, either.

Chocolate is a $60 billion global industry today. The average American consumes 12 pounds of chocolate per year (58 million pounds are sold around Valentine's Day alone). And the Swiss, Austrians, Germans, Irish, British, Norwegians, Danes, Belgians, Swedes, and Australians all eat more than we do.

The confection has a long and storied history. Mesoamericans first cultivated cacao beans more than 3,000 years ago. The Mayans made it into a sacred drink, offered it in tribute to kings, and placed it in the tombs of the nobility so they could savor it in the afterlife. Common folk enjoyed it, too. Five hundred years ago, Spanish historian Oviedo y Valdes wrote, "It is the habit among Central American Indians to rub each other all over with pulpy cocoa mass and then nibble at each other." (No word about the resulting population explosion.) By the time Columbus arrived, cacao beans were the coin of the realm. And it wasn't long before Europeans back home were clamoring for it.

Today, the world produces over 3 million tons of cacao beans a year. But the crop—called "the elixir of the gods" by Swedish botanist Carolus Linnaeus and (ahem) my wife—is demanding. It requires a long rainy season and deep, rich soil within 20 degrees of the equator. And, like many of its advocates, cacao can be fickle. It requires high humidity, constant pruning, and protection against pests.

But it's worth it. And not just for the flavor. It turns out that, chemically speaking, chocolate is a near-perfect food.

A 2006 Johns Hopkins study showed that eating a little bit every day is good for your health. Cacao helps the body process nitric oxide, a compound for healthy blood flow and blood pressure. It contains antibacterial agents that fight tooth decay. The cocoa butter in chocolate contains oleic acid, a monounsaturated fat that raises good cholesterol. Chocolate also contains phenyl ethylamine (a mild mood elevator) and flavonoids that keep blood vessels elastic. Studies show that eating a little bit of chocolate once a week can reduce your risk of stroke by 25 to 45 percent.

Milk chocolate, however, is high in calories, saturated fat, and sugar. If you're eating it solely for health reasons—and whom are you kidding?—stick with dark chocolate. It contains more cacao and less sugar.

Cacao is a storehouse of natural minerals. It's a source of copper in our diet and an antioxidant on the order of green tea, protecting against heart disease and helping alleviate stress. Dark chocolate is rich in polyphenols, as is red wine. Chocolate can provide an energy boost, too. It is an easy way to fuel up before, and during, intense activity.

Plus, there are psychological benefits. Chocolate increases serotonin production and releases endorphins. It contains phenylethylamine, the same chemical that is released in the brain when we fall in love. Eating chocolate gives many women a natural "high," a feeling of ecstasy.

Some researchers even believe chocolate slows the aging process. (I'm skeptical but what have you got to lose?)

We shouldn't take these health claims too far, of course. Physicians rarely say "take a candy bar and call me in the morning." There is no such thing as prescription-strength chocolate.

But perceptions are changing. When I was a kid, conventional wisdom was that chocolate made you fat, gave you pimples, and ruined your teeth. Modern science is tempering this view.

And the rewards aren't just physical. They are also aesthetic. Chocolate is the final touch of elegance at the end of a good meal—or a special treat to be savored.

Even in tough times, chocolate is a luxury you can afford. Pastry chef Norman Love points out that "You can buy two bars of the best chocolate in the world for $5. The queen of England can't buy any better chocolate than you can."

Premium chocolate is only slightly less nuanced than fine wine. It is recognized by its aroma, strength, and balance of taste sensations and interesting textures. It is a reminder to slow down, look, smell, taste, and take your time. Be grateful, one French gourmet says, "for what God and 2,000 years of civilization have allowed to land on your tongue."

Chocolate is something we all associate with the best part of childhood. It provides a feeling of well-being. It has clear health benefits. It doesn't just taste good. It helps you live longer. No wonder women find it only slightly less vital than oxygen.

So, instead of flowers or champagne, next time try bringing home a three-and-a-half-ounce bar of Ghirardelli Intense Dark Twilight Delight. And then step back. You don't ever want to stand between a woman and her chocolate.

That sort of thing never ends well.

An Incandescent Drop of American Fire

A few months ago, my family and I moved into a new home near Charlottesville, and a friend gave us the best housewarming gift ever: a hummingbird feeder.

It doesn't require much, just a place to hang it and a simple solution consisting of one cup of sugar to four cups of water. But the return on investment is large. Hummingbirds are a joy to watch. They are also opportunistic feeders. Once they discover what's on offer, they are there all the time, a continual source of enchantment.

With an ordinary feeder you may get bored with the same birds day after day—or grow tired of the Cold War with the local squirrel population. But hummingbirds never cease to delight.

These are not just the world's smallest birds. They are the smallest warm-blooded creatures on the planet. The largest species, the Giant Hummingbird, weighs seven-tenths of an ounce; the smallest, the Cuban Bee Hummingbird, just seven-hundredths.

They are marvels of miniaturization. Hummingbird nests are the size of half a walnut shell. A penny will almost cover the inside diameter. The two eggs in a typical clutch are the size of tic tacs.

And there is a good reason these birds spend so much time at my feeder. They have the highest metabolic rate of any creature on earth. Hummingbirds live their lives on the brink of starvation. They are able to store only enough energy to survive overnight.

Consider . . . a hummingbird flaps its wings up to 200 times a second. It takes up to 300 breaths a minute. Its resting heart rate is 600 beats a minute. And when a hummer flies, its heart may beat twice that fast.

Since they burn calories so furiously, hummingbirds must constantly refuel, often consuming more than twice their weight in small insects and nectar each day. A hungry hummer may visit more than 2,000 flowers between dawn and dusk. (This constant search is why it doesn't take them long to discover a new feeder.)

Researcher Crawford Greenewalt calculates that if a man used energy at a hummingbird's rate, he would need to eat 40 ten-pound sacks of potatoes or more than 1,000 Quarter Pounders a day. Remember that the next time someone remarks that you "eat like a bird."

Hummingbirds are fliers par excellence, moving at up to 35 mph and diving at nearly 60 mph. They can hover precisely for long periods of time, balancing perfectly, as if floating. No other bird can fly backwards.

You'd imagine that a creature that weighs a fraction of an ounce, has a tiny beak, and dines on nectar is a cream puff. Not so. Hummingbirds are highly territorial and protect their food supply with ferocity. I witness aerial dogfights in my backyard every day in the summer. Hummers won't hesitate to dive bomb other birds, butterflies—even unsuspecting humans—who wander too close to the feeder.

And the little buggers are fearless. They will buzz down for a sugar-water fix even if I'm eating lunch six feet away. If I don't see them or hear their distinctive high-pitched chirp, I know they have arrived when those beating wings make a sound like The Bumblebee from Hell has suddenly appeared behind my back.

With the days growing shorter, the hummingbirds will soon be off. By late October, they begin a nearly 2,000-mile migration to Central America. That includes a 500-mile marathon over the Gulf of Mexico, an 18-hour ordeal across open water, with no place to stop and nowhere to feed until landfall.

Ranging only from Alaska to the Andes, these are distinctly American birds. If you live east of the Mississippi, the ones you see outside your window are all ruby-throats. (Only the males have the characteristic red marking.) But you'll find several other species—of the nearly 350 known to exist—in the western United States.

On a trip to Telluride a few summers ago, a friend invited me over to his house one afternoon. Just beyond his back patio, he had strung a long line of hummingbird feeders. A great cloud of multicolored hummers swarmed around us, glittering in the sun. It was like entering Wonderland. I could hardly pay attention to the conversation.

Of course, hummingbirds have captivated men and women for hundreds of years. A Mayan legend says the hummingbird is actually the sun in disguise, here to court the moon. The Aztecs believed that every hummingbird was the spirit of a fallen warrior. And when early Spanish explorers encountered them, they called them *joyas voladoras,* flying jewels.

Hummingbirds have often captured the imagination of poets, too. In "Ode to the Hummingbird," Pablo Neruda rhapsodizes about a "flying spark of water, incandescent drop of American fire, flaming resume of the jungle, rainbow of celestial precision . . . a golden thread, a green bonfire . . . small, superlative being, you are a miracle, and you blaze."

What's so great about hummingbirds, really? It depends on who's looking, I suppose. To me, hummingbirds are magic in the air. I admire their energy and intensity, their vitality. There's something irresistible about these tiny creatures, speeding back and forth and then suddenly pulling up in midair, shining like an emerald.

Hummingbirds are one of Nature's most eye-catching creations, testimony that the universe is more mysterious and sublime than it needs to be. They are also a small reminder that life is rich, the most beautiful and exotic things can't be owned—and it's pretty darn great to be alive.

THE MOST CIVILIZED
THING IN THE WORLD

A few nights ago, my brother Carter invited me to a reception at the R. R. Smith Center in Staunton, Virginia to hear author James Gabler speak on my favorite American, Thomas Jefferson, and one of his great passions: wine.

Jefferson is best known as the nation's third president, the author of the Declaration of Independence, and the founder of the University of Virginia. But he was much more, a true renaissance man, fascinated by the whole range of human experience.

When wine entered his galaxy of interests, as it did on a trip to France in 1784, he began acquiring a depth of knowledge and appreciation of wines that no American of his time would rival.

He called wine "a necessity of life." Yet his interest went far beyond drinking it. Jefferson investigated grape varieties, soil, climate, fermentation, storage, shipment, and every other facet of viticulture. He exchanged hundreds of letters with horticulturalists, scientists, and wine dealers. He planted vineyards at Monticello and experimented with grape growing in his Paris garden on the Champs-Elysees.

Jefferson loathed what he called "ardent spirits" and believed whiskey was a pox on American families. He insisted that wine promoted good health and predicted that America, someday, would make wines every bit as good as those of France. He was right on both counts. Two hundred years later, it is well documented that moderate wine consumption increases "good" cholesterol and may help prevent heart disease and certain forms of cancer.

And the Paris Wine Tasting of May 24, 1976, shook the world. That was the day French judges did a blind tasting of top-quality chardonnays and cabernet sauvignons from France and California and rated the California wines best in both categories.

The United States is now one of the world's leading wine-producing, wine-consuming, and wine-exporting countries. All 50 states have commercial wineries. Jefferson's own Virginia bristles with more than 80. (I heartily recommend spending a fall afternoon at the King Family Vineyard near Charlottesville. Set at the foot of the Blue Ridge Mountains, it offers not only majestic views and some of the state's best wines but everything from picnic grounds to polo matches.)

Jefferson was hardly alone among the Founding Fathers in his love of wine:

- Benjamin Franklin, a notorious ladies' man and bon vivant, had a cellar of over 1,100 bottles.
- George Washington had a preference for Madeira and spoke of "that hilarity which a glass of good Claret seldom fails to produce."
- John Adams was another enthusiastic wine drinker. His letters show he ordered 500 bottles of French wine just before receiving word that he had been appointed America's first minister to England.
- And when James Monroe was elected to the presidency in 1817, Jefferson spent all but five lines of his congratulatory letter discussing recommendations for the new president's wine cellar.

Jefferson understood the importance of wine and entertaining. His account books reveal that during his eight years as president, he purchased over 20,000 bottles from Europe. Indeed, he spent $7,597 on wine in his first term alone, a substantial sum given that his annual presidential salary, including expenses, was $25,000.

Jefferson's fondness for wine did not diminish in retirement. Records from Monticello show that in the two-year period beginning in January 1822, Jefferson and his guests consumed more than 1,200 bottles. Although Jefferson drank wine daily, there is no evidence that he was ever accused of intoxication during his lifetime. (Although the scandal sheets accused him of plenty else.) By all accounts, he was a temperate drinker.

Jefferson was a champion of native grape varieties—more than 200 species grew wild in the woods around his home. But, due to the ravages of nature and his long absences, his vineyards at Monticello were a constant disappointment. Yet he never gave up on his wine experiments. In a letter to a friend he explained, "tho' an old man, I am but a young gardener."

No one had a more profound impact on the future of American viticulture than Jefferson. But he was no wine snob. Nor did he buy wine as an investment. He drank wine for pleasure. And he liked sharing his pleasure with others.

As a leader of the American Revolution, Jefferson helped bring freedom to his countrymen. In his tireless promotion of the benefits and enjoyment of wine, he was determined to bring them something else: civility, sophistication, and refinement.

Wine is the product of thousands of years of agricultural and cultural experimentation. It is older than recorded history, emerging from the early mists of civilization. Ancient Greek poets lavished praise on local wines. The Pharaohs' tombs in Egypt are filled with depictions of men and women drinking and carrying wine. Archaeological digs reveal wine drinking in the Mediterranean as far back as 6,000 BC. And it may have been enjoyed in China 1,000 years earlier.

Winemaking is old, in part, because it is simple. Ripe grapes are picked and crushed, and the juice is stored in an airtight container. Tiny one-celled organisms (yeasts) that exist naturally within the grapes gradually convert the sugar in the juice into alcohol, a process called fermentation. This simplification downplays the knowledge and skill a great winemaker brings to the process. But when conditions are right, there is no arguing the outcome: liquid art.

Galileo said wine is "sunlight, held together by water." Robert Louis Stevenson called it "bottled poetry." Omar Khayyam wondered what vintners buy that is one half so precious as the stuff they sell. And legend has it that when Dom Perignon experienced his first sip of champagne, he shouted, "Come quickly! I am tasting the stars!"

Fine wine is made for discriminating tastes. And it improves with age. (The older you get, the more you like it.)

A bottle of wine is made for sharing. The same can hardly be said of a bottle of beer. (And, unless you're Keith Richards, a bottle of liquor isn't meant for polishing off in a single evening.)

You don't have to be an expert to appreciate wine, any more than you need to master music theory to enjoy Beethoven's Ninth. It is simply one part of the good life. The right wine can make any get-together a special occasion. It can turn a good meal into a symphony. It makes every table more elegant, each day more civilized. It promotes relaxation, contentment, and the free flow of ideas.

Jefferson understood that wine could be as powerful an expression of culture as literature, painting, or music, and that drinking good wine with good food in the presence of good friends is one of life's most civilized pleasures.

It isn't necessary to find a fabulous vintage or buy some exorbitant bottle. As the British wine writer Oz Clarke observed:

> To pontificate, to let opinions rule your appreciation of wine and to be unable to feel, as the candles gutter and the moon rises on a warm summer night, that the wine on the table, however unsung and lacking in renown, is, for that short moment, perfection itself, is to miss the whole heart of wine—and of life too.

How to Eat Like a Zen Master

Two weeks ago, I suffered a home invasion—and not for the first time.

I had plopped down to watch Duke play Virginia, having just fixed a toasted ham and Swiss on rye, and a few minutes later, to my astonishment, my plate was bare except for a few crumbs and a spot of pickle juice.

The sandwich thief had struck again!

How clever of him to enter my home in broad daylight, steal the sandwich and dill spear right under my nose, then vanish without a trace. Wiping the Dijon mustard from my lips, I considered the suspects. . . .

Seriously now, how many meals have you eaten this way, so consumed by your plans for the day, the conversation at the table, or—worst of all—the drone of the Tube that you never really tasted the food?

Thich Nhat Hanh would not approve.

Who is he? Nhat Hanh is an expatriate Vietnamese monk and Buddhist Zen master who has spent his life advocating non-violence, setting up relief centers for refugees, ministering to the needy, establishing monastic centers, and authoring more than two dozen books on what he calls "mindful living." In 1967, Dr. Martin Luther King nominated him for the Nobel Peace Prize, telling the committee, "I do not personally know of anyone more worthy of this prize than this gentle monk from Vietnam."

Nhat Hanh insists that most of us in the West live mindlessly. We spend our days on autopilot, reminiscing about the past or, more often, endlessly planning for the future, even if that's only 10 minutes from now. By doing this, we miss our appointment with life. Because the only time we can be fully alive is in the present moment.

To change, we need only recognize that it is always now—and increase our awareness of what is going on within and around us. Sounds simple enough. But few actually do it. Instead, we live in a near-constant state of distraction, even when we sit down to eat. (And some, you'll notice, don't even bother to sit.)

Nhat Hanh says we can change this and turn mealtime into an art, a spiritual discipline, simply by following the Seven Practices of a Mindful Eater:

1. *Honor the food.* Start by unplugging all your daily distractions. Turn off the TV, your cell phone, and the laptop. Then take a moment to consider that everything you are about to consume—even the contents of your salad bowl—was recently alive and is about to provide your sustenance. Be grateful, too, for the many people who made this meal possible: the farmer who grew and harvested the food, the trucker who transported it, the shopkeeper who offered it, and your spouse or other individuals who may have worked hard to prepare it.

2. *Engage all your senses.* Before eating, make a practice of pausing. Notice the color, the smell, and the texture of the food. With your first bite, take an extra moment to savor each nuance.

3. *Serve modest portions.* Nhat Hanh recommends using a small dinner plate no larger than nine inches across. Modest portions are not only healthier, they are less wasteful and a small step toward a more responsible use of the planet's resources. It's hard to believe, but over 16,000 children in

the developing world still die every day from starvation, malnutrition, or hunger-related illnesses.

4. *Savor small bites.* This allows you to better enjoy the taste of the meal. It also improves digestion since the process begins with enzymes in your mouth breaking down the food.

5. *Eat slowly.* This will make you feel pleasantly satisfied sooner and help you avoid overeating. There is a big difference between feeling you have had enough and swearing you cannot eat another morsel. Set your fork down between bites. (Few people do this, I've noticed. Try it in a restaurant, and more often than not your server will try to whisk your plate away.)

6. *Eat regular meals.* Skip a meal and you're more likely to yield to fast-food restaurants and vending machines. Planning and sticking to regular meals—at least as much as your schedule allows—will enable you to eat more nutritious food, enjoy more satisfying company, and settle your body into a consistent rhythm.

7. *Eat a plant-based diet.* Buddhists like Thich Nhat Hanh claim this isn't just healthier, it is also easier on the environment and more compassionate toward animals. To the extent you do eat meat, studies show it's better to favor fish and poultry. My good friend Dr. John Reed, head of the Sanford-Burnham Medical Research Institute, loves a good steak. But he told me recently that he has given up red meat altogether. He says the increasing evidence of a connection between red meat and colon cancer is pretty scary.

To eat like a Zen master, you don't need years of training or hours spent in cross-legged meditation. You need only recognize your mindless habits and make an effort to change them.

Dine this way and you'll find that not only are your meals more enjoyable, you'll eat less, too. And studies show that caloric restriction is an important source of longevity.

Eating mindfully allows you to appreciate your food and its connection to the rest of the world. It makes you look and feel better. And it helps you live longer, too.

So try this Zen master's guidelines. See if you can make them second nature. And, who knows, you might never fall prey to the sandwich thief again.

THE SUBLIMEST ACTIVITY
OF THE HUMAN MIND

Like most investment analysts, I spend hours each day reading news articles, blogs, earnings reports, financial columns, and corporate websites. Ordinarily, I move through these as quickly as possible, scanning for a new insight here or a piece of evidence for or against an investment idea there.

It's not pleasure reading. My goal is to extract the information I need as quickly as possible.

Time spent this way is the very opposite of reading a poem. Great poetry forces you to slow down. It's not a race to the finish. It's a moment of leisure, a time to smile, brood, think, or reminisce.

Poetry is language at its most distilled and powerful, a way to draw the universal from the particular. Samuel Johnson called it "the art of uniting pleasure with truth." William Hazlitt said poetry is "all that is worth remembering in life." Carl Sandburg described it as "an echo, asking a shadow to dance."

But at the pace we live, who among us really has time for poetry? Not many, apparently. The National Endowment for the Arts released a report showing that in 2008 just 8.3 percent of adults in the United States had read any poetry in the preceding 12 months, the lowest tally in 16 years.

Some will argue that the problem is modern poetry itself: inaccessible, irrelevant, or just plain bad. That may be so in some cases. But you don't have to go for the new stuff. Most of us have read only a tiny fraction of the best poems ever written. Yet as strapped as we are for time, is it worth even bothering with these? After all, a poem won't make you stronger, fitter, richer, or better looking. It won't help you grow your business, cut your taxes, or beat the S&P 500.

However, it might deliver something else. U.S. poet laureate Kay Ryan said, "I like to think of my poems as cute mousetraps: innocent looking, but if you get too close you'll get your head snapped off."

That describes the feeling I got the first time I read James Wright's "Lying in a Hammock at William Duffy's Farm in Pine Island, Minnesota":

> Over my head, I see the bronze butterfly,
> Asleep on the black trunk,
> blowing like a leaf in green shadow.
> Down the ravine behind the empty house,
> The cowbells follow one another
> Into the distances of the afternoon.
> To my right,
> In a field of sunlight between two pines,
> The droppings of last year's horses
> Blaze up into golden stones.
> I lean back, as the evening darkens and comes on.
> A chicken hawk floats over, looking for home.
> I have wasted my life.

The reader gets a similar surprise when he reaches the end of Shelley's classic "Ozymandias":

> I met a traveller from an antique land
> Who said: "Two vast and trunkless legs of stone
> Stand in the desert. Near them on the sand,
> Half sunk, a shattered visage lies, whose frown
> And wrinkled lip and sneer of cold command
> Tell that its sculptor well those passions read
> Which yet survive, stamped on these lifeless things,

The hand that mocked them and the heart that fed.
And on the pedestal these words appear:
'My name is Ozymandias, King of Kings:
Look on my works, ye mighty, and despair!'
Nothing beside remains. Round the decay
Of that colossal wreck, boundless and bare,
The lone and level sands stretch far away."

All is vanity, indeed.

Congratulations, by the way. You're now part of the 8.3 percent.

(And if you haven't seen the superb film *Il Postino,* about the poet Pablo Neruda, do yourself a favor and check it out. Then be sure to watch the director's commentary afterwards, if you don't mind getting your head snapped off twice.)

A surprisingly high percentage of the world's greatest literature is verse. Much of the Bible is written in poetry, from the Psalms to the Prophets, from Job to Ecclesiastes.

We have Homer's epics *The Iliad* and *The Odyssey,* the sonnets of Shakespeare, Virgil's *Aeneid,* Dante's *Divine Comedy,* Milton's *Paradise Lost,* and Whitman's *Leaves of Grass.*

W. Somerset Maugham said, "The crown of literature is poetry. It is its end and aim. It is the sublimest activity of the human mind. It is the achievement of beauty and delicacy. The writer of prose can only step aside when the poet passes."

If you're new to poetry, don't feel you have to struggle with Ovid's *Metamorphoses* or the often-inscrutable poetry of John Donne. In fact, you can start with the simplest: haiku. Using simple everyday imagery, haiku creates crystalline images that heighten our awareness and remind us to pause and be present. Here are just a few favorites:

Bright moon—
strolling around the pond
all night long
                    —*Basho*

A bush warbler—
and of a hundred men
not one knows it's there.
                —*Ryokan*

Sun rising
over the mountain path—
scent of plums.
                —*Basho*

Bitter morning:
sparrows sitting
without necks.
                —*James W. Hackett*

Barn's burnt down—
now
I can see the moon.
                —*Masahide*

Millions claim they have no time or taste for poetry. But I disagree. Wallace Stevens said, "A poet looks at the world the way a man looks at a woman."

Who doesn't have time for that?

DRUNKEN MONKEY ICE CREAM . . . AND THE WISDOM OF THORNTON WILDER

Last week I spoke at an investment conference in New Orleans that fell smack in the middle of the Jazz & Heritage Festival. This was not exactly a coincidence. My colleagues and I, along with a few hundred thousand other music fanatics, had showed up four days early to soak up the sun and the sounds.

The festival—and New Orleans itself, of course—is best known for jazz. But that's just a starting point, really.

We heard pop (James Taylor), gospel (Mavis Staples), blues (Johnny Winter), reggae (Third World), zydeco (Thomas Fields, "The Big Hat Man"), rock (Sonny Landreth), bluegrass (Del McCoury), funk (Galactic), R&B (Erykah Badu), alt-country (Wilco), swamp (Tab Benoit), soul (Booker T), folk (Pete Seeger), and Cajun (Bruce Daigrepont), not to mention a few unclassifiables like The Creole Wild West Mardi Gras Indians, The Ebony Hillbillies, and Big Chief Monk Boudreaux.

We also heard every kind of jazz, from swing, bebop, and fusion to brass bands, ragtime, and Dixie. There was only one kind of music we didn't hear this week: bad. Most of it, in fact, was astonishingly good. If you had a butt, it was moving.

107

The concert performances were only part of the attraction, however. My personal Jazz Fest motto is "Come for the Music. Stay for the Food."

Generally, at outdoor events with over 50,000 spectators, the concession stands offer the usual fare: hot dogs, hamburgers, French fries, maybe Polish sausages with peppers and onions.

Not Jazz Fest. Your fast food choices include sautéed trout smothered with blue crab, alligator pie, quail-pheasant-andouille gumbo, Cajun duck po-boy, or grilled chicken livers with pepper jelly. Walking around the fairgrounds wearing polka-dotted shorts and suspenders is tolerated. Ordering a corn dog is not.

At the end of each day, of course, we found ourselves back in the city, where there is still more music. It rises up from lone musicians on street corners. Second-line bands parade around the French Quarter. Jazz and blues spill out of clubs, saloons, and restaurants all over town.

It's as if the whole city breathes in a minor key. Perhaps especially after Hurricane Katrina. New Orleans is bouncing back, however. Locals tell me business is picking up again. And the visitors, of course, are in heaven. One festival-goer's T-shirt summed it up nicely:

I Like New Orleans Broken Better Than Any Other City Fixed

There is a lot to like here, even if you're not a music lover. You can gallery hop the Arts District, ride the Canal Street ferry, take a streetcar tour of the Garden District, relax at the Sculpture Garden in City Park, people watch on Bourbon Street, visit Saint Louis Cathedral in Jackson Square, or just sit on the shore and watch the mighty Mississippi roll past. (Total cost: approximately zero.)

Then there are all those terrific restaurants: Commander's Palace, Bayona, Brennan's, Herbsaint, Stella, or NOLA, to name just a few.

And if you visit NOLA, for instance, do you order the shellfish stew made with seared mahi mahi, jumbo gulf shrimp, homemade chorizo sausage, and garlic black mussels? Or should you go with the hickory-roasted duck with whiskey caramel sauce, saving room, of course, for the White Chocolate Bananas Foster Bread Pudding with Drunken Monkey Ice Cream?

It's a tough call.

After dinner, it's worth visiting the newly refurbished Rock n' Bowl on Carrollton Avenue, a favorite place to eat, drink, dance, bowl, or just hang out and hear great musicians. (Trust me. There isn't a jukebox in the whole town.) On Wednesday night, we stopped in to bowl a few frames and hear Nathan and the Zydeco Cha-Cha's.

The band was exceptional that night. And so was the bowling performance of my friend Steven King. His skills are not finely honed. (Indeed, his game score rarely rises above the low double digits.) Still, I've never seen gutter balls thrown with such power and consistency. The ball appears to seek the trough even before leaving his hand. It was, in its own way, impressive to watch.

Later, we stopped to listen to a brass band at the corner of Bourbon and Canal, where my friend Maura Taylor danced with a homeless man in the street for 20 minutes. "Except for the smell," she said, "it was lovely."

What does all this have to do with the search for the good life?

Perhaps Thornton Wilder said it best. "My advice to you is not to inquire why or whither, but just enjoy your ice cream while it's on your plate."

Especially if it's Drunken Monkey.

THE LOST ART OF CONVERSATION

According to A. C. Nielsen Co., the average American watches more than four hours of TV each day. That's two months of non-stop television per year.

In a 65-year life, that person will have spent nine years glued to the tube. The same study found that the amount of time per week that parents spend in meaningful conversation with their children is 3.5 minutes. The average time children spend watching TV each week? 1,680 minutes.

Parents often wonder how they can better relate to their kids, how they can combat the coarsening effects of modern culture. May I suggest the off button?

Surrounded by cable television, DVDs, CD players, cell phones, personal digital assistants (PDAs), iPods, iPads, satellite radio, video games, and the Internet, a young person might reasonably ask what adults did before the age of electronic media.

In truth, we spent more time visiting friends and neighbors, took long walks, learned musical instruments, gave dinner parties and dances, went fishing, and played chess or checkers. And we read.

We read to become informed. We read to be entertained. We read as a noble intellectual exercise. And because reading is to the mind what exercise is to the body, we thought better, expressed ourselves more clearly, and wrote with greater style and refinement.

This kind of literacy can turn everyday communication into a kind of poetry. (Compare the Lincoln-Douglas debates, for example, to the current quality of political discourse.)

We also engaged in the lost art of conversation. In language filled with wit and intelligence, we spent time talking about our interests, argued the pressing issues of the day, wondered aloud about great mysteries, told each other our dreams, and let those around us know how we felt about them.

As an example of both the higher sentiments and greater literacy of an earlier age, here is a letter from Sullivan Ballou, a 32-year-old soldier in the Union Army, to his 24-year-old wife:

July 14, 1861
Camp Clark, Washington

My very dear Sarah:

The indications are very strong that we shall move in a few days—perhaps tomorrow. Lest I should not be able to write again, I feel impelled to write a few lines that may fall under your eye when I shall be no more. . . .

Sarah my love for you is deathless, it seems to bind me with mighty cables that nothing but Omnipotence could break; and yet my love of Country comes over me like a strong wind and bears me irresistibly on with all these chains to the battle field.

The memories of the blissful moments I have spent with you come creeping over me, and I feel most gratified to God and to you that I have enjoyed them for so long. And hard it is for me to give them up and burn to ashes the hopes of future years, when, God willing, we might still have lived and loved together, and seen our sons grown up to honorable manhood, around us. I have, I know, but few and small claims upon Divine Providence, but something whispers to me—perhaps it is the wafted prayer of my little Edgar, that I shall return to my loved ones unharmed. If I do not my dear Sarah, never forget how much I love you, and when my last breath escapes me on the battle field, it will whisper your name. Forgive my many faults and the many pains I have caused you. How thoughtless and foolish I have often times been! How gladly would I wash out with my tears every little spot upon your happiness. . . .

But, O Sarah! If the dead can come back to this earth and flit unseen around those they loved, I shall always be near you; in the gladdest days and in the darkest nights . . . always, always, and if there be a soft breeze upon your cheek, it shall be my breath, as the cool air fans your throbbing temple, it shall be my spirit passing by. Sarah do not mourn me dead; think I am gone and wait for thee, for we shall meet again . . .

Ballou was killed a week later in the first battle of Bull Run.

WHAT SUCCESS REALLY MEANS

I was shocked and saddened to learn that one of my favorite singers died this month, jazz singer Kenny Rankin.

Never heard of him? Maybe that's because, unlike a pop star like Michael Jackson, there was no saturation coverage or candle-light vigils for him. Kenny never won a Grammy. He didn't sell millions of albums. In fact, two of his best—*Because of You* and *Hiding in Myself*—are no longer in print.

Kenny didn't have an outlandish personal life to splash onto the front page of the Entertainment section. Although he struggled with drugs and alcohol at one point in his career, he was a soft-spoken, salt-of-the-earth type. And he didn't pack stadiums and arenas. He played mostly small clubs and bars, rarely filling those.

Whenever Kenny came to town, I would call friends and invite them to come out and hear him.

"I don't know," they'd typically say. "Who is this guy?"

"Just trust me," I'd say.

As much as I looked forward to Kenny's performances, what I really enjoyed was watching jaws hit the floor as soon as he opened his mouth to sing. One buddy was completely flabber-gasted. "What is this guy doing playing a bar with 20 people in it?"

"Worse," I said, "I invited 15 of them."

Sometimes Kenny would just sit in the middle of us with his guitar and take requests. He was happy to play whatever we wanted to hear. And when he took a break between sets, he rarely disappeared backstage. More often than not, he'd just amble back to the bar, sit down, and chat.

As far as I could tell, the man didn't have a pretentious bone in his body. Not that he didn't have the talent and more than a few high-profile fans. Johnny Carson was bowled over by Kenny, booking him on the *Tonight Show* 20 times. He even wrote the liner notes for his debut album.

Paul McCartney was another admirer. "No one can sing 'Black-bird' like Kenny Rankin," he once remarked. In fact, McCartney asked him to sing it when he and John Lennon were inducted into the Songwriters Hall of Fame.

Saxophone great Stan Getz was another devotee, describing Kenny's pristine tenor as "a horn with a heart."

Kenny was a fine guitarist, too. (He played on Bob Dylan's landmark 1965 album *Bringing It All Back Home*.) He wrote beautiful compositions performed by Peggy Lee, Mel Torme, Georgie Fame, Carmen McRae, and many others. But he was best known for his interpretations of others' songs.

He rarely changed the lyrics. But, like most jazz artists, he would often radically rework a song. Those who felt he strayed too far from the melody missed the point.

"My interpretation of the song is purely emotional," he once said. "We've all experienced disappointment and heartache, and that's what I draw on . . . I'm really hurting for the people in the song. When I sing I'm feeling, not thinking."

Despite his tremendous talents, Kenny spent most of his career in relative obscurity, garnering attention primarily from jazz aficionados and fellow musicians. But while Kenny never won the widespread acclaim or financial rewards of more commercial artists, he experienced one important success: He spent his life exercising his talents, doing exactly what he wanted to do.

"I just feel privileged that I've been allowed to continue in my craft," he said. "When someone tells you a song changed their life, or inspired them to look at things in a slightly different way, well, you can't ask for a better reward than that."

Kenny died of complications only a few months after his initial cancer diagnosis. But his music lives on through his recordings and the memories of those who heard him.

I encourage you to join that circle. A good starting place is *The Jazz Channel Presents Kenny Rankin.* And especially his heartrending version of "While My Guitar Gently Weeps." (Watch the DVD once and you'll have to own it.) This is what it means to have a "gift." Kenny Rankin never had a singing lesson his entire life.

WHAT ARE YOUR SINS OF OMISSION?

I recently viewed the History Channel series on the seven deadly sins, that 1,600-year-old inventory of our universal shortcomings: pride, anger, envy, greed, gluttony, sloth, and lust.

I was surprised to learn that most philosophers and theologians consider sloth the single most insidious vice. I'd always thought sloth was one of the more amiable weaknesses. Does lounging in front of ESPN with a bag of Doritos really constitute a great moral failure?

But the spiritual meaning of sloth is not laziness. It's apathy, hardness of heart, moral indifference, blindness, complacency, and "smallness of soul." Poverty, injustice, and suffering exist, in part, because we don't act. Sloth is the category that encompasses everything we should do but don't.

That's a big one. Few of us spend time reflecting on the ethics of inaction. We are interested in all sorts of things—friends, family, work, Angelina Jolie. But our personal moral failings? Not so much.

We already know it's wrong to lie, cheat, kill, or conk a woman on the head and run off with her purse. Sins of commission are easy to identify. But sins of omission? That's trickier.

For example, it's clearly wrong to drown someone. But our legal system will not prosecute you for letting someone drown. Killing a child elicits universal condemnation. But permitting thousands of children to die each day from starvation is different.

Or is it? As Dennis Ford writes in *Sins of Omission* (Fortress Press, 1990), "Every three days more people die from malnutrition and disease than from the bombing of Hiroshima. Every year more people die from preventable hunger than died in the Holocaust. Somewhere along the line, moral reflection and outrage have lost their audience."

I'm one of those missing in action. Most days I go about my business, do my work, chip away at my problems, and hardly give a thought about the rest of the world's.

But does our failure to act make us morally culpable? Is the misery of others ever the product of our own indifference? Is doing "too little" morally reprehensible? And why is it uncomfortable to even consider these questions?

No doubt it's partly because the world is so full of problems, we're wary of letting them drag us down. Ayn Rand once received a letter from a reader who was inspired by her writings but found the world such a mess he said he didn't know where to begin to change it. Rand responded that if a doctor showed up at a battlefield and hundreds of soldiers lay wounded and dying, he wouldn't despair that he couldn't save them all and drive off. He'd identify the most urgent situation and get to work.

Yet whether the issue is feeding the poor, protecting the environment, or caring for the elderly, few of us are committed enough to inconvenience ourselves for change. Why are we unmoved? How do we sustain and legitimize our apathy?

I recently put these questions to Dr. Craig Shealy, a professor of graduate psychology at James Madison University and the executive director of the International Beliefs and Values Institute, a nonprofit organization that studies ethics and how they are linked to actions and practices around the globe.

His research reveals that our decisions about whether to act are based on a combination of upbringing, personal values, and culture. Western culture, in particular, provides a significant headwind. With Madison Avenue bombarding us daily with countless messages about what to wear, where to eat, and what to drive, even the most eloquent pleas for helping others can sound shrill or preachy.

In our do-your-own-thing society, we don't want anyone laying a guilt trip on us. Moralizing or sanctimonious appeals from "do-gooders" often backfire, causing us to feel irritation and resentment, not compassion.

Ours is a culture of individualism. We come into this world with a self-centered perspective and quickly learn that we can pursue our advantage by figuring out what is best for us, not what is best for everyone. And it works. Individual initiative and hard work generally lead to economic, material, and social rewards.

As a nation of individualists, freedom is our highest ideal. But it can also mean the freedom to bully the weak, shun the disadvantaged, despoil the environment, ignore the suffering of animals, or turn our backs on the oppressed, the sick, and the dying.

Our indifference is reinforced by the popular perception that "people get what they deserve." We like Horatio Alger stories, tales of individuals rising from humble circumstances to overcome adversity and make a great success of their lives.

But that isn't always possible. In some parts of the world, the odds are stacked against you. (And if you believe everyone in the United States starts out with an equal opportunity, you might rent the movie *Precious*. It's fictional, but boot-strappers will find it eye-opening.)

Even if you've achieved your success through a lifetime of education, persistence, and hard work, you may owe a bigger debt of gratitude than you realize. Nobel Prize–winning economist and social scientist Herbert Simon estimates that "social capital" is responsible for at least 90 percent of what people earn in wealthy societies.

Sound far-fetched? Consider living in a society without modern infrastructure, communications, or a reliable power supply. Imagine there is no free-market system to incentivize you, no police force to protect you, no court system to enforce contracts or protect your rights. As Warren Buffett once remarked, "If you stick me down in the middle of Bangladesh or Peru, you'll find out how much this talent is going to produce in the wrong kind of soil."

Fortunately, we don't have to sacrifice every day to survive. The beauty of capitalism is that it promotes the general welfare when we pursue our self-interest. (We get what we want when we deliver the goods and services others want.) But excellence at moneymaking doesn't necessarily translate into excellence of character.

I have my favorite charities, but like you, perhaps, I am vaguely haunted by the feeling that I don't give enough, do enough, engage enough. I suspect that my problem is sloth.

What's the solution? I'm not sure there is one. However, Dr. Shealy offers this bit of advice to activists and fund-raisers who would encourage others to lend a hand:

1. Understand that everyone, depending on his or her personal beliefs and background, interprets a plea for help differently.
2. Recognize that getting someone involved generally requires you to touch an emotional center, not just an intellectual one.
3. When you offer donors the possibility of making a contribution, give them the space to reflect on what you're asking them to do. Allow them the opportunity to respond from a deep place, not just a sense of obligation.

There's probably no cure for dyed-in-the-wool moral indifference. (At least, not one that doesn't involve trampling people's freedoms or making yourself obnoxious.) It would be nice to believe that we only need someone to tickle our conscience and our behavior will change. But I'm not so sure.

Immanuel Kant said two things filled him with awe: the starry skies above and the moral universe within.

Yet you'll notice the stars are always there.

THE BEAUTY OF SLOWING DOWN

I have a number of friends who are financially independent but certainly not wealthy. Why? Because their schedules are packed, their days are overloaded, and they regularly carp that they have no free time.

What kind of affluence is that? They have money but not the time to enjoy it. They have financial freedom but choose to relentlessly pursue more instead. They are victims of mindlessness, ambition, or distraction. In many ways, their lives are more impoverished than those who have far less.

Of course, it's not easy to find the right balance between achievement and enjoyment. But when things are out of whack, the symptoms are pretty obvious. The people around us are talking, but we aren't listening. We're divided between what is happening here and what is happening somewhere else. Or we're thinking about what will happen tomorrow . . . or 15 minutes from now. In the process, we miss a lot.

Modern society puts a premium on speed and efficiency, too. We figure we can accomplish more by doing two or three things at once.

But this distraction often comes at a price.

John Freeman, editor of *Granta* and author of *The Tyranny of E-mail* (Scribner, 2009), writes:

We will die, that much is certain; and everyone we have ever loved will die, too, sometimes—heartbreakingly—before us. . . . Busyness numbs the pain of this awareness, but it can never totally submerge it. Given that our days are limited, our hours precious, we have to decide what we want to do, what we want to say, what and who we care about, and how we want to allocate our time to these things within the limits that do not and cannot change. In short, we need to slow down.

He has a point. And there are basic practices that can assist you:

- Doctors say slower breathing is one of the simplest ways to better health. Deep breathing lowers stress and reduces systolic blood pressure. It allows oxygen to get down to the smallest airways in our lungs, the alveoli, where the oxygen exchange is most efficient. Quick, shallow breathing causes your body to release less nitrous oxide, so your organs and tissues are less oxygenated.
- Eat more slowly and you will eat less. There is a lag time between when the stretch receptors in your stomach signal it is time to stop eating and your brain gets the message. If you slow your intake, you won't just savor your meals more. Researchers at the University of Rhode Island discovered that people who eat more slowly consume 70 less calories per meal. Multiply that by three meals a day and you'll drop 20 pounds over the next year.
- Slowness won't hurt your love life. Mae West once remarked that anything worth doing is worth doing slowly . . . very slowly. Marriage counselor Lori Buckley of Pasadena agrees, "Often, the first thing to disappear from a marital relationship is the long, lingering, teasing kiss."
- Slowing down prevents accidents. It's impossible to calculate the number of motorists killed or injured each year because they were in a rush. Insurance companies have found that the overwhelming majority of job-site accidents can be traced to hurrying.

- Slowness is even part of successful money management. Some folks realize late in life that they haven't saved enough for retirement. To make up for lost time, they often decide to roll the dice by trading risky derivatives (futures and options), penny stocks, or hot tips from friends and colleagues. Big mistake. When it comes to meeting long-term investment goals, starting early, investing regularly, and reacting slowly—or hardly at all—is a winning combination.

- A more deliberate pace enhances your quality of life. There's an old Chinese saying, "Man in hurry cannot walk with dignity." A constant flurry of activity does not present an attractive image. And it creates stress and anxiety, causing you to miss a lot of what is going on around you. As the philosopher Lin Yutang noted, the wise man is not hurried and the hurried man is not wise.

Deep down, most of us realize this. But it never hurts to be reminded, and perhaps take things down a notch. More than 150 year ago, clergyman and Transcendentalist William Henry Channing described the slower, more relaxed life as his "Symphony":

> To live content with small means; to seek elegance rather than luxury, and refinement rather than fashion; to be worthy, not respectable, and wealthy, not rich . . . to study hard, to think quietly, act frankly, talk gently, await occasions, hurry never; in a word, to let the spiritual, unbidden and unconscious, grow up through the common—this is my symphony.

We all have obligations and deadlines. But hurry and extreme future-mindedness impoverish the present. What we value most are love, friendship, solace, beauty, and humor. Yet these things are best appreciated or communicated face to face in a calm, relaxed setting.

Slowing down enhances your sense of gratitude, improves your mental and physical health, allows you to gain control of your life, lets you appreciate beauty, and enables you to reconnect with those around you.

Sometimes the best way to spend a day is savoring what you've got before it's gone.

WHEN ENTERTAINMENT BECOMES ART

I just returned—again—from my annual trek to Jazz Fest in New Orleans. As always, the music—and the food—was righteous.

Of course, it's tough to call an event a jazz festival when it features everyone from Simon & Garfunkel to Pearl Jam. But jazz is what brings most of us back. (That and the quail and pheasant gumbo.)

A lifelong collector and aficionado, my favorite music is "anything good." (Unfortunately, that qualifier eliminates just about everything on the charts today, in my view.) It wasn't until my mid-30s, however, that I developed a passion for jazz and, in particular, a near obsession with the music of John Coltrane.

Prior to that, I had no taste for it. Jazz seemed too complicated, too fussy. All I heard was a lot of honkin' and skronkin'. "Where is the melody?" I'd complain.

However, everything changed one rainy night in 1992 when, with absolutely nothing else to do, a friend and I bought tickets, 10 minutes before showtime, to see the Wynton Marsalis Septet at a local auditorium.

The scalper who sold them to us out front—for five bucks each—probably didn't know or care that the seats were front-row center. That's not the best place to be, acoustically speaking, but—as it turned out—the ideal location for what I was about to witness.

Marsalis was touring behind a trio of fine albums he'd recently recorded called *Soul Gestures in Southern Blue*. I didn't know this at the time, of course, because I'd never listened to him, indeed had never owned a jazz record unless you stretched the definition to include fusionists like Jeff Beck or Weather Report. (And if you're one of those lost souls who thinks Kenny G makes jazz albums, please . . . stop reading now and go say 10 Hail Marys.)

The Marsalis band was made up of six other young men, including a phenomenally gifted blind pianist named Marcus Roberts, all wearing impeccably tailored suits with rich-looking shirts and ties, complete with stickpins. As the applause died down after the introduction, they began to play. And I was entranced.

The sound emanating from the stage was the bluest, swingingest, most majestic thing I'd ever heard. It wasn't just music. It was stories told without words. I heard joy. I heard sadness. I heard disappointment, jealousy, and off-color jokes.

With each piece, the band established a slow, sweaty groove, played the head (what jazz musicians call the melody), and then took turns improvising. Wynton would step up to the microphone for a solo, then the tenor saxophonist, then the trombonist, then the altoist, each creating something new but building on what the player before had said.

Behind each soloist, the other musicians listened intently, nodding their heads, smiling at each other and occasionally making surprised faces, frowning in disbelief, or even laughing at what they heard.

It was clear these men loved the music, loved improvising, and loved each other. Behind them, all the while, the rhythm section simmered. It was sheer magic. Everything made perfect sense. I couldn't have been more astonished if I were attending a lecture in Swahili and suddenly understood every word.

I fell in love with jazz that night. And that led me into a world that I never knew existed, peopled by giants like Louis Armstrong, Jelly Roll Morton, Duke Ellington, Ella Fitzgerald, Charlie Parker, Billie Holiday, Bill Evans, Miles Davis, Thelonious Monk, Dizzy Gillespie, and countless others.

This isn't just music. It's not just entertainment. It's distinctly American art. Yet according to the National Endowment of the Arts, few people are listening:

- Less than 7 percent of adult Americans attended a live jazz performance last year.
- Even among college-educated adults, the audience for jazz is diminishing, to 14 percent last year from 19.4 percent in 1982.
- And not only is the audience shrinking, it's getting older. The median age of adults in America who attended a live jazz performance in 2008 was 46. In 1982, it was 29.

That's a shame. When friends tell me they can't fathom the music and have no taste for it, I understand. It wasn't long ago I felt the same way. (George Foreman once remarked that jazz is like boxing. The better it is, the less people appreciate it.) But a little exposure can make a world of difference. At a recent conference in New York, for instance, I took a handful of colleagues down to the Village Vanguard—the closest thing to a shrine in the world of jazz—to hear saxophonist Joe Lovano. They were delighted.

"Now I get it," one friend gushed after the show. "It's like baseball. You have to be there."

Jazz is essentially a performing art. But there are mountains of great recordings to ease your way into the genre. The Miles Davis classic *Kind of Blue* is one of the most accessible jazz albums. If you prefer vocals, you could do worse than to pick up a copy of *Ella and Louis*.

Why should you? Because great jazz can transform your environment, change your life. Put it on in your home or car and—instantly—you are enveloped in an atmosphere of style and sophistication. It's good for Sunday morning, great for a dinner party, perfect with a glass of wine. It's beautiful . . . and it's fun.

Yet when I take a peek at friends' music collections, I usually see the same old stuff: Billy Joel, Jimmy Buffett, the Eagles, and *Dark Side of the Moon*. It reminds me of children who only eat pizza, chicken fingers, and spaghetti. Hey, I like those, too. But would you really want to eat nothing else for the rest of your life?

If you're American, jazz is part of your heritage (although it's much more appreciated today in Europe and Japan). It was invented here. Scholar Gerald Early insists that 2,000 years from now, America will be remembered for three timeless innovations: the Constitution, baseball, and jazz.

Jazz delivers a sonic slice of life, with improvisations on the most universal of human themes, what Duke Ellington called "the world's greatest duet, a man and a woman going steady."

Marsalis says, "Jazz is the art of timing. It teaches you when. When to start, when to wait, when to step it up, and when to take your time—indispensable tools for making someone else happy."

In his book *Moving to Higher Ground* (Random House, 2008), he writes:

> It's not easy to find words for the kinds of emotions that jazz musicians convey. You don't have a name for the feeling of light peeking through the drapes in your childhood bedroom. Or how the teasing by classmates hurt. You don't have a name for the feeling of late-night silence on a car ride with your father or how you love your wife's smile when you tease her. But those feelings are real, even more real because you can't express them in words. Jazz allows the musician to instantly communicate exactly how he or she experiences life as it is felt, and the instant honesty of that revelation shocks listeners into sharing and experiencing that feeling too.

Like the best fare in New Orleans, jazz is a delicious stew. Yes, it's based on the blues. (Tenor saxophonist Johnny Griffin once remarked that jazz is music made by and for people who have chosen to feel good in spite of conditions.) Yet, like Walt Whitman, it contains multitudes, including camp-meeting shouts, church hymns, fiddlers' reels, Negro spirituals, minstrel ditties, vaudeville tunes, American standards, ragtime, parlor music, European classical music, and romantic ballads.

So shake up your impoverished music collection. Pick up a copy of *Solo Monk* or *Giant Steps*. If you're looking for something different to do this weekend, stop in a club and hear some local jazz musicians. You'll be pleasantly surprised.

As Plato pointed out a couple thousand years ago, "Music gives soul to the universe, wings to the mind, flight to the imagination, and life to everything."

◼ Do You Have a Secret?

Why do we find secrets so fascinating?

Everyone has them. Yet we hanker to learn more, to be in the know. Just about everywhere, people want news that is privileged, unpublished, classified, scandalous, or personal—information, above all, that is not widely known.

Marketers know this. That's why newsstands everywhere are papered with magazines offering diet secrets, sex secrets, success secrets, celebrity secrets, and fitness secrets. Investment-letter copywriters churn out endless marketing based on "secrets of great wealth." My book publisher, John Wiley & Sons, even suggested that I title my previous collection of essays *The Secret of Shelter Island*.

What is the secret of Shelter Island? Can you keep a confidence? Good. So can I.

Frank Warren can't, however. He's kept almost none of the thousands of secrets he's been told. And that's a good thing. Six years ago, Warren launched the PostSecret project, an ongoing community art project in which people anonymously mail him a personal secret on a homemade postcard. No restrictions are made on the content of the secret, only that it must be truthful and never have been spoken before.

A lot of us, apparently, can't wait to spill the beans. Warren has received more than 400,000 postcards, each revealing a sender's hope, fear, desire, or epiphany. Some cards appear as though they were created during an impulsive moment. Others are invested with painstaking detail and look like sacred objects.

128

Warren displays the best of them on www.postsecret.com (updated weekly) and his many PostSecret books. I recently stumbled on his exhibit at the American Visionary Art Museum in Baltimore and was taken with it.

What's the big deal about secrets—some heartbreaking, some insightful, some just plain nutty—from anonymous folks? You be the judge. I jotted down a few of my favorites to share with you. I quickly discovered, however, that typed words on a page don't deliver the emotional wallop of the handwritten cards themselves. (This is an art project after all.) But here are a few of the Post-Secret musings I found especially thought provoking:

I'm scared I will be killed in the line of duty . . . and NO ONE will tell my son how much I loved him.

If my dog were a human, I think he'd look like Brad Pitt.

Sometimes when my Dad starts telling me stories I've already heard, I can't help but think about how much I'll miss hearing them when he's gone.

I had my dream wedding with the wrong person.

I went to the museum to meet chicks. I found out I was a chicken.

My goal in life is to have crow's feet and deep laugh lines when I'm old.

I cannot tell my family that grandpa FAKED his deathbed conversion to make them all feel better. He was a lifelong atheist, and one of the kindest, most decent and generous men I've ever met.

I look for examples every day that prove there is more good than evil in the world. I always find them.

❧

I tell everyone I take the stairs to be environmentally friendly, but I'm really just afraid of elevators.

❧

I am the type of person that I complain about.

❧

Sometimes I sit in the rain because I feel it washes away my mistakes.

❧

I am thankful for your absence at the table this year.

❧

I spent my childhood wishing I was an adult and now I spend my adulthood wishing I was a child.

❧

I'm starting to LOVE my pear shape!

❧

My wife is pregnant and I'm over the moon.

❧

I hate everything about dance. I wish they would kick me out.

❧

As a child on my aunt and uncle's farm, I fed a chicken nugget to a chicken. I still feel guilty about that.

❧

I drink from a martini glass and pretend that I'm fabulous.

❧

Sometimes I let my children eat cheese puffs for breakfast.

❦

I told my depressed ex-girlfriend that I didn't care anymore. That she might as well jump off a bridge. And she did.

❦

Dad was extra mean to the waitress. I think it's 'cause she looked like you.

❦

I no longer know where my life is heading. But I don't care as long as she's riding shotgun.

❦

I ignored the doorbell and just ate the candy myself. Happy Halloween!

❦

I have always wanted to find a baby on my doorstep (and keep it).

❦

I trashed my parents' house to look like I had had a party while they were out of town . . . so my Mom would think I had friends.

❦

All my life I wanted to look like Liz Taylor. Now Liz Taylor is starting to look like me.

❦

I don't feel beautiful anymore because you stopped saying it . . .

❦

I can't remember your voice. I miss you, Mom.

❦

I used your toothbrush to clean the sink.

❦

My last mortal thought will be, "why did I take so many days—just like this one—for granted?"

❦

I recommend visiting Warren's exhibit at the American Visionary Art Museum if you get a chance. It's a soulful experience. Each card is individual, and yet, at a deeper level, this community of confessions reveals our connections, even when we find the thoughts expressed surprising or appalling. The voices speaking through them offer us the opportunity to recognize our own secrets, to realize we are not alone.

(Incidentally, if you are interested in participating in Frank Warren's community art project, feel free to mail your secret on a handmade postcard to PostSecret, 13345 Copper Ridge Rd., Germantown, MD 20874.)

In his latest PostSecret book, Warren writes, "This project has shown me that art can be like a new tongue that allows us to speak and pray in ways that might otherwise be impossible. And if we listen, we may come to understand that we are always on a spiritual journey—even when we feel most lost."

Are You Amusing Yourself to Death?

I've often said that the first step to becoming a better investor is an easy one: Turn off the TV. CNBC—and its competitors—will only make you dumber and poorer.

This comes as a surprise to many. After all, financial channels offer a steady stream of well-credentialed experts, men and women with impressive titles from prestigious firms. Most have PhDs, years of experience, or manage large sums of money. They look good. They sound sharp. They have insightful opinions and reams of arcane investment data tripping off their tongues. How could listening to them possibly make you a worse investor?

Because the unstated premise behind these shows—which exist, of course, to sell advertising—is that investors should be in a near-constant state of reaction:

- "The market is selling off hard today. What should investors do now?"
- "The Fed has raised interest rates a quarter of a point. What should investors do now?
- "GDP growth was revised down to 2.8 percent last quarter. What should investors do now?"

They bring on one analyst with a bullish view and another with a bearish one—on stocks, bonds, currencies, commodities, interest rates, or the economy—let them square off for a few minutes, then cut to commercials. A few minutes later, they come back and do it some more. And this goes on day after day, week after week, year after year.

Near the market bottom in 2009, I was playing tennis with a friend who was badly upset about the market's belly flop.

"I tell you," he said in utter disgust, "I'm really tempted to just turn off CNBC and sell all my stocks."

"There is something else you can do," I reminded him.

"What's that?" he asked.

"Just turn off the TV."

Lately, I've been thinking that what's good for investors is not a bad idea for the rest of us. Why do so many bright, talented, educated people spend countless hours staring blankly at the tube?

The short answer, of course, is we enjoy it. But do we, really? Is watching TV more fulfilling than what you'd be doing if you weren't? If you get specific about it, you may feel a little ridiculous. For example, have you ever told yourself something like:

- Gee, I really need to get more exercise, but *Dancing With the Stars* is on in 10 minutes. (Maybe I'll just watch them exercise instead.)
- I promised my daughter I'd teach her how to play chess, but these *Seinfeld* reruns are really funny.
- I really should stop in to visit my aging grandmother, but I can't miss the playoffs!
- I promised myself I'd learn to play the piano this year, but this is the finals of *American Idol*.
- I really do want to plant that garden. But I can't miss my soaps.

If we're challenged, of course, we have plenty of rationalizations. Let a TV critic tell you that most of the programming is mindless junk and you'll point to the educational stuff on the History Channel, Discovery, or National Geographic, even if that's only a fraction of what you watch.

If he replies that you're still being subjected to hours of commercials each week, you tell him you record the shows on your DVR and fast-forward through the ads.

If he counters that taping only allows you to consume even more television, you can always play your trump card: Mind your own business.

After all, you're an adult. It's your life to live. You can spend it any way you want. But, between *South Park* and *Grey's Anatomy,* do you ever reflect on how you're spending it?

Last week, I read journalist David Lipsky's recently published collection of conversations with David Foster Wallace, the brilliant young writer whose *Infinite Jest* made the *Time* list of 100 All-Time Greatest Novels. (Wallace battled depression for years and, tragically, hanged himself in 2008. It was a tremendous loss for his family and friends, but also for contemporary fiction.)

At one point in the interviews, Wallace says, "I'll zone out in front of the TV for five or six hours, and then I feel depressed and empty. And I wonder why. Whereas if I eat candy for five or six hours, and then I feel sick, I know why. . . . One of the reasons that I feel empty after watching a lot of TV is that it gives the illusion of relationships with people. It's a way to have people in the room talking and being entertaining, but it doesn't require anything of me. I receive entertainment and stimulation without having to give anything back but the most tangential kind of attention. And that is very seductive."

Bingo. No matter how good the programming is—and some of it is excellent—or how rapidly you fast-forward through the commercials, the hours you spend in front of the tube is time you haven't spent pursuing your goals, living out your dreams, or just interacting with another human being.

If you're elderly and alone, or housebound for some other reason, you may have a valid reason. But that doesn't describe the majority of us.

Twenty-five years ago, Neil Postman warned of our consuming love affair with television in *Amusing Ourselves to Death* (Viking, 1985). In the book—a jeremiad about the danger of turning serious conversations about politics, business, religion, and science into entertainment packages—he argues that TV is creating not the dystopia of George Orwell's *1984* but rather of Aldous Huxley's *Brave New World:*

> Spiritual devastation is more likely to come from an enemy with a smiling face than from one whose countenance exudes suspicion and hate. In the Huxleyan prophecy, Big Brother does not watch us, by his choice. We watch him, by ours. There is no need for wardens or gates or Ministries of Truth. When a population becomes distracted by trivia, when cultural life is redefined as a perpetual round of entertainments, when serious public conversation becomes a form of baby-talk, when, in short, a people become an audience and their public business a vaudeville act, then a nation finds itself at risk.

He concludes that we'd all be better off if television got worse, not better.

According to A. C. Nielsen, 99 percent of American households have a television. Two-thirds have more than three. These sets are on an average of 6 hours and 47 minutes per day.

Forty-nine percent of Americans polled say they spend too much time in front of the TV. It's not hard to see why. The average viewer watches more than four hours of TV each day. That's two months of nonstop TV-watching per year. In a 65-year life, that person will have spent nine years glued to the tube.

You already know how little you gain by watching so much TV. But have you also considered what you lose?

■ In Praise of Idleness

Americans idealize hard work, duty, industry, and self-sacrifice. We know this by how many terms we have for those who lack these qualities: loafer, idler, shirker, slacker, goof-off, deadbeat, bum, goldbrick, layabout.

As children, we're taught that idle hands are the devil's workshop. Idleness is synonymous with laziness—or worse. But other cultures take a different view. The Japanese have the highly ritualized tea ceremony. Some Brits still have afternoon tea, a relaxing half hour with Earl Grey, cucumber sandwiches, and genteel conversation. Mexicans dispense with tea altogether and just take a siesta. (As the Spanish proverb says, "How beautiful it is to do nothing, and then rest afterwards.")

Successful lives are not always measured by achievement. Too much time at the grindstone can leave us culturally impoverished, spiritually indigent. We should know how to cultivate leisure, to use it to rise to higher levels of grace and intellectual repose.

No sensible life is without periods of indolence. Besides, idleness can be a noble attribute, a virtuous pastime. Consider that culture itself is a by-product of leisure. Idleness leads to contemplation, creativity, and inventiveness. These, in turn, resolve themselves in literature, poetry, music, philosophy, and art.

Idleness reflects our status as free men and women. It is an expression of liberty. True idleness is not doing nothing. It is being free to do anything.

Downtime is an energizing force, too. It clears our heads and gives us strength. Without it, our concentration is lessened, our immune systems are stressed, our reasoning skills are diminished. We get tired and cranky.

Yet, in today's society, indolence is hard work. Family will poke and prod you. Colleagues will try to motivate you. Even a night on the town comes crashing down when your companion utters those regrettable words, "I really ought to be going. I need to get an early start."

Yet work is not always required. There is such a thing as sacred idleness. Aristotle said, "The great-souled man will not compete for the common objects of ambition . . . He will be idle and slow to act."

Mark Twain, whose characters Tom Sawyer and Huck Finn are among the most resourceful loafers in all literature, once wrote, "I have seen slower people than I am—and more deliberate . . . and even quieter, more listless, and lazier people than I am. But they were dead."

Ronald Reagan, a master of inactivity, once remarked, "It's true that hard work never killed anybody, but I figure why take the chance?"

Yet, once ingrained, it's hard for many of us to break free of the Calvinist work ethic, to return to that natural and blessed state of inactivity. In short, we feel guilty. But we shouldn't. One can even argue that idleness has a divine sanction. In his Sermon on the Mount, Jesus said, "Consider the lilies of the field, how they grow; they toil not, neither do they spin. And yet I say unto you, that even Solomon in all his glory was not arrayed like one of these." (Matthew 6:28–29)

Hebrew sages taught that when you are first welcomed into heaven, a record is revealed to you of all the many times in your past when you could really have been happy and enjoyed some moment but failed to do so. And then you are called to repent of each and every one of those moments.

The best lives are not lived in a hurry. Why pursue wealth if not to purchase a bit of leisured contentment? The great end of living is the true enjoyment of it.

Winston Churchill understood this. British historian Paul Johnson recalls the time as a boy when he met the Prime Minister in October 1946:

> He gave me one of his giant matches he used for lighting cigars. I was emboldened by that into saying, "Mr. Winston Churchill, sir, to what do you attribute your success in life?" and he said without hesitating: "Economy of effort. Never stand up when you can sit down, and never sit down when you can lie down."

With those words, he stepped into his limo and pulled away.

THE TYRANNY OF THE NEW

Imagine picking up today's newspaper and finding music critics swooning over a sensational new artist, insisting that his work not only expresses the deepest and most profound human emotions but also represents the highest point that beauty has reached in the sphere of music. Would you not be tempted to listen?

Or imagine a trusted source who tells you about a fabulous new author, one who writes more originally and comprehensively than anyone before, whose rendering of characters is uncanny, and who tells you nothing less than what it means to be human. Would you not be tempted to read him?

Well, I have good news. These examples are not hypothetical. These artists are real, and you would gain a lot by becoming more familiar with their work.

Unfortunately, there is no one to entice you. There is no hype surrounding them, no media buzz. They don't have PR agents. No agency is marketing them. And the audiences they attract are minuscule compared to top-selling commercial artists.

How can this be? Because I lied. They are not new. They are old. Their names are Mozart and Shakespeare.

Disappointed? You shouldn't be, because if you haven't experienced the best of their work, they are still new to you. But no publisher, talent agency, or record company has much incentive to bring their work to your attention.

And that's too bad. Of the billions who have inhabited this globe, only a few thousand men and women ever achieved greatness in the arts. Of these, just a few hundred created something truly magnificent. And among these, only a handful created staggering works of genius that represent the pinnacle of human achievement.

In music, for instance, Mozart shares the limelight with names like Beethoven, Bach, Handel, and Haydn. In Western painting, Michelangelo, Picasso, Raphael, da Vinci, and Rembrandt are engraved on Mt. Olympus. In literature, Shakespeare—the category killer—is joined by Goethe, Dante, Virgil, and Homer, among others.

People around the world and throughout history have been entertained, enlightened, and astounded by these individuals' achievements. At least some familiarity with their work is a hallmark of a liberal arts education. Yet once our formal education ends, so does our interest, it seems. Instead, we start taking our cue from contemporary culture and begin pursuing what is new or hot or "buzz-worthy," even as we imagine ourselves largely immune to the siren song of Madison Avenue.

I'm not dismissing contemporary art and entertainment. I enjoy them as much as the next guy and hold more than a few strong opinions. For instance, you wouldn't want to get into an argument with me that *Get Yer Ya-Ya's Out* is *not* the greatest rock and roll album ever.

But I'm talking about something higher. Only a tiny amount of what is written or composed or painted in any generation is recognized as truly great by succeeding ones. Recognizing this doesn't make you a snob, only aware that opinions about what is "lastingly valuable" rarely persist.

Science and technology follow a steady path of progress and improvement. The arts do not. No one today is writing plays better than Shakespeare or composing music better than Bach or painting pictures better than Titian. There are plenty of talented artists in the world. But as Schopenhauer noted, talent is hitting a target no one else can hit; genius hitting a target no one else can see.

We are adults for only a few decades. Is it not worthwhile to get to know the best that has ever been composed or painted or written?

Classic literature, in particular, presents, in the poet Matthew Arnold's words, "the best that is known and thought in the world."

Your access has never been easier. The local library offers all the world's greatest books—with no waiting list. (If you're unsure where to begin, pick up a guide like *The New Lifetime Reading Plan*.) Most enduring works can be downloaded for free. For a few dollars, you can own high-quality, digital recordings of the world's greatest music performed by the finest symphony orchestras. Visit any major city and you can marvel at paintings and sculptures that the world's richest men and women cannot own, even if they could afford them.

Some will find this view elitist, so let me be clear. If the paintings of Mark Rothko or the novels of Stephen King or the music of Jay-Z are what really turn you on, knock yourself out. It's your life to spend enjoying what you please, and don't let anyone ever tell you otherwise.

But if you truly believe their work will endure through the centuries or that the masterworks that generations of men and women have called immortal is not worth your time, I wear the elitist label proudly.

We all would like to experience the best that life has to offer. Yet few of us can afford the finest French wines, the best Italian sports cars, or life in Pacific Palisades. (And these would do little to change your quality of life, anyway.) But few in the West are so impoverished that they cannot afford to experience the greatest products of the human imagination.

Emily Dickinson said it about the printed word, but it could as easily apply to the other arts as well:

> There is no frigate like a book
> To take us lands away,
> Nor any coursers like a page
> Of prancing poetry.

> This traverse may the poorest take
> Without oppress of toll;
> How frugal is the chariot
> That bears a human soul!

WHY YOU SHOULD KNOW "THE INDISPENSABLE MAN"

Over the holidays, I had some friends and neighbors over for a dinner party, and a number of guests asked about the painting hanging over my fireplace.

It is a large oil-on-canvas replica of the famous 1851 painting by Emanuel Leutze that depicts Washington crossing the Delaware. It was, you may recall, Washington's first move in his successful surprise attack against Hessian forces on Christmas Day, 1776.

Although the original painting—like my replica—is striking, it is riddled with historical inaccuracies. For starters, the crossing took place in the dead of night. But that wouldn't have made a particularly inspiring work of art. The flag shown—the original "Stars and Stripes"—did not exist at the time of his crossing. The boats are wrong. They were larger with higher sides. The men did not bring horses. It was raining. Washington was, in all likelihood, not standing, and certainly not in such a heroic fashion. The Delaware at what is now called Washington Crossing is far narrower than the river in the painting. It was not filled with icy crags. And, not incidentally, Washington and his men are heading in the wrong direction.

Chuckling at these artistic liberties, one neighbor asked why I had the painting hanging over my mantel. That is a story I never tire of telling.

George Washington was one of Virginia's wealthiest men (and, like virtually all plantation owners of his day, a slaveholder). Yet few risked more in defying tyranny than he did. When the revolutionary leaders pledged their lives, their fortunes, and their sacred honor, these were more than just fine-sounding words. This was treason. The founders knew that if the king's soldiers caught them, they would be hanged. Yet Washington left his comfortable, aristocratic life and led a ragtag band of ill-trained, poorly clothed, underfed soldiers against the armed forces of the king of England and won our independence.

That's not the reason I own the painting, however.

Washington was unanimously elected president and served two terms. In 1787, he presided over the Convention that drafted the American Constitution, the document that not only limited his power, but became a model and inspiration for free people everywhere. Many historians regard Washington as "The Indispensable Man," the crucial founding father and one of the two or three greatest presidents ever.

But that's not why the picture is over my mantel, either.

Washington's greatest act, the one that made him internationally famous, was his resignation as commander in chief after the war.

Following the signing of the peace treaty and British recognition of American independence, Washington stunned the world when he surrendered his sword to Congress and retired to his farm at Mount Vernon.

In all of history, this was something completely new. Read the stories of Julius Caesar, Alexander the Great, Napoleon, and other famous generals. Conquerors had always made sure they received political and material rewards commensurate with their achievements. And far from giving up the powers they possessed, they pressed on to acquire more.

Yet Washington took nothing, asked for nothing. This was simply not how the world worked.

Thomas Jefferson was not exaggerating when he declared in 1784, "The moderation and virtue of a single character . . . probably prevented this revolution from being closed, as most others have been, by a subversion of that liberty it was intended to establish."

News that Washington had voluntarily relinquished power—as he would again when he resigned the presidency without asking for so much as a pension—traveled far and wide. People around the world were simply agog.

No one was more disbelieving than George III. Upon hearing that Washington—having risked everything, suffered much, and defeated the most powerful army on earth—had turned the nation over to his countrymen and gone back to Mount Vernon, he declared, "If that is true, he'll be the greatest man who ever lived."

That is why his image is over my mantel.

A REVELATION AT 4,500 FEET

I've just returned from an investment conference at the Four Seasons Resort in Costa Rica, followed by a real estate expedition to Agora's beautiful Rancho Santana development on the Pacific coast of Nicaragua.

Our trip took an adventurous turn, however, when a small group of us traveled on to the Totoco Eco-Lodge on Ometepe, an island formed by two volcanoes rising from Lake Nicaragua, the biggest lake in Central America and home to rare freshwater sharks that—I am not making this up—get there by leaping salmon-like up the rapids of the San Juan River.

What is an eco-lodge, exactly? It's not the Waldorf, I can tell you that. The first night I slept under mosquito netting in a bunk bed in an open room (without doors or windows) with a dozen or so other intrepid travelers, many of whom were terrific snorers.

We were smack in the middle of a nature preserve—and Ometepe is home to hundreds of howler monkeys, small primates with an outsized roar that sounds like a cross between an elephant seal and someone getting violently ill.

Howlers get particularly noisy around daybreak, which in Nicaragua arrives at an unspeakable hour. Lying in bed listening to them—you have no other choice—you'd swear the forest is full of lions and tigers. It's not, of course, but the howlers certainly lend a touch of authenticity to the experience.

Our first day there, we noticed that men and women returning from a hike up the nearby Maderas volcano were absolutely encased in mud. "How careless can you get?" we laughed.

We had no idea what we were talking about.

Early Sunday morning, five of us—and a local Nicaraguan guide—embarked on the vigorous nine-hour round-trip hike up the volcano, which soars 4,500 feet above sea level. Maderas is dormant. It hasn't been active since the 13th century. But Concepción, smoldering ominously next door, erupted violently last year.

Our hike was idyllic at first. Crisscrossing the rainforest, we passed coffee, plantain, and cacao trees. The bushes were filled with exotic flowers, butterflies, fork-tailed hummingbirds, and bright-green parrots. We passed under troops of white-faced and howler monkeys and marveled at ancient petroglyphs—rock engravings left by indigenous Indians dating to 300 BC.

A couple miles up, we entered a cloud forest and the dirt path turned into a soggy climb through mud and clay. Often, the only way to advance was by grabbing rocks or tree branches and pulling yourself up the trail. We landed on our rear ends more than once, but before long the shrieks and groans turned into peals of laughter. Our clothes and shoes were ruined, but we pressed on.

Hikers on their way down rhapsodized about the view from the peak and told us about a beautiful lagoon in the center of the caldera. "Unfortunately, the water is too cold to swim," they said.

When we got there, of course, we swam anyway.

My friend and colleague Dave Fessler was the first to step in and immediately sank to his knees in muck. He took another step forward and he sank to the top of his thigh—and kept going. Before long, the others splashed in behind him.

Listening to them shouting and waving, it was depressingly clear that I, too, was about to experience the frigid water and the most disgusting lake bottom imaginable (and I grew up in a small town, swimming in ponds).

Relieved to be off the trail, my buddies cavorted about, covering themselves with muck and acting like giddy teenagers. You wouldn't know it from my photos, but this was an alcohol-free afternoon.

Refreshed at last, we toweled off, made short work of a bag of chicken salad sandwiches and climbed back up to the rim.

The view from the peak, across the rainforest, beyond towering Concepción and out to the blue waters of Lake Nicaragua, was simply spectacular.

"Woo-hoo," yelled one companion, "What a sight!"

"What a day!" shouted another.

"What a life!" chimed in a third, summing up what the five of us were feeling.

Despite our long trek, it was only noon. Dave looked down at his watch. "My brother is in church right now," he said.

Then, shading his eyes and gazing out across the horizon, he added, "And so am I."

PART THREE

KNOWING AND BELIEVING

A few years ago, a friend and I were hiking along the rim of the Grand Canyon when I spotted a hawk circling high above us.

"Wow," I said, shading my eyes. "Imagine the view he has up there."

"Too bad he doesn't see it," my buddy replied.

"What do you mean?" I asked.

"His eyes are focused like a laser on any movement—a mouse, a snake, a rat—that could provide his next meal. He has the best view in the world. But he doesn't begin to see it."

He was right, of course, and I've often thought that many of us aren't much different. Head down and nose to the grindstone, we miss the big picture. We're blind to the magnificent vista that surrounds us. We are not really awake.

I wrote these essays because I am passionate about the battle of ideas. I want to know which ones are true, which ones work. And while I'm always interested in political, economic, and scientific ideas, the most important ones are ideas about how to live.

The libraries, of course, are full of books by authors pretending to tell us just that. But where do you start? Whom do you trust? How do you know who's right?

You can spend a lifetime studying and arguing those questions. But, speaking for myself, I can't accept a proposition that is not supported by reason and reliable evidence. If—for whatever reason—these two basic tests cannot be met, I am happy to consider an idea without embracing it. One should never be ashamed to say, "I really don't know."

Buddha famously said, "Do not believe anything simply because you have heard it. Do not believe traditions because they have been handed down for many generations. Do not believe anything because it is spoken and rumored by many. Do not believe anything because it is written down in religious books. Do not believe in anything merely on the authority of your teachers and elders. But after observation and analysis, when you find that anything agrees with reason and is conducive to the good and the benefit of one and all, then accept it and live up to it."

These are extraordinary words for a founder of a major religion, and a reminder that profound thinkers down through history still speak to us today. It doesn't matter that culture and technology are far beyond what they could have imagined a few hundred or a few thousand years ago. Human beings are still the same. We grapple with the same weaknesses and temptations.

Yet great men and women inspire and ennoble us. They remind us that millions have struggled with the same things we face: fear, disappointment, frustration, failure, illness, even death. Most of us are too busy in our workaday worlds to devote serious time to their words. To be economically successful, you generally need to put in a lot of hours and obtain a high level of specialized knowledge. Doctors need to know medicine. Pilots need to know aviation. Attorneys need to know the law.

It is time consuming just to simply keep up with developments in your own field. Yet economic success sometimes interferes with success in the rest of your life. And if you learn all the important life lessons the hard way—by trial and error—you are going to suffer a lot of unnecessary setbacks. Worse, you'll be well into the back nine before you discover what you need to know.

Here is a sampling of thoughts from some of the individuals who have most inspired me. My hope is that an essay or two here may act as a launching pad that leads you on to further exploration.

■ Tolstoy's Forbidden Book

Russian writer Leo Tolstoy was one of the greatest novelists of all time. His two masterpieces, *War and Peace* and *Anna Karenina,* are widely regarded as the very pinnacle of realist fiction.

In many ways, Tolstoy had it all. By his mid–40s, he was rich, in perfect health, and at the height of his fame. He was also wracked with despair. Despite his worldly success, Tolstoy felt that his life was meaningless. No matter what he achieved, he asked himself, "What is it for? What does it lead to?"

Over time, these "moments of perplexity" turned into a full-blown crisis. He contemplated suicide. Yet from this internal struggle grew the book that Tolstoy believed was his greatest accomplishment. He called it *A Calendar of Wisdom.*

Over 15 years, Tolstoy read, researched, and compiled the greatest spiritual thoughts of all time, creating a circle of reading that included Epictetus, Marcus Aurelius, Lao-Tzu, Buddha, Pascal, Schopenhauer, and the New Testament, among others.

What could be more precious, he asked, than to communicate daily with the wisest souls who have ever lived? For months at a time he avoided newspapers and magazines, reading nothing but the world's wisdom literature. In his diary he wrote, "I became more and more astonished by the ignorance, and especially by the cultural, moral ignorance of our society . . . All our education should be directed to the accumulation of the cultural heritage of our ancestors, the best thinkers of the world."

Yet too often today, we experience just the opposite. The media bombards us daily with heartbreak, misery, and cynicism. Much of what we read is depressing, even rattling. We tire of hearing about wild-eyed terrorists, drug-addled celebrities, ethically challenged businessmen, and crooked politicians.

Thoughts meant to inspire, uplift, or ennoble are as welcome as a cold glass of water on a July afternoon. And with the publication of his *Calendar of Wisdom* in 1912, Tolstoy achieved his goal.

After the Russian Revolution, however, its publication was forbidden under the new Soviet regime, due to the book's spiritual orientation and numerous religious quotes.

Rereading it this week, however, I was struck by one overriding theme: We are here for a short time. Knowledge is limitless. Therefore, the most critical knowledge is not a particular skill or discipline, but rather wisdom about "How to Live."

Here is a brief sampling of Tolstoy's thoughts on the subject:

- There are only two ways to live: either without thinking of death . . . or with the thought that you approach death with every hour of your life.
- The more upset you are with other people and circumstances, and the more satisfied you are with yourself, the further you are from wisdom.
- Don't compare yourself with others. Compare yourself only with perfection.
- It is not the place we occupy that is important, but the direction in which we move.
- When you want to escape from rage, do not walk, do not move, do not speak. Your rage cannot be justified by anything. The reason for your rage is always inside you.
- Speak only when your words are better than silence. For every time you regret that you did not say something, you will regret a hundred times that you did not keep your silence.

- There are two ways not to suffer from poverty. The first is to acquire more wealth. The second is to limit your requirements. The first is not always in our power. The second is.
- You do not have the right to be unhappy with your life. If you are not satisfied, see this as a reason to be unsatisfied with yourself.
- The more strictly and mercilessly you judge yourself, the more just and kind you will be in the judgment of others.
- Strive for goodness without any expectations for rapid or noticeable success. For the further you progress, the higher your ideal of perfection will rise. Yet it is the process itself, this striving, that justifies our lives.

Not your typical banned book, needless to say. But then the Soviet regime was about obedience to the state above all else.

Tolstoy believed in a higher ideal. And while he swore he couldn't define it or explain it, it cured his existential despair, gave him direction, and imbued his life with meaning.

In his *Calendar,* he wrote, "Nobody knows where the human race is going. The highest wisdom, then, is to know where *you* are going."

A SHAMELESS VENERATION OF HEROES

Although he is considered—along with Adam Smith and John Maynard Keynes—one of the world's most influential economists, Karl Marx was dead wrong.

Not just because his theories failed to lift people out of poverty and create prosperity. Not just because Marxist governments have systematically denied citizens their most basic human rights. (And not just because millions around the world have risked their lives to escape these societies.)

Karl Marx was also wrong because he distrusted exceptional men and women, envied superior talent, and instead exalted those who tilled the soil, cut the cloth, and swept the floors.

Don't get me wrong. There is nothing wrong with a day's work for a day's pay. Work gives meaning and dignity to life. Our society couldn't run without the numberless men and women who quietly and competently go about their daily business. But the real history of civilization is the story of extraordinary individuals. They are the ones who excite and inspire us. Is there any emotion that rivals the one we feel when we say, "I can't believe a human being did that"?

In the summer of 1941, for example, Sergeant James Allen Ward was awarded the Victoria Cross for climbing out onto the wing of his Wellington bomber in midflight to extinguish a fire in the starboard engine. Secured only by a rope around his waist, he smothered the fire and managed to crawl back into the cabin.

Winston Churchill, a great admirer of swashbuckling exploits, summoned the soldier to 10 Downing Street. Struck dumb with awe in Churchill's presence, however, Ward struggled to answer even the most basic questions. Surveying the unhappy hero, Churchill said, "You must feel very humble and awkward in my presence."

"Yes sir," stammered Ward.

"Then you can imagine how humble and awkward I feel in yours," replied Churchill.

The British prime minister got it exactly right. We should never lose our shameless veneration of heroes: the soldiers who spilled onto the beach at Normandy in June 1944, the New York firefighters who rushed into the Twin Towers on 9/11, Captain "Sully" Sullenberger landing his disabled jetliner on the Hudson River. These are the men and women who change our conception of who we are and what is possible.

It's not just about raw courage and bravery, however. History shows that heroism comes in all shapes and sizes. We owe an enormous debt of gratitude to rational thinkers like Plato and Aristotle, groundbreaking scientists like Newton and Einstein, and great moral leaders like Confucius, Socrates, and Jesus.

In *The Greatest Minds and Ideas of All Time* (Simon & Schuster, 2002), historian Will Durant wrote:

> I see men standing on the edge of knowledge, and holding the light a little farther ahead; men carving marble into forms ennobling men; men molding people into better instruments of greatness; men making a language of music and music out of language; men dreaming of finer lives—and living them.

How different our lives would look without political innovators like Locke and Jefferson, inventors like Edison and Marconi, or business pioneers like Henry Ford and Andrew Carnegie.

Novelist Ayn Rand once said the motive and purpose of her writing was not philosophical enlightenment, beneficial influence, or the reader's intellectual development, but rather "the projection of an ideal man."

In *The Romantic Manifesto* (World Publishing, 1969), she writes:

Since man's ambition is unlimited, since his pursuit and achievement of values is a lifelong process—and the higher the values, the harder the struggle—man needs a moment, an hour or some period of time in which he can experience the sense of his completed task, the sense of living in a universe where his values have been successfully achieved. It is like a moment of rest, a moment to gain fuel to move further.

Her books and the work of artists she particularly admired—men like Victor Hugo and Sergei Rachmaninov—provide that. But what motivates individuals like these?

Scholar and social scientist Charles Murray has spent years studying excellence in the arts and sciences from 800 BC to 1950. He compiled inventories of more than 4,000 men and women who have been essential to literature, music, art, philosophy, and the sciences and ranked them according to their eminence.

His research reveals that these individuals had—almost without exception—a strong sense that this is what they were put on earth to do. This zest, this life-affirming energy turns out to be an essential prerequisite to great achievement.

In *Human Accomplishment* (HarperCollins, 2003), Murray writes:

If human beings with the potential for excellence generally have done best in cultures where people believe the universe to have transcendental meaning, one must ask why. The easy answer is that the giants of the past were deluded. They imagined that what they were doing had some transcendental significance, and, lo and behold, their foolishness inspired them to compose better music or paint better pictures. But this line of thought can become embarrassing when one confronts just what those self-deluded people accomplished. Is it not implausible that those individuals who accomplished things so beyond the rest of us just happened to be uniformly stupid about the great questions? Another possibility is that they understood things we don't.

This truth crossed Karl Marx's head at 30,000 feet. He envisioned life as a meaningless trial based on social forces and "class struggles." Yet without intellectual, political, and religious freedoms, how can we realize our potential as individuals or live the best possible life?

Marxist philosophy fails us utterly here. Heroes don't. They provide us with vivid examples of excellence. They show us how the human spirit expresses itself most gloriously. They inspire us, galvanize us. Without them, our lives are impoverished.

We should study them, contemplate their actions, warm ourselves by their fire, and pursue some modest form of discipleship True, we may never lead like George Marshall, write like Jane Austen, or paint like Rembrandt. But exceptional men and women like these provide brilliant stars to steer by.

A Path to Personal Freedom

Has there ever been a professional athlete whose fall from grace was more sudden or severe than Tiger Woods'?

He is back playing PGA Tour events now, but a great deal of skepticism remains about his highly public rehabilitation. Many insist he is simply cultivating an image recommended by his handlers and lawyers. Some even doubt the sincerity of his attempt to reconnect with Buddhism, the religion of his youth.

But that may be too cynical. Buddhism is growing in the West, but this is still a solidly Judeo-Christian nation. So this particular revelation hardly plays to the gallery.

And several other professional golfers have recently credited their success to Buddhist teachings. Adherents include Thailand's Thongchai Jaidee, currently ranked 44th in the world, and Y. E. Yang, who became the first Asian to win a major when he beat Tiger in the 2009 PGA Championship. English golfer Justin Rose climbed to sixth in the world in 2007 after spending two years meditating with Buddhist swing coach Nick Bradley. And Vijay Singh, who has earned more money than any golfer on the current Tour except Tiger, says Buddhist philosophy puts him "on a peaceful plane."

Buddhist principles may or may not make Tiger Woods a better golfer, but they do stand a chance of making him a better person.

Buddhism is more than just a 2,500-year-old Eastern religion. It is a philosophy, a code of ethics, a way of life. The Dalai Lama refers to it as a science of the mind.

The Buddha, who recommended a middle way between extravagance and asceticism, never claimed to be a deity or savior. According to Buddhist tradition, he was an ordinary human being who attained enlightenment and taught others how to live with wisdom and compassion.

He taught that wisdom begins with recognizing Four Noble Truths:

The First Noble Truth:	There is suffering in every life.
The Second Noble Truth:	Our suffering is caused by our attachments and cravings.
The Third Noble Truth:	If we end our attachments and cravings, our suffering will end.
The Fourth Noble Truth:	This can be achieved by following the Noble Eightfold Path to Enlightenment.

Eventually, we all must grapple with aging, pain, economic and personal setbacks, the loss of family and friends, and, ultimately, our own passing. The first two Noble Truths describe anguish and its origins, the second two its remedy.

And the Noble Eightfold Path? Here are the basics:

Wisdom Training

Step 1: Right View—See life as it really is, not just as it appears. Everything is impermanent. In the Prajna Paramita Sutras, the Buddha says, "Regard this fleeting world like the stars fading at dawn, like bubbles on a fast moving stream, like morning dewdrops evaporating on blades of grass, like a candle flickering in a strong wind. . . ."

Step 2: Right Intentions—Approach others with compassion and understanding.

Ethics Training
Step 3: Right Speech—Speak the truth in a nonhurtful way.

Step 4: Right Action—Behave so as to harm no one. (Many Buddhists extend this to animals and the environment, as well.)

Step 5: Right Livelihood—Earn your living in a legal, nondeceitful way.

Personal Mastery
Step 6: Right Effort—Strive to improve your behavior and character.

Step 7: Right Mindfulness—Recognize that it is always now. Be awake to the present moment and act from a clear conscience.

Step 8: Right Concentration—Use meditation, a sense of dignity, and personal willpower to act with integrity and overcome cravings.

What are these cravings, exactly? It varies. Your craving might be a Maserati Quattroporte Sport GT. Your sister's might be fresh-baked chocolate chip cookies. (I think we all know what Tiger's is.) A craving, simply put, is any unhealthy desire, insatiable hunger, psychological fixation, or addictive behavior.

Buddhism challenges us to understand the nature of our anguish and practice a more skillful way of living. If we fail to do this, we may drift through life in the grip of habitual impulses, living in a way that is both ignoble and undignified.

The Noble Eightfold Path represents a road to personal freedom. The goal is to break out of your routine and ask, "What am I here for? Am I living so that I can die without regrets? How much of what I do is compromise?"

In particular, Buddhists believe that by meditating on death we become more conscious of life. In particular, you are encouraged to consider: Since death alone is certain and the time of death is uncertain, how shall I live?

It's a sobering question, one that requires you to confront your mortality and recognize that not all of your desires are reasonable or even obtainable.

It's important to have goals to work toward, of course. But, according to the Dalai Lama, once our basic needs are met, we don't necessarily need "more money, we don't need greater success or fame, we don't need the perfect body or even the perfect mate—right now, at this very moment, we have a mind, which is all the basic equipment we need to achieve complete happiness."

Buddhism teaches that contentment is determined more by your state of mind than by external circumstances. Many of us fail to recognize how much our happiness is determined by the way we choose to perceive our situation.

And the solution is often simple: Let go. (There is a Zen saying: Knowledge is learning something every day. Wisdom is letting go of something every day.) To be free from delusions, fear, ignorance, pride, anger, envy, and hatred is to be free from suffering.

None of these principles is incompatible with other religious beliefs, incidentally. This philosophy is not about accepting a particular creed or dogma but rather about integrating a higher level of awareness into your daily life. The objective is to bring about an inner transformation, to perfect your heart and train your mind.

That's why Buddhism is often referred to not as a religion but as an ethical philosophy, a spiritual practice, or simply a path to inner peace and personal freedom. It offers nothing to believe and everything to discover.

Of course, whether Tiger Woods accepts these timeless principles and acts on them is up to him. But his PGA competitors should be worried. When he gets his personal life together, he's likely to be a holy terror on the links again.

■ YOUR GREATEST RISK

Ask someone what he or she wants out of life and you're likely to hear a familiar litany: a great job, a loving family, a nice home, a comfortable retirement, and so on.

But what are you living for? Of all the things you might pursue in life, which is the most valuable?

"Most people have trouble naming this goal," writes William B. Irvine, Professor of Philosophy at Wright State University. "They know what they want minute by minute or even decade by decade during their life, but they have never paused to consider their grand goal in living. It is perhaps understandable that they haven't. Our culture doesn't encourage people to think about such things; indeed, it provides them with an endless stream of distractions so they won't ever have to. But a grand goal in living is the first component of a philosophy of life. This means that if you lack a grand goal in living, you lack a coherent philosophy of life."

There was a time when great thinkers sought to answer these questions. But no longer. Modern philosophy has evolved into a specialized academic discipline that pursues arcane questions of no real interest to the general public. When was the last time you read or heard anything from a living philosopher?

Yet the ancient Greeks and Romans obsessed over these questions. They strove to learn what was most important and how to achieve it. In sum, they wanted to discover how best to live.

Their answers evolved into stoicism, a philosophy that is not widely understood today.

The word *stoic* is used to describe someone unmoved by joy or grief, someone without passion. Yet that is not the Stoic philosophy. Stoicism is about pursuing a life that is both meaningful and fulfilling. It's about healing the inevitable suffering in life and achieving tranquility.

How is this done? Ancient Stoic philosophers advised:

- Contemplating the transitory nature of the world around you
- Living in the present without fear of the future
- Banishing negative emotions
- Living according to your own nature
- Pursuing virtue
- Seeking courage and wisdom
- Living simply and frugally
- Mastering desire, to the extent that it is possible to do so

Sounds simple enough. But that's deceptive, really. These tenets require work.

Living in the present without fear of the future, for instance, may seem impossible when we consider all the sad and tragic news that surrounds us. Yet the Stoic philosopher Epictetus reminds us that most worldly events are beyond our control. What disturbs our minds then is not the events themselves but merely our judgments about them. And we can change these.

After all, there is little you can do to stop nuclear proliferation, global warming, the specter of terrorism, or an economic downturn. Yes, you can speak your mind, cast your vote, organize. But worry? That solves nothing.

Likewise, the Stoic advice to live simply and frugally could have saved millions of Americans who overreached a ton of heartache in recent years.

Limiting your material desires and craving for luxury enables you to save and invest more of your after-tax income. Paradoxically, the shortest route to financial freedom is to fight the acquisitive instinct and the desire to appear wealthy.

Too many imagine that if they just earn enough they can finally fulfill—and ultimately eliminate—their desires. Yet nothing ever does. New desires spring up to take the place of old ones. Recognize this and at least you can make honest choices in your life.

This point was made 1,700 years ago in a well-known dialogue between Alexander the Great and the Greek philosopher Diogenes:

Alexander: Diogenes, you are a man of great repute. Yet you spend your days untroubled, unperturbed, indulging in conversation and the pleasures of life.

Diogenes: Tell me what is so much better about the life of Alexander the Great?

Alexander: I am a conqueror of nations!

Diogenes: So, conqueror of nations, what are you going to do next?

Alexander: I will conquer Greece!

Diogenes: Yes . . . then what?

Alexander: I will conquer Asia Minor!

Diogenes: Alright . . . then what?

Alexander: I will conquer the rest of the world!

Diogenes: And then?

Alexander: Then . . . I plan to relax and enjoy life.

Diogenes: So why not relax and enjoy it now?

He must have made an impression. The great conqueror once observed, "Were I not Alexander, I would be Diogenes."

Diogenes lived according to his own nature, caring little for reputation, luxury, or material possessions. Few would subscribe to his brand of extreme asceticism. But at least he had philosophy of life—and lived it.

Most of us never take the time to consider our grand goal. Instead, we choose society's default position: the pursuit of affluence, social status, and pleasure.

That is your perfect right, of course. But the risk is that you may mislive. Instead of pursuing and enjoying what matters most, you could wake up one day to find that confusion and distraction have caused you to squander your life.

And that is the greatest risk of all.

ARE YOU PART OF "THE GREAT CONVERSATION"?

A few weeks ago, John Mackey, founder and CEO of Whole Foods, invited me to a social event at his ranch west of Austin.

Wandering through his home, I couldn't help admiring the beautiful artwork on the walls, much of it depicting Eastern mystical traditions. I asked John if he had an interest in oriental philosophy.

"Some," he said, adding at one point, "I'm a perennialist."

What a thought-provoking self-description, one you seldom hear these days. Perennialists believe you should learn—and pass along to your children and students—those things that are of everlasting importance to all people everywhere.

What are those things? Humanity's best ideas about how to live.

Some will insist, of course, that we've hit a snag right out of the gate. After all, the world is full of divergent views. People simply don't agree on these matters.

But perennialists counter that enlightened people everywhere agree on certain core principles. These are handed down from generation to generation, through the ages, and across nations and cultures.

The phrase *Philosophia Perennis*—the Perennial Philosophy— was coined by the German mathematician, philosopher, and polymath Gottfried Leibniz (1646–1716). In more recent years, Aldous Huxley, Mortimer Adler, and Huston Smith, among other writers, carried the perennialist torch, beckoning us to take part in what they call "The Great Conversation."

It's a broad discussion about what constitutes the best life, one that encompasses everything from the *Analects* of Confucius to Aristotle's *Nicomachean Ethics*—the sound, practical, and undogmatic ethics of common sense—to the mystical truths of the world's great religious traditions.

The conversation is ongoing and evolving, never static. The best ideas about how to live are hardly new, of course. But discoveries are sometimes made, and old ideas are enlarged or restated for a modern audience. Recent books that touch on the perennial philosophy include Roger Walsh's *Essential Spirituality,* Karen Armstrong's *The Great Transformation,* and Robert Wright's *The Evolution of God.*

Perennialists understand the connection between compassion and successful living. They offer, for example, that:

- Everything worthwhile in life is created as the result of love and concern for others.
- Humanity is one great family. Our similarities are deep, our differences superficial.
- The Golden Rule, expressed in some way in every society, is the cornerstone of human understanding.
- The giving of time, money, support, and encouragement can never be detrimental to the giver.
- Character development—the path from self-absorption to caring and consciousness—is paramount.
- Problems are life's way of getting the best out of us. They are opportunities to grow.
- It is important to nourish your mind with the thoughts of history's wisest thinkers.
- Courage and self-awareness are required to live fully and follow your heart.
- You should develop the ability to reason accurately and independently rather than accepting ideas based solely on authority or tradition.

- Our egos cause us to cherish opinions, judge others, and rationalize our beliefs. Perennialists ask "Would you rather be right or be happy?"
- We should exercise humility. Not because others find it attractive (although they do) but because, if we are honest with ourselves, we have much to be humble about.
- We should practice forgiveness. When we forgive others, we find that others forgive us—and that we forgive ourselves.
- Moral development comes from strengthening our impulse control, prioritizing personal relationships, and fostering social responsibility.
- Our lives are immeasurably improved by expressing gratitude and generosity.
- Development of the heart is essential. Our actions are the mirror of our inner selves.
- Whenever we act, we are never just doing. We are always becoming. If we aren't growing, we are diminishing.
- Integrity is everything.

Rather than quarreling over sectarian differences, perennialists are interested in the nuggets of truth at the heart of every great tradition.

Two years ago, for instance, a friend and I bumped into Nassim Nicholas Taleb, author of *The Black Swan,* at a bookstore in Vancouver. (This was no great coincidence. All three of us were speaking at an investment conference at the Fairmont down the street.)

Taleb indicated that he was planning to write a book on religion, whereupon my friend and he got into a brief dispute about whether a particular theological point "was true."

Like many conversations of this nature, more heat was shed than light. Frustrated at one point, Taleb waved an arm toward the fiction section. "How about all those books over there. Are they true?"

"Of course not," my friend said. "They're novels."

"But they are full of universal truths," I added.

Taleb turned and jabbed a finger in my direction. "Exactly!"

Consciously or not, he was advocating the perennial philosophy. Perennialists seek enlightenment wherever they can find it. It doesn't matter whether the source is ancient, modern, mythical, foreign, mystical, or verified by the latest scientific findings. It only matters that it works, that it has some practical application for more skillful living.

As the historian Will Durant wrote in *The Greatest Minds and Ideas of All Time* (Simon & Schuster, 2002):

> We are born animals; we become human. We have humanity thrust upon us through the hundred channels whereby the past pours down into the present that mental and cultural inheritance whose preservation, accumulation and transmission place mankind today, with all its defectives and illiterates, on a higher plane than any generation has ever reached before.

What is that higher plane? An upward spiral of caring—from *me* to *us* to *all of us*.

It doesn't always come naturally. And for some, unfortunately, it doesn't come at all.

But perennialists try to absorb as much as they can of our 3,000-year heritage and take an occasional moment from their hectic lives to ask, "Am I becoming the kind of person I want to be? Am I part of The Great Conversation?"

A 2,600-Year-Old
Manual for Living

In my former life as a money manager, I found that many investors—
often aided and abetted by their advisors—use a blinkered approach
to the stock market.

They believe a successful strategy starts with a hunch about the
economy. Based on this, they make an educated guess about what
lies ahead for the stock market. This, in turn, leads to a theory
about which stocks to buy. But a theory that's based on a guess
that's based on a hunch may not be the best foundation for your
investment portfolio.

Investors hate uncertainty. And history shows that they will pay
brokers, money managers, and investment gurus a lot of money to
eliminate it.

The problem is they can't. Count yourself a sophisticated investor the
day you wake up and say, "Given that no one can tell me with any
certainty what the economy or financial markets will do, how should
I run my portfolio?" This is the beginning of investment wisdom.

When my publisher, Julia Guth, first heard me describe my
market-neutral approach more than a decade ago, she referred to
it as "the Tao of the Dow." (I think she liked saying this, in part,
because Tao is also pronounced "Dow.")

I had never considered my approach a Taoist one, but as I learned
more about the philosophy, I was struck by the similarities. Consider,
for example, the following verses from China's ancient *Tao Te*

Ching. They could be aimed squarely at economic forecasters, market timers, and metaphysical speculators:

> The ancient Masters
> didn't try to educate the people,
> but kindly taught them to not-know.
> When they think that they know the answers,
> people are difficult to guide.
> When they know that they don't know,
> people can find their own way.

Or consider this verse:

> Not knowing is true knowledge.
> Presuming to know is a disease.
> First realize that you are sick;
> then you can move toward health.

Or even more simply:

> Those who know don't talk.
> Those who talk don't know.

The venerable *Tao Te Ching* is not an investment guide, of course. It is a 2,600-year-old collection of 81 brief poems that describe a vision of what our lives would be like if we lived in harmony with the way things are.

It is among the most translated books in the world, exceeded only by the Bible and the Bhagavad-Gita. The Tao itself represents a transcendent mystery, something we cannot name or even imagine. Interpreted literally, it is "the way" of the universe, an explanation of life.

It contains no moral code, however. In fact, the *Tao Te Ching* is rarely about taking action. More often, it is about the wisdom of inaction and accepting what you cannot change, be it the state of the economy, the death of a loved one, or the behavior of your adult children.

Tradition tells us the author is Lao Tzu, a keeper of the imperial archives in the ancient capital of Luoyang, who lived around 600 BC. But more likely he didn't exist at all. Like Homer, Lao Tzu is probably a combination of many ancient sages—and the Tao is a compilation of wisdom that came into being over a great period of time. (The words *lao tzu* literally mean "old philosopher.")

Taoist philosophy challenges you to embrace paradoxical thinking. For example, you may believe an affront requires a forceful response. Lao Tzu encourages you to consider humility instead. A problem needs an effective solution? Consider the benefits of nonaction first.

The ancient symbol of the Tao shows the two phases of the moon conjoined. This represents the yin and yang of the world: masculine and feminine, darkness and light, weakness and strength, action and inaction. In the West, we tend to think that opposites contradict. The Oriental view is that they complement each other—and it is only when we change our ingrained ways of thinking that we begin to change our world.

Taoist philosophy requires an open mind and considerable reflection to be fully appreciated. It reminds us, for instance, that we may be so busy trying to get rich, change the world, or improve ourselves that we miss life's essence. Verse 8 says:

> Fill your bowl to the brim
> and it will spill.
> Keep sharpening your knife
> and it will blunt.
> Chase after money and security
> and your heart will never unclench.
> Care about people's approval
> and you will be their prisoner.
> Do your work, then step back.
> The only path to serenity.

Taoism offers an alternative view of abundance, one that values maintaining dignity over acquiring social position, and enjoying free time over acquiring possessions.

Culture, society, and technology have changed a great deal over the past few thousand years. But the Taoist philosophy remains relevant. For example:

Knowing others is intelligence;
knowing yourself is true wisdom.
Mastering others is strength;
mastering yourself is true power.

Or consider this timeless nugget:

Wise men don't need to prove their point;
Men who need to prove their point aren't wise.

Lao Tzu said we should have a nature like water. Water can be forceful, yet it is always the first to yield, moving quickly around obstacles and relentlessly seeking the simplest path. With time and persistence, water will wear away the tallest mountains and transform the landscape.

People who are confrontational—who remain dogmatic—never learn this lesson. They are more interested in being right than moving forward. The *Tao Te Ching* says:

People are born gentle and weak;
at their death they are hard and stiff.
All things, including the grass and the trees,
are soft and pliable in life;
dry and brittle in death.
Stiffness is thus a companion of death;
flexibility a companion of life.
An army that cannot yield
will be defeated.
A tree that cannot bend
will crack in the wind.
The hard and stiff will be broken;
The soft and supple will prevail.

One of the classics of Oriental literature, the *Tao Te Ching* is both simple and profound—and easy to follow. The secret is not to complicate it.

The Tao encourages you to stop feeding your ego and enjoy the fruits of your labor. It teaches that the experience of inner peace is the true gauge of accomplishment.

The *Tao Te Ching* deals with many of the most basic human experiences: birth, death, loss, gain, dignity in the face of challenge, how to judge the character of a person, when to move forward, when to retreat, how to deal with good fortune or ill fate. There is even sage political advice: *Governing a large country is like frying a small fish. You spoil it with too much poking.*

Despite his wisdom, Lao Tzu expected skepticism. He seemed to know his message would not always be well received:

> When a superior man hears of the Tao,
> he immediately begins to embody it.
> When an average man hears of the Tao,
> he half believes it, half doubts it.
> When a foolish man hears of the Tao,
> he laughs out loud.
> If he didn't laugh,
> it wouldn't be the Tao.

Our lives are full of responsibilities and obligations. Technology and the pace of modern life add even more pressure and anxiety. Yet it is possible to gain understanding from the *Tao Te Ching*, a 2,600-year-old discourse on the nature of existence.

Taoism teaches that to be truly free we must be able to work with change rather than against it. We should be humble, flexible, and detached from most worldly concerns. The art of abundance is often a matter of recognizing, appreciating, and celebrating life as it is:

> If you look to others for fulfillment,
> you will never be truly fulfilled.

If your happiness depends on money,
you will never be happy with yourself.

Be content with what you have;
rejoice in the way things are.
When you realize there is nothing lacking,
the whole world belongs to you.

IF YOU KNEW WHAT JIM BROWN KNOWS

Jim Brown is arguably the best all-around athlete ever.

He was a track star, one of the nation's finest lacrosse players, averaged 38 points per game on his high school basketball team, and broke NFL records as a running back for the Cleveland Browns. In 2002, the *Sporting News* named him the greatest football player of all time.

He was pretty handy with a tennis racquet, too. And he liked to wager on his matches. At a Las Vegas tennis club in 1979, Brown was frustrated when his opponent canceled a money match at the last minute.

A stranger with a young boy approached him. His proposal, delivered in a thick foreign accent, was preposterous. He bet Brown that his nine-year-old son—short and scrawny even for his age—could whip him in tennis. And he was cocky about it. He offered to put up his house.

We can only imagine what ran through Brown's mind as he sized up the half-pint. After all, this wasn't a bet. It was an insult.

The stranger had chosen the wrong man to outrage. Brown wasn't just an athletic phenom. His NFL career could be summed up in his oft-quoted remark, "Make sure when anyone tackles you he remembers how much it hurts."

He countered that they should make the bet an even $10,000.

The club owner tried to warn Brown. And while he did reduce his wager, he wouldn't be talked out of the match, insisting, "The man needs to be taught a lesson." And so Jim Brown strode off to the courts—with Mike Agassi and his young son Andre in tow.

It didn't take Brown long to recognize his error. He had been hustled.

We seldom deliver lessons in humility. More often than not, we wind up on the receiving end. This is especially true in my bailiwick, the investment arena, where high confidence and big egos are routinely taken down like the Berlin Wall.

Every successful investor develops an abiding sense of humility, a deep respect for the unknown and the unknowable. What will happen tomorrow or next week is always an open question.

And if you don't know who you are, the stock market is an expensive place to find out. Just ask Victor Niederhoffer.

A professional trader and former finance professor, Neiderhoffer established his reputation as hedge fund great George Soros' partner, managing his fixed income and foreign exchange investments from 1982 to 1990.

Niederhoffer is a smart guy and an unorthodox thinker, drawing on many disciplines—including psychology, philosophy, and advanced mathematics—to make his trading decisions. His 1997 book, *The Education of a Speculator,* was a *New York Times* best seller.

But in the fall of that same year, he got his postgraduate degree. Viewing the Asian market meltdown as a once-in-a-lifetime buying opportunity, Neiderhoffer loaded up his hedge fund with Thai bank stocks, confident the government would never let them fail. He was wrong. His fund quickly lost more than three quarters of its value and he was forced to close its doors.

Niederhoffer is an experienced, insightful guy. But I wish he'd written *The Education of a Speculator* after he took his hedge fund nose down, not before. That would have been a book worth reading.

Niederhoffer is hardly alone, of course. History has not been particularly kind to all manner of experts and their definitive pronouncements:

- Anglican Archbishop James Ussher (1581–1656) researched the dates of Biblical events and painstakingly subtracted all the Old Testament generations. When he finished his calculations, he proclaimed that the earth was created on October 23, 4004 BC at nine o'clock in the morning. (He missed his mark by 4.6 billion years or so.)
- In 1899, Charles H. Duell, commissioner of the United States Patent and Trademark Office proposed shuttering the office. "Everything that can be invented has been invented," he declared.
- In 1927, *The New York Times* heralded Philo T. Farnsworth's new creation, the television, with a front-page article and this subhead: "Few Commercial Possibilities Seen."
- Walter Lippman, one of the twentieth century's most respected journalists and thinkers, wrote in a column dated April 27, 1948, "Among the really difficult problems of the world, the Arab-Israeli conflict is one of the simplest and most manageable."
- In 1962, a little-known Liverpool group called The Beatles auditioned for Tony Meehan of Decca Records. They performed 15 songs in just under an hour. Decca sent them packing, saying "guitar groups are on the way out" and "the Beatles have no future in show business."

It's not just the "experts" who flounder, of course. In many ways, life is one long lesson in humility. Our perceptions deceive us. Trust gets misplaced. Knowledge grows and opinions change. Even when the truth is with us, there are usually exceptions.

It's natural to seek out experts who can guide us. But outside of physics and chemistry, predictions are best taken with a whole shaker of salt.

We all swim in a vast sea of the unknown. The sooner we recognize this—and embrace it in our personal and business lives—the better our chances of staying afloat.

THE NOBLEST EXPRESSION
OF THE HUMAN SPIRIT

Here's a riddle.

What is the secret of eloquence, the standard of virtue, the basis of moral authority, the object of philosophy, the most formidable power on earth, the noblest expression of the human spirit, and beauty itself?

Thoreau said it was better than money, love, or fame. The New Testament proclaims it is the basis of freedom (John 8:32). Schopenhauer observed that it is first ridiculed, then violently oppressed, then accepted as self-evident.

The answer, of course, is truth. Yet you'll notice that the supply often exceeds demand.

The other day, for instance, a friend forwarded me a political e-mail filled with dubious accusations and misstatements of fact. You would think a message that is unsigned, printed in three colors, and written in ALL LARGE CAPS might engender a bit of skepticism. Yet it resonated with him so strongly that he eagerly accepted it.

We all want to believe that we are in possession of the truth. Even when we're uncertain, we like to feel that we're evaluating information rationally and will surely recognize the truth when we see it.

But as Winston Churchill observed, "Men occasionally stumble over the truth, but most of them pick themselves up and hurry off as if nothing ever happened."

We all walk around with a picture in our heads that we believe reflects the world as it truly is. We depend on this image. It governs our thoughts, feelings, and behavior. But is it accurate?

With today's radio, cable TV, and Internet, you can watch, read, or listen to whatever kind of news pleases you, and indulge your political, social, and scientific theories, whether sophisticated or naive, extremist or pedestrian, grounded in reality or so far out you're floating in the asteroid belt.

It's called selective exposure. Rather than dealing with the unpleasant sensation of having our beliefs tested, we simply steer clear of information that contradicts what we think we know. We carefully select the messages we consume. As a result, we're not just arguing over what we should be doing. We're arguing over what is happening. We're no longer just holding different opinions. We're holding different facts.

We don't have time to investigate everything ourselves, of course. So we rely on conventional wisdom and the opinions of others. We draw generalities from specific circumstances. We accept things we hear or read if they sound credible—and especially if they appeal to our personal prejudices. As we grow older, we even forget or misremember our own experiences.

We are creatures of culture, too, brought up to accept certain narratives about how the world is. Yet these preconceptions harden and make us resistant to opposing points of view. They prevent us from opening our eyes . . . or our minds. And out of politeness or political correctness, we are reluctant to ask questions or voice dissent. We fall back on what is generally accepted rather than doing the heavy lifting and thinking for ourselves.

That should make us consider from time to time whether our version of reality—our truth—is correct.

Social scientists observe that what we believe—what we accept as true—is highly dependent on our upbringing and the society we live in. We are all caught in a web of cultural context.

Postmodernists and deconstructionists have taken this to extremes, claiming that there is no such thing as objective truth, only culturally based worldviews and opinions, none any more valid than another.

What a depressing thought, for what are we all pursuing if not objective truth? Yet Oxford biologist Richard Dawkins effectively skewers the postmodern position in *River Out of Eden* (Basic Books, 1995):

> Show me a cultural relativist at thirty thousand feet, and I'll show you a hypocrite. Airplanes built according to scientific principles work. . . . Airplanes built according to tribal or mythological specifications don't. If you are flying to an international congress of anthropologists, the reason you will probably get there—the reason you don't plummet into a ploughed field—is that a lot of Western scientifically-trained engineers have got their sums right.

It is not possible to thoroughly investigate every claim we accept. But not all modes of knowing are equal. In fact, most of our beliefs are derived in one of three ways.

The first is *tradition*. These are beliefs that are handed down from grandparents to parents to children and so on. The problem here, of course, is that if a particular fact or story or folk remedy was in error to begin with, it's as untrue today as it was originally, no matter how many generations have passed it along.

The second source is *authority*. If a teacher, public official, or religious leader tells us something is true, we're more inclined to accept it. This can be a valid shortcut. But, regardless of their credentials, experts are often mistaken. Just because information comes from someone important, it doesn't guarantee its reliability.

The third source of belief is *reason and evidence*. Here we are on firmer ground. Historians use documents, letters, and photographs to piece together the past. Judges base their opinions on physical and circumstantial evidence, eyewitness testimony, and confirmed facts. Scientists construct hypotheses, test them by observation and experiment, share their methods, and offer the results for acceptance or rejection.

Scientists, like historians and judges, are far from perfect and their claims are always subject to revision. Yet the scientific method, with its double-blind methodology and rigorous peer-review process, is based on a fine understanding of human fallibility. It is designed to weed out erroneous conclusions.

In 1989, for example, Martin Fleischmann, then one of the world's leading electrochemists, and Stanley Pons announced their discovery of cold fusion—nuclear fusion near room temperature. But their results could not be replicated, and their "discovery" was soon dismissed for lack of evidence.

The success of science in the modern era has given it a powerful aura. Indeed, some have tried to make it the unquestionable authority and final arbiter of truth and knowledge. That can be a mistake.

Scientists are egotistical, ambitious and biased, too. Even the peer-review process, as we saw in the ClimateGate scandal, can fall prey to ideological conflicts and personal vendettas.

Science has plumbed the depths of the ocean, the hinterlands of space, and the recesses of the atom. It has increased our understanding of life immeasurably. But it does not tell us why we're here or imbue life with meaning.

Science does an excellent job of telling us what is. It cannot tell us what ought to be.

That is left for theologians, poets, and philosophers. Some important truths we have to discover for ourselves.

THE ART OF LIVING CONSCIOUSLY

One of the benefits of attending and speaking at Mark Skousen's FreedomFest each year—billed as "The World's Largest Gathering of Free Minds"—is getting to know a lot of smart, interesting people. One of them is Dr. Nathaniel Branden.

A long-time psychotherapist and corporate consultant, Branden is a leading authority on self-esteem, a field he pioneered more than 40 years ago. His many books include *Honoring the Self* and *The Six Pillars of Self-Esteem*.

Branden believes our greatest calling is to live consciously. This is not pop psychology. Branden is a serious thinker who argues that true satisfaction and peace of mind are found only when our values, interests, goals, and behavior are in alignment.

A young father, for instance, may say that his relationship with his children is a high priority and watching TV is a low priority. But if he spends several hours a week in front of the Tube and very little time interacting with his kids, his values and behavior are out of whack. The result, among other consequences, is a feeling of disharmony.

Living consciously means taking a close look at your life and perceiving your situation clearly. It means opening yourself to the possibility of errors in your thinking. Indeed, it requires an eagerness to discover your mistakes, candor about admitting them, and a willingness to correct them.

This isn't always easy. By the time we are adults, many of our thoughts and beliefs have crystallized. Having discovered and settled on "the truth," many of us aren't interested in exposing ourselves to contradictory evidence or opposing points of view.

Yet as Transcendentalist Ralph Waldo Emerson noted 150 years ago, "God offers every mind the choice between truth and repose. Take which you please—you can never have both."

Living consciously means accepting that whatever is, is. Our desires don't obliterate uncomfortable facts about the way things are. No matter how much we may wish things were different, reality is intransigent. Acknowledging this is part of growing up.

Conscious living also means being present to what you are doing while you are doing it. When you are in the office, you focus on your work, not the golf course. When you are playing golf, you concentrate on your game rather than fretting about business. When you are playing with your grandkids, you are not mulling over the real estate contract on your desk or reflecting on the last homeowner's meeting. You are aware, open, and receptive to the present moment. This is a challenge for all of us. But greater mindfulness creates more effectiveness in every area of our lives.

Conscious living also entails finding creative solutions to our problems. And Branden has developed a fascinating way to uncover them: sentence completion exercises.

It's a simple but powerful technique to expand personal effectiveness. The procedure requires you to take a sentence stem and write down 6 to 10 endings rapidly, without pausing to think. There is no censoring your thoughts or worrying about whether a particular ending is reasonable or significant. The objective is to generate insights by avoiding inhibitions and quickly jotting down whatever enters your mind.

For example, the sentence stem "If I bring 5 percent more consciousness to my work . . ." might generate responses like:

- I'd learn more about my business.
- I'd procrastinate less.

- I'd think more about my priorities.
- I'd spend less time on e-mail.
- I'd stay focused on important issues.

The idea is to increase your awareness, change your behavior, and improve your results. Imagine, for example, how your business might change if you gave 6 to 10 reflexive answers to these sentence stems:

- If I think about how I set my priorities . . .
- If I want to have a more effective team . . .
- If I look at how I spend my time . . .
- If I want my employees to trust and admire the company . . .
- If I want to keep a customer for life . . .

Branden provides more examples and describes this practice in detail in *The Art of Living Consciously* (Simon & Schuster, 1997). What most surprises me about these exercises is how quickly and efficiently they reveal exactly what you need to do. Nobody has to tell you. You already have the answers, right below the surface of your distracted mind.

The beautiful thing about Branden's technique is how it works in virtually every area of life. For example, it's hard to imagine someone who wouldn't benefit from completing these stems:

- If I commit myself to raising my standard of living . . .
- If I approach my work as an opportunity for self-development . . .
- If I take full responsibility for my choices and actions . . .
- If I am fully accountable for my relationships with others . . .
- If I reflect on what it means to use everything I know . . .
- If I bring 5 percent more consciousness to my daily activities . . .

Branden calls this technique "a shot of adrenaline to the psyche," and it's tough to disagree.

He even uses sentence completion exercises in relationship counseling. Branden says he typically asks each partner to tell him what might be hard about being married to him or her. He then has them face each other and complete such stems as:

- One of the ways I can be difficult is . . .
- Sometimes I can be frustrating when I . . .
- Sometimes I make you angry when . . .
- Sometimes I hurt you when . . .
- One of the things you want from me and don't always get is . . .

No one likes having someone else point out his or her personal shortcomings. But when you cough them up yourself, it's pretty enlightening.

He also suggests that couples can increase their feeling of intimacy by completing these stems:

- One of the things we enjoy about each other is . . .
- One of the things we have in common is . . .
- I appreciate it when you . . .
- I feel especially loved when you . . .
- I feel most connected to you when . . .

In his practice, Branden found that couples who remain deeply in love over many years operate at a high level of mindfulness. Instead of taking each other for granted, they communicate respect and caring, even in situations where they cannot accommodate.

Individuals who don't live consciously, however, tend to be bored, conflicted, burned-out, anxious, unhappy in their careers, and disappointed in their relationships. Unfortunately, they seek the causes outside themselves. This conveniently absolves them of responsibility—and prevents them from discovering the truth.

Branden even argues that one of the reasons some of us fear death as much as we do is our secret knowledge of how incompletely we have lived. The solution? Greater consciousness.

This means harmony between what we profess and what we do. It's about living purposefully rather than just drifting through life. It means identifying what is important, recognizing your possibilities, honoring and fighting for your highest potential.

In *Self-Esteem Every Day* (Fireside, 1998), Branden writes that conscious living "is a noble pursuit, even a heroic one . . . to strive for greater clarity of perception and understanding, to move always in the direction of heightened mindfulness, to revere truth above the avoidance of fear or pain is to commit ourselves to spiritual growth—the continuing development of our ability to see."

How to Let Your
Life Speak

I had never been a Peeping Tom before, but last week the clerk at a local bookstore in Nantucket suggested I walk a few blocks over to see the historic Parliament House, a Quaker Meeting House built in the 1700s and now situated at 10 Pine Street.

Since the front door was locked and no one answered, I walked around the building and stood on my tiptoes, peering in the windows. Only later that day did I learn that the Parliament House is no longer a museum but rather a private residence and that I'm lucky no one called the authorities to report a tall, middle-aged man outside with his nose pressed against the windowpane.

Oops.

I was on Nantucket as a break from an investment conference on Cape Cod 29 miles north. The ferry ride over is an easy trip, and poking around the downtown art galleries, museums, and bookshops is a fine way to spend a late summer afternoon.

The island is beguiling and full of history. (If you go, don't miss the Nantucket Whaling Museum, listed by international travel writer Andrew Harper as "One of 10 U.S. Places to Visit before You Die.") Nantucket has one of the highest concentrations of pre–Civil War structures in the United States. Both its mid-nineteenth century charm and architectural beauty are well preserved.

The first settlers to formally organize on Nantucket were Quakers. Let me confess that, unless I'm looking at a box of oatmeal, I don't generally think much about Quakers. But they have a fascinating history.

Quakerism originated in mid-seventeenth century England. Members called themselves the Society of Friends, since they were "Friends of one another, Friends of Truth, and Friends of God."

Their religious practices conflicted with the Church of England, however, and they were aggressively prosecuted. Their leader, George Fox—who believed all people are guided by an "Inner Light" and don't need a minister or priest to act as a spiritual intermediary—survived eight imprisonments and numerous beatings.

Many Quakers left for the New World in search of religious freedom. But they didn't find it, at least not initially. Puritans and other New England Protestants, many of whom had arrived to escape their own persecution, were highly intolerant.

And not just for theological reasons. Quakers refused to take oaths. They wouldn't serve in the militia. They wouldn't pay taxes to the established church. They wouldn't remove their hats except for worship. And because of their belief that every person is of equal worth, they refused to bow in deference to aristocrats and public officials.

When two Quaker women appeared in Boston in 1656, Governor John Endicott ordered them searched for signs of witchcraft. He let them go, but laws were soon passed to keep Friends away. First-time Quaker visitors to Boston were "whipped out." If they had the audacity to return, they were to be hanged. (And some were.) Fines were imposed for even communicating with them.

Nantucket, however, was remote, tolerant, and secular. Quakers there were free to manage their affairs—and to leave their stamp on the island.

On Fair Street, I visited a Friends Meeting House from 1864 preserved by the Nantucket Historical Association. These Quaker places of worship are famous for their austerity and simple grace. Aesthetically, they are about as far from St. Peter's Basilica as you can get—and yet there is something enormously appealing about them.

Quakers practice an unadorned simplicity in all outward things, including modesty and plainness in dress. Meetings are mostly silent.

The quiet atmosphere is meant to lead to a shared state of spiritual community. When a member of the assembly rises to speak, it is to share his or her "Inner Light."

What do Quakers believe? Despite their Christian roots, that's not an easy question to answer. According to Robert Lawrence Smith, author of *A Quaker Book of Wisdom* (William Morrow, 1998):

> Quakerism is the only faith that is most commonly explained in a cascade of negatives. Quakerism has no theology, no body of religious dogma, no sacred books, no written creed. Traditional Quaker worship does not involve a minister, priest or other religious leader. There is no liturgy. There are no crucifixes or other religious images in Quaker Meetinghouses or homes.

Quaker wedding services are a simple exchange of vows between bride and groom. When Quakers bury their dead, the term *funeral* hardly applies. No prayers are offered, no pastor presides, and only a few quiet words of gratitude for the life of the deceased are spoken. Mourners do not speculate on the afterlife. For Quakers, death is the end of life as we know it. What comes after remains a mystery. It is enough that a life has brought joy and love.

By the 1820s, the number of Quakers on Nantucket had declined sharply. The Revolutionary War and the War of 1812 were disastrous for the Society of Friends, not because of casualties but because they refused to participate. Strict pacifists, they cited the words of their Peace Testimony: We utterly deny all outward wars and strife, and fighting with outward weapons, for any end, or under any pretense whatsoever.

This can be an appealing notion when a nation is caught up in a senseless or futile war. But not all wars are senseless. As historian Bruce Thornton notes, "Pacifism is the transitory luxury of a people whose security has been earned by the bravery and militarism of earlier generations." Most Quakers today would probably agree. More than half of all draft-eligible Quaker men in the United States served in the Second World War, a conflict that inspired a clear moral choice.

It is estimated that there are less than 120,000 Quakers in the United States today, and roughly 250,000 in other parts of the world. It is doubtful that theirs will ever be more than a small religious denomination. Yet there is food for thought here. Quakers believe we should search within for truth and reach out to help others, that we should be more forgiving of others' shortcomings and less forgiving of our own.

They stress a commitment to truth. Living honestly means you don't have to wrestle with your conscience. You don't have to make up excuses. You don't have to worry about your reputation. Aside from issues of morality, honesty simplifies your life. As Mark Twain pointed out, if you stick to the truth, you don't have to remember anything.

The pursuit of truth also means Quakers never view scientific inquiry as a threat. It is simply another part of the search for greater understanding. Quakers also emphasize that as we age we grow in wisdom and are often in a position to share it with those around us. We shouldn't miss those opportunities.

As George Fox said, "Let your life speak." The Quaker leader taught that your true self is not what you profess or what you believe. It's the way you conduct yourself in your public and private affairs—the way in which, for better or worse, you let your life speak.

We can all benefit from the sustenance that Quaker wisdom provides. In a culture where success is often judged by what you own, what you wear, or what you drive, its advocacy of conscience, simplicity, truth, and silent contemplation provides a timeless framework, a guideline for living.

Quaker wisdom reminds us to focus on the essential, keep first things first, and live to the point. How? By setting an example . . . and letting your life speak.

■ A Legacy of Inspiration

In January 1948, Mohandas Gandhi was shot three times by a Hindu assassin as he walked through a garden in New Delhi to take evening prayers. He died instantly.

Today he is remembered as an anticolonialist, an advocate of nonviolence, a pioneer of civil disobedience, and the father of the world's largest democracy. Believers in his vision used Gandhi's tactics during America's civil rights movement, to end apartheid in South Africa, and, at Tiananmen Square in 1989, to challenge China's autocratic government.

He achieved a great deal as a political leader, working against discrimination, poverty, and the caste system. He ended "untouchability." He expanded women's rights, religious tolerance, and economic self-reliance. For all these things, Gandhi is rightly honored. But in the long run, Mahatma (literally "Great Soul") may be best remembered for his contribution to humanity's inner life.

Gandhi advocated a simple and unassuming lifestyle. He lived modestly, wore the traditional Indian dhoti and shawl, and ate plain vegetarian food. He said it did not require money to be neat, clean, and dignified.

He undertook long fasts, sometimes for self-purification, other times as social protest. And he had a sense of humor. Asked once what he thought about Western civilization, Gandhi replied, "I think it would be a good idea."

Gandhi suffered many hardships in his life. He was imprisoned several times and for many years in both South Africa, where he first employed nonviolent civil disobedience as an expatriate lawyer, and in India. During these periods, he took the time to write down his key principles. Here are just a few of his thoughts:

- In matters of conscience, the law of the majority has no place.
- All of your scholarship, all your study of Shakespeare and Wordsworth would be in vain if at the same time you did not build your character and attain mastery over your thoughts and your actions.
- A man is but the product of his thoughts. What he thinks, he becomes.
- The only tyrant I accept in this world is the "still small voice" within.
- Strength does not come from physical capacity. It comes from an indomitable will.
- I do not want to foresee the future. I am concerned with taking care of the present.
- What a great thing it would be if we, in our busy lives, could retire into ourselves each day, for at least a couple of hours, and prepare our minds to listen to the voice of the great silence.
- Experience has taught me that silence is a part of the spiritual discipline of a votary of truth. Proneness to exaggerate, to suppress or modify truth, wittingly or unwittingly, is a natural weakness of man, and silence is necessary to surmount it. A man of few words will rarely be thoughtless in his speech. He will measure every word.
- True happiness is impossible without true health, and true health is impossible without rigid control of the palate. All the other senses will automatically come under our control when the palate has been brought under control. And he who has conquered his senses has really conquered the whole world.

More than 60 years after his death, Gandhi is still viewed as one of the world's great spiritual leaders.

He dedicated his life to the purpose of discovering Truth—something he insisted could be revealed only to those with a deep sense of humility—and believed the most important battle is overcoming our own fears and insecurities. The difference between what we do and what we are capable of doing, Gandhi insisted, is sufficient to solve most of our problems.

"He was driven to help the poor, the sick, and the downtrodden and to free them from colonialism no matter the cost to himself," said Archbishop Desmond Tutu. "In the end it cost him his life. However, he left us a legacy of inspiration that is remarkable in its sincerity and love of humanity."

Gandhi taught tolerance and love for all people. Albert Einstein offered that "generations to come will scarce believe that such a one as this ever in flesh and blood walked the earth."

Gandhi asked that his writings be cremated with his body. He wanted his life to be his message, not what he had written or said. In the end, he believed that words are meaningless. Actions alone show our true priorities. Or, as he famously said:

You must be the change you wish to see in the world.

THE ONLY THING NEW IN THE WORLD

At a recent investment conference, a young man in the audience told me he lacked the confidence to invest in anything right now.

"Why?" I asked.

"Because our country has never faced a more perilous future," he said.

I disagree. In the 1930s, for example, world trade had contracted by two thirds. Businesses failed in record numbers. One in four workers was unemployed. People lost their homes, their savings, and their dignity, and depended on charity to survive. Stock prices plunged 89 percent from peak to trough. Skilled workers and former business executives walked the streets selling apples or shining shoes to earn money for bread.

Homeless people built shacks out of old crates and formed shantytowns called "Hoovervilles" out of bitterness toward President Herbert Hoover. Farmers were hit particularly hard. Crop prices collapsed. Yet consumers still couldn't afford them.

Nature piled on, too. Beginning in 1930, a severe drought spread across the Great Plains. Topsoil turned to dust that was carried away by strong winds, piling up in drifts against houses and barns. The "Dust Bowl" covered large parts of Kansas, Oklahoma, Texas, New Mexico, and Colorado. The drought destroyed the livelihood of hundreds of thousands of small farmers. Many set out in search of a better life in California and lost everything along the way.

These were bleak times. But they were only a prelude to what lay just ahead. By early 1942, Hitler's armies were nearly to Moscow. German submarines were sinking our oil tankers off the coasts of New Jersey and Florida, within sight of the beaches, and there was not a thing we could do about it.

We had almost no army and scarcely any air force. Half our navy had been destroyed at Pearl Harbor. Army recruits were drilling with wooden rifles. Britain was badly bloodied. And there was no guarantee the Nazi war machine could be stopped. Yet Americans rallied. And so did our allies. As Winston Churchill declared, "We have not journeyed across the centuries, across the mountains, across the prairies, because we are made of sugar candy."

I'm not shrugging off the many political and economic struggles we face today. But a sense of history puts things in perspective. The affluence and easy prosperity of the past few decades was never the historical norm. Yet Americans have always risen to meet the challenges we faced. History reminds us of the great sacrifices and amazing triumphs of those who came before us.

During the American Revolution, for example, General Washington's ragtag volunteer army fought right through the winter, without warm clothes, with shoddy or no shoes, with little food, and none of the comforts of home. "Posterity who are to reap the blessings," wrote Abigail Adams to her husband John Adams, "will scarcely be able to conceive the hardships and sufferings of their ancestors."

Americans should know this—and appreciate it. Historical illiteracy is not just ignorance. It's a form of ingratitude.

Pulitzer Prize–winning historian David McCullough recently gave a lecture at an Ivy League college. He asked the audience, "Who knows who George Marshall was?" Not a single hand in the audience went up. Not one. We cheapen the lives of those who came before us when we can't be bothered to learn about their sacrifices, when we take our liberties for granted, or imagine that Americans have never faced more trying circumstances than today.

True, many are now enduring the toughest economic times of their lives. Some, including my own family, also have loved ones away serving in the armed forces. But, as a nation, we have faced far tougher times.

The future is always fraught with uncertainty. But history gives us a sense of proportion. It tells us who we are and where we've been. It enlarges our view. And while we sometimes fall short of our ideals, it reminds us how they have guided us in the past . . . and should still lead us today. Without history, we lose our story—and our bearings. We forget who we are and what it has taken to come this far. A sense of history is a strong antidote to self-pity or self-importance. It inspires courage and humility. History reinforces what we believe in, what we're willing to stand up for.

It's not that the Founding Fathers or heroes of other generations were godlike. They weren't. They were fallible human beings, just like us. Sometimes they made terrible mistakes or used shockingly poor judgment, just as we do. But if we take the time to read and to listen, the wisest and bravest among them will reach through the past—across the centuries—with voices that warn us, guide us, and lift our spirits.

Their chief lesson, especially in times like these, is that courage and patience and determination matter. And that character matters most of all. These qualities may not always guarantee success. But they guarantee you deserve it.

THE UNIVERSITY ON YOUR SHELF

A few months ago, a couple in our Florida neighborhood invited my wife, Karen, and I over to tour their newly redecorated home.

Wine glasses in hand, we wandered from room to room as our hosts showed us the latest colors and fabrics, new lighting and furniture, flooring, wallpaper, cabinets, counters, and window treatments. The house was beautiful. Yet something was missing.

As we were leaving, it finally dawned on me. There weren't any books!

Books do more than decorate a room. They make it inviting. They give it personality. A home without books is like a body without a soul. Books are friends, comforters, and counselors; repositories of wisdom; sources of ideas. A good collection of books is a university in itself. If I visit a home without them, I feel cheated.

Why? Because I can spend three minutes looking at your book-shelves and learn more about your taste and interests than I could in a half-dozen leisurely dinner conversations. Your personal library (ahem) speaks volumes.

At a glance, your guests know whether your interests run toward classics or best sellers, history or politics (or both), literary fiction or travel, fly-fishing or golf, art or engine repair. A wildly eclectic mishmash says a lot about you, too.

And forget the secret ballot. Your political views are right there in plain view. It doesn't matter whether you've had the chance to read your Chomsky or Hayek selections. The mere intent is evidence enough.

Your core beliefs also sit on your bookshelf. The family Bible says one thing, the entire "Left Behind" series another. Titles by C. S. Lewis and G. K. Chesterton reflect a subtle theology; Karen Armstrong or the Dalai Lama, a cosmopolitan view.

Of course, not everyone who loves books has them on display. Some, for instance, grow tired of carting them from one address to the next. This may lead to tough choices. (Robert B. Parker can be safely jettisoned, for instance. But P. G. Wodehouse? Never.)

Others have given up reading for cable. Fortunately, I grew up in an era when watching television wasn't terribly appealing. Transmission and reception were equally bad. And while my childhood home was thick with books, today my parents use the library almost exclusively. The few books they buy are either immediately passed on (if they're any good) or unceremoniously tossed out (if they're not).

Then there is my friend Jimmy, who insists he's done with paper and cloth. He's hooked on his Kindle. It's a neat gadget—I have one myself—but there's something about the tactile experience of handling a book that I'll never give up. Who really wants to curl up in front of the fire with an electronic reader?

We all know the value and pleasures of reading. But a personal library affords endless opportunities for something equally important: rereading.

My uncle, Beau Puryear, is a military historian who has spent a lifetime studying character and leadership. After interviewing more than 150 four- and five-star generals over a 40-year period, he concluded that the greatest leaders, without exception, were avid readers.

In his book *Marine Corps Generalship* (CreateSpace, 2009), he quotes a radio broadcast by Yale University professor William Lyon Phelps in 1933:

> The habit of reading is one of the greatest resources of mankind; and we enjoy reading books that belong to us much more than if they are borrowed. A borrowed book is like a guest in the house; it must be treated with punctiliousness, with a certain considerate formality. You must see that it sustains no damage; it must not suffer while under your roof. You cannot leave it carelessly, you cannot mark it, you cannot turn down the pages, and you cannot use it familiarly. And then, someday, although this is seldom done, you really ought to return it.
>
> But your own books belong to you; you treat them with that familiar intimacy that annihilates formality. Books are for use, not for show; you should own no book that you are afraid to mark up or afraid to place on the table, wide open and face down. A good reason for marking favorite passages in books is that this practice enables you to remember easily the significant sayings, to refer to them quickly, and then in later years, it is like visiting a forest where you once blazed a trail. You have the pleasure of going over the old ground, and recalling both the intellectual scenery and your old earlier self.
>
> Everyone should begin collecting a private library in youth; the instinct of private property, which is fundamental in human beings, can here be cultivated with every advantage and no evils. One should have one's own bookshelves, which should not have doors, glass windows, or keys; they should be free and accessible to the hand as well as the eye. The best of mural decorations is books; they are more varied in color and appearance than any wallpaper, they are more attractive in design, and they have the prime advantage of being separate personalities, so that if you sit alone in the room in the firelight, you are surrounded with intimate friends. The knowledge that they are in plain view is both stimulating and refreshing. You do not have to read them all.
>
> There are, of course, no friends like living, breathing, corporeal men and women; my devotion to reading has never made me a recluse. How could it? Books are of the people, by the people, for

the people. Literature is the immortal part of history; it is the best and most enduring part of personality. But book friends have this advantage over living friends, you can enjoy the most truly aristocratic society in the world whenever you want it. The great dead are beyond our physical reach, and the great living are usually almost as inaccessible: As for our personal friends and acquaintances, we cannot always see them. Perchance they are asleep, or away on a journey. But in a private library, you can at any moment converse with Socrates or Shakespeare or Carlyle or Dumas or Dickens or Shaw or Barrie or Galsworthy. And there is no doubt that in these books you see these men at their best. They wrote for you. They "laid themselves out," they did their ultimate best to entertain you, to make a favorable impression. You are as necessary to them as an audience to an actor, only instead of seeing them masked, you look into their inmost heart of hearts.

Today, we swim in a sea of media information. We are surrounded by data, by trivia. Where is wisdom to be found? In books.

Warren Buffett's business partner—and fellow multi-billionaire—Charlie Munger says, "In my whole life, I have known no wise people who didn't read all the time—none, zero."

Author Seth Lerer observes, "We live not with books themselves but with our memories of books: the bits and pieces we recall, the pages we dog-ear; the lines we highlight." Reading parallels life. It readies us for it. There simply isn't time to learn everything the hard way.

Whether you're seeking the practical, the spiritual, the theoretical, or the aesthetic, great books—with their mysterious enticements and timeless wisdom—are always there.

And, just occasionally, so are curious guests.

▨ We Are All
Greeks Now

Right now, I'm steaming across the Mediterranean aboard the *Royal Princess* with a group of investors, adventurers, and *Spiritual Wealth* readers.

We're smack in the middle of our "Cradle of Civilization" tour to Greece, Turkey, Israel, Egypt, and Rome—and having a large time.

We kicked things off in Athens last week, touring the city and its ancient ruins, consuming heaping portions of souvlaki and Greek wine, and realizing just how far the greenback goes in a euro-based economy. (Not very.)

We've all seen, heard, learned (and eaten) a lot. But if there is one overwhelming impression, it is the enormous debt of gratitude we owe the ancient Greeks. More than 2,400 years ago, they founded Western civilization.

How? Modern drama, poetry, literature, competitive sports, politics, architecture, and philosophy all evolved from Greek ways. Their way of life, their emphasis on reason, their ideals still shape every aspect of life in the West.

Rational inquiry, individualism, private ownership of property, the idea of a middle class, civilian control of the military, political freedom, equal justice before the law, constitutional government, even democracy itself—these are all Greek inventions.

The Athenians discovered a new way of looking at the world. Observation and experimentation trumped tradition and superstition.

Ideas were investigated and tested, not merely accepted as received wisdom. (The Greeks had a vivid and well-developed mythology, of course. But there was no state religion, no official doctrines, and no powerful priestly caste sanctioning views or punishing heretics.)

Ancient Greece was filled with discoverers and innovators.

- Thales of Mileters strove to understand the natural forces that regulate the universe and gave birth to the scientific method.
- Pythagoras proved that the universe operates according to mathematical laws.
- Archimedes calculated the value of pi—the ratio of a circle's circumference to its diameter—and demonstrated the principle of leverage. ("Give me a place to stand," he famously said, "and I will move the earth.")
- Euclid wrote treatises on geometry, optics, and music theory.
- Ptolemy attempted to diagram the heavens, laying the foundation of modern astronomy.
- Socrates, Plato, and Aristotle founded Western philosophy with their sophisticated inquiries into metaphysics, epistemology, and ethics.

Alexander set out to conquer the world and created the largest empire in history up to that time. His conquests, of course, were really nothing more than one immense raid for plunder. But he was also the great disseminator of Greek culture. And that turned out to be a good thing.

The Greeks invented the idea of freedom. Historically, personal freedom belonged solely to royalty, aristocracy, or the strongest male warriors. The Greeks expanded personal and political freedom to the majority. As Pericles wrote, "In Athens, we live exactly as we please." This notion existed nowhere else in the ancient world.

True, the Greeks owned other Greeks as slaves. Women were denied basic rights. And political freedom was limited to male citizens. But remember, this was the ancient world. It was a start.

Perhaps the defining feature of Athenian culture was intellectual freedom. The Greeks were the first to idealize the development of the mind, not for the good of the government or the state but for the benefit of the individual.

Everything was open to argument and discussion, including religion and government. The Greeks' curiosity, relentless questioning, and intellectual rigor led to enormous achievements in logic, physics, mathematics, rhetoric, and analysis. They made rational inquiry—rather than the pronouncements of authority—the royal road to truth.

Empirical research and the application of mathematics liberated us from myth and magic, leading to unimaginable progress in science, technology, engineering, and medicine.

Today, we bemoan our fast-paced, technology-dominated lives. But no one wants to return to the era of chronic pain, early death, malnutrition, disease, superstition, and everyday suffering that was our ancestors' destiny, and the fate of billions in the Third World today.

Yes, there have been countless contributions from other cultures along the way. But it is the Greek legacy of reason, investigation, and individual freedom that led to the remarkable ascendancy of the West. As the British poet Percy Shelley observed, "We are all Greeks."

Man does not live by bread alone, of course. It was both the Greek emphasis on reason and the Judeo-Christian emphasis on ethical monotheism that gave the Western mind its distinctive shape. A world where science, technology, and our fellow human beings were freed from moral constraints would not be one worth living in.

To investigate this chapter in our development, however, we must turn from ancient Greece to Jerusalem. Fortunately, that's just where we'll be tomorrow.

I'll pass along my observations in my next letter. . . .

■ THE WISDOM OF HILLEL

After spending five days in Athens, the Greek Isles, and Turkey, our "Cradle of Civilization" tour landed at Haifa last week on Israel's Mediterranean coast.

Piling into our coach, we visited Nazareth and the Mount of Beatitudes, enjoying a sumptuous lunch—complete with excellent Israeli wine (who knew?)—on the Sea of Galilee. We then traveled past the Dead Sea, alongside the Jordan River and through the controversial West Bank settlements, finally arriving in Jerusalem.

This is an endlessly fascinating city with more history than some continents. Home to dozens of sacred sites—and a perennial destination for millions of religious pilgrims—the walled Old City has been besieged, desecrated, burned, and rebuilt many times over the past 4,000 years.

The locals, in fact, are still wailing. Arriving on the Jewish Sabbath, we stopped to see the men and women gathered for prayer at the Western Wall, a remnant of the Second Temple complex destroyed by the Romans in 70 AD. Just a stone's throw away is one of the world's most beautiful shrines, the magnificent Dome of the Rock with its 24-karat-gilded cap.

Nearby, too, is the Church of the Holy Sepulchre. Tradition holds that it is built over the sites where Jesus was crucified, buried, and resurrected.

It's a bit surprising to see three of the holiest sites of Judaism, Christianity, and Islam practically on top of each other. But then, the world's three great monotheisms share common roots. Judaism is based on the Old Testament, Christianity on both the Old and New Testaments, and Islam on the Old and New Testaments and the Qur'an.

Over the past 1,000 years, of course, the faithful have often been at daggers drawn, an unfortunate and depressing history for the Holy Land. But there have always been those who imagined things differently. In a famous Talmudic story, the great rabbi Hillel (c. 80 BC −30 AD) was approached by a pagan who promised to convert to Judaism if Hillel could teach him the entire Torah while standing on one leg. Hillel replied, "What is hateful to yourself, do not to your fellow man. That is the whole of the Torah, and the remainder is but commentary. Go and study it."

Hillel argued that any interpretation of scripture that bred hatred or disdain for others—whatever their beliefs—was illegitimate. The world could use more of his approach.

At its best, religion aligns us with a moral axis. It allows us to live with realities that don't have easy explanations and problems that can't be solved: mortality, pain, grief, despair, and outrage at injustice, poverty, and cruelty.

Some modernists claim that faith is incompatible with the philosophical rationalism of the ancient Greeks. Not so. Students did not visit Socrates to learn anything—he always insisted he had nothing to teach them—but to have a change of mind.

As religion historian Karen Armstrong writes in *The Case for God* (Knopf, 2009):

> Socrates, Plato and Aristotle, the founders of Western rationalism, saw no opposition between reason and the transcendent. They understood that we feel an imperative need to drive our reasoning powers to the point where they can go no further and segue into a state of unknowing that is not frustrating but a source of astonishment, awe and contentment.

This is possible only when we cultivate a receptive, listening attitude. It requires us to set aside doctrinal quarrels, put our core beliefs into practice, and develop what Confucius called "human-heartedness."

People want to live richly and intensely. They want peace and serenity in the midst of pain and loss. They want lives filled with significance, with a sense of the divine. They want to honor the ineffable mysteries of life. Many find this in ritual, prayer, and practice. Yet true religion is always a call to change.

Our actions mirror our thoughts and beliefs. We need look no further than an individual's outer behavior to see the degree of his inner achievement.

Jerusalem's great Abrahamic traditions have enabled millions to find meaning in the face of pain and injustice. They allow us to overcome the thoughtlessness, greed, and self-preoccupation that threaten to undo our best efforts.

True, we will always fall short as nations and individuals. But the quest for spiritual attainment—a sense of the transcendent—is Jerusalem's greatest legacy, its unique gift to the West.

Meditations of the Philosopher-King

At the Roman Forum two weeks ago, economist and FreedomFest founder Mark Skousen was delivering his "Persuasion vs. Force" talk—an eloquent plea for freedom and tolerance—when a passerby stopped to heckle him loudly.

Skousen continued unperturbed, asking only that the heckler hold his remarks until the end—which was fitting. The Forum was one of the first places in ancient times where ordinary citizens had the right to stand up and publicly voice their opinions, even unpopular ones.

Our group endured the heckler because we were wrapping up our "Cradle of Civilization" tour and, as Freud noted, the first human to hurl an insult instead of a rock was the founder of civilization.

Visiting these ancient ruins gave us a chance to reacquaint ourselves with Rome's history and one of its great philosophers, Marcus Aurelius.

Marcus was emperor of Rome for two decades before succumbing to the plague in 180 AD. He was the most powerful man of his day, ruling an empire that stretched from Western Europe to the Middle East and Africa. During his reign, he defended Rome against barbarians, invading tribes, pestilence, and plague at every border.

Yet, in those quiet moments of leisure when he was able to take off the mantle of emperor, he also composed one of the world's great works of Stoic philosophy, known today as his *Meditations*.

The book is essentially an inner dialogue. Marcus wrote solely for himself, not posterity. His goal was to face up to the world, define the good life, and develop a manual for daily living.

His words still resonate today. Here is just a sampling:

- If you are pained by any external thing, it is not this that disturbs you, but your own judgment about it. And it is in your power to wipe out this judgment now.
- Be like the jutting rock against which waves are constantly crashing, and all around it the frothing foam then settles back down. Say not "Oh, I am so unfortunate that this has happened to me." But rather "How fortunate I am that, even though this has happened to me, I continue uninjured, neither terrified by the present nor in fear of the future."
- Never consider anything to be beneficial to you, which could ever compel you to violate your faith in yourself, to abandon your modesty, to hate anybody, to be overly suspicious, cursing, disingenuous, or to lust after anything which must be hidden behind walls or veils.
- Wisdom and right action are the same thing.
- Whenever you notice someone else going astray, immediately turn and examine how you yourself have gone astray, for example, esteeming money, pleasure, reputation, or something else, as if it were the highest good. Examine yourself in this way and you will quickly forget your anger.
- People seek retreats for themselves in the country, by the sea, and near the mountains, and you too are especially prone to desire such things. But this is a sign of ignorance, since you have the power to retire within yourself whenever you wish. For nowhere can a person retire more full of peace and free from care than into his own soul.
- Kindness is unconquerable, so long as it is without flattery or hypocrisy. For what can the most insolent man do to you if you continue to be kind to him?
- The noblest way of taking revenge on others is by refusing to become like them.

- If someone is able to show me that what I think or do is wrong, I will happily change, for I seek the truth, by which no one ever was truly harmed.
- Someone else may ask: "How may I possess that?" But you should ask: "How may I not covet that?" Someone else asks: "How can I be rid of him?" But you: "How can I not wish to be rid of him?" Another: "How may I not lose my little child?" But you: "How may I not dread the loss of my child?" Turn your prayers around entirely, and see what happens.

On every page, Marcus Aurelius shows extraordinary insight and humility, his words transcending the boundaries of time and place. No wonder his *Meditations* are among the best-known and most widely read works of antiquity.

The message is simple and direct, but powerful. Marcus values inner strength, dignity, and self-respect. He reminds us that life can end at any moment, that the past and the future are inaccessible, that we are made better by confronting difficult conditions with resolution and courage, and that our most important goal is our own private quest for perfection.

Over the past 1,800 years, his words have helped millions face up to the setbacks, cravings, triumphs, and disappointments that are the lot of every human life.

Marcus wastes no time on airy theories or speculations. The measure of a philosopher, he believed, was not his discourses, but his way of living.

As he writes in the *Meditations*, "Stop philosophizing about what a good man is and be one."

PART FOUR

MATTERS OF LIFE
AND DEATH

When I first agreed to write a weekly column called *Spiritual Wealth*, a friend sputtered at the news.

"You?" he said, finding the notion comical. "What qualifies you to write about anything spiritual?"

"I don't know," I said, "what *disqualifies* me?"

"Maybe if you made it to church a little more often," he said with a chuckle.

"So you're saying if I went to synagogue, for instance, I couldn't write about spirituality?"

"Well, yes," he said, amending his words. "Perhaps if you were a little more active in the Judeo-Christian community, you'd be better suited to the task."

"So it wouldn't be possible then for a Muslim to say anything about spirituality?"

He paused. "Well, Islam *is* part of the great Abrahamic tradition," he said, sounding a tad more uncertain.

"How about Gandhi?" I asked. "His faith wasn't based on the Old or New Testaments. He was a Hindu. Was he not spiritual?"

"Well, hmm . . . yes, I suppose," he stammered.

"Or how about the Dalai Lama? Buddhists don't follow the Bible or even posit a God. Is the Dalai Lama not spiritual?"

He said yes, he thought the Dalai Lama was a spiritual leader, but he wasn't sure why, except that he represented a particular faith and advocated compassion.

"Well, how about a compassionate person who doesn't follow any organized religion?" I added. "Is it not possible for him or her to be spiritual?"

From the pained look on his face, you would have thought I'd tied his brain in a knot. Yet are these not the most elemental questions for people of faith? I was surprised that he hadn't considered them.

My own background is unexceptional. I was born into a Christian household, grew up in the Episcopal church, and try to practice the virtues I learned. (Although I still struggle with that "judge not" stuff.) I've spent several decades reading, thinking and writing about religion and spirituality. I find them inexhaustible and endlessly fascinating subjects. I can't learn enough. But this seems to be a minority viewpoint. Most of my friends and colleagues are either secular and have no interest in religion or are religious and have little interest in the subject outside their tradition. Or even within it, for that matter. Ask the average Christian what happened at the First Council of Nicaea and you are likely to get a blank stare.

I have tried to pass along my interest in world religions to my kids. When my daughter, Hannah, was in elementary school, I explained how—from time immemorial—human beings have yearned to understand their origins and how best to live. This impulse led to the rise of different religions in different times and places.

Hannah and I read and discussed them, starting with ancient Egyptian religions and moving up the timeline through Zoroastrianism, Greek religion, Roman religion, Norse religions, Celtic religions, Hinduism, Jainism, Buddhism, and Sikhism. Eventually, we reached Judaism and Christianity. Then we moved on to more recent religions.

"Why in the world would you do *that*?" a relative asked in mild disbelief. She believes the study of comparative religions is a good way to become comparatively religious.

But what is there to fear in knowledge? Recent research from the independent Pew Forum on Religion and Public Life found that Americans by all measures are a deeply religious people, but they are also deeply ignorant of religion. Three thousand, four hundred people randomly selected to answer a 32-question survey about the Bible, Christianity, and world religions missed on average half the questions and generally flubbed even questions about their own faith. The group that scored highest in religious literacy was—I'm not kidding—atheists and agnostics. Clearly, there is room for improvement here.

Judging by my inbox, however, my most controversial thoughts were not the ones endorsing religious pluralism but rather modern science. A significant percentage of the population feels their faith is under attack today and, in particular, that science undermines it.

I don't understand this point of view. We don't think twice about stepping on a plane and hurtling across the Pacific Ocean at 600 mph. Why? Because we know science works. If we wind up in the hospital, physicians may inject us with solutions, hook us up to an IV drip, or put us under for surgery. We submit to these treatments because we know science solves our problems. It gives us real-world answers.

But when it comes to modern cosmology or evolutionary biology, many pretend that scientists don't know what they're talking about.

Genuine faith is belief in the absence of evidence, not belief in spite of the evidence. The religious impulse is supposed to be, at least in part, a search for truth. When it comes to understanding the history of the cosmos or human origins, are we really going to accept ancient texts over reason, evidence, and the scientific method?

Some will answer with an enthusiastic yes. But as Ralph Waldo Emerson wrote, "The religion that is afraid of science dishonors God." Read on and see if you don't agree.

Discovering a New Sense of the Sacred

On March 6, 2009, NASA launched the Kepler Space Telescope to discover planets outside our solar system.

Named after Johannes Kepler, the famous mathematician who devised the laws of planetary motion, it will monitor 100,000 stars similar to our sun for four years, keeping a lookout for habitable, Earth-sized planets.

Already, Kepler has found 15 extra solar planets (beyond the 510 already known to exist) and identified up to 1,235 other candidates. Fifty-four of these are the right size and orbit a "habitable zone"—the goldilocks region neither too close to a sun nor too distant—where liquid water might pool on the surface of a planet.

It's a fantastic start, especially since Kepler has telescoped only a small part of the galaxy. Scientists believe that if we can find a planet with Earthlike conditions, we may ultimately find signs of extraterrestrial life.

No one can know the odds at this stage, but Dr. Alan Boss of the Carnegie Institution of Science estimates there may be 100 billion habitable planets in the Milky Way. Astrophysicist Duncan Forgan of Edinburgh University suggests there could be thousands of intelligent civilizations in our galaxy alone. And the Hubble Space Telescope has uncovered over 100 billion other galaxies. It's enough to boggle the mind.

I spoke to a neighbor about these developments this week. He was not amazed or elated, however. He was angry.

"They are not going to find life on other planets," he insisted. "I don't care how favorable the conditions are. Life didn't arise 'naturally' on earth, so it can't arise 'naturally' somewhere else."

"I thought we were talking about science," I said.

"The truth is the truth," he said in a huff and strode off.

He's right about one thing. Scientists can't yet explain how life arose. What's more, we may never find life beyond our planet. But if I were a betting man . . .

Four hundred years ago, Galileo's observations through his telescope proved that the Earth moved. In his *Dialogue Concerning the Two Chief World Systems,* he claimed that the sun and the planets did not circle the earth, as was commonly believed. Rather, the Earth and the planets revolve around the sun.

This finding did not sit well with the Church. Galileo's pronouncements contradicted official Christian doctrine, specifically Chronicles 16:30, Psalm 93:1, Psalm 96:10, Psalm 104:5, and Ecclesiastes 1:5.

Galileo was hauled before the Inquisition, forced to recant, and found "vehemently guilty of heresy." His offending Dialogue was banned, and he was sentenced to formal imprisonment (later commuted to house arrest, which he remained under for the rest of his life).

In a letter to Kepler, Galileo complained that many of those who opposed his doctrines refused to look through his telescope, "even though I have freely and deliberately offered them the opportunity a thousand times."

The same prejudice persists in certain quarters today. Some don't like what microscopes, particle accelerators, spectrometers, and space telescopes tell us about the universe we live in. They huff and puff about the "arrogance" of science.

But the scientific enterprise is not just about discovery. It is also about humility. We strive to understand because we know that we don't know.

Science promotes knowledge and critical thinking. Conclusions are based on observation, experimentation, and replication. Beliefs that aren't supported by testable evidence aren't necessarily untrue. They just aren't science.

A few weeks ago, my grade-schooler brought home a worksheet describing the scientific enterprise. A scientist, it said:

- Shows curiosity and pursues answers to questions about the world
- Maintains a balance of open-mindedness and skepticism by entertaining new ideas and challenging information not supported by good evidence
- Respects the importance of reproducible data and testable hypotheses
- Tolerates complexity and ambiguity
- Persists in the face of uncertainties

What is there to oppose here? In science, a fact is something confirmed to such a degree that it would be unreasonable to withhold assent. Conclusions are never final. Findings are always subject to revision.

Albert Einstein said, "All our science, measured against reality, is primitive and childlike—and yet it is the most precious thing we have."

Isaac Newton said, "I do not know what I may appear to the world, but to myself I seem to have been only like a boy playing on the seashore, and diverting myself in now and then finding a smoother pebble or a prettier shell than ordinary, while the great ocean of truth lay all undiscovered before me."

Conceding what you don't know, admitting when you're wrong—these are strengths, not weaknesses.

Pope John Paul II understood this. During his reign, he made over 100 public apologies for the Catholic Church. In 2000, he apologized for its persecution of Galileo. (Better four centuries late than never.)

Today's Kepler mission is part of the centuries-old quest to expand our horizons and discover new worlds. It has generated intense interest and popular excitement. And why not?

Space exploration gives us a sense of awe and wonder. It is also a reminder that we belong to a planet, a galaxy, a cosmos that inspires devotion as much as discovery.

THE HIGHEST OF ARTS

Many would describe my friend John as the picture of success.

He enjoys good health, a loving family, a high-paying job, and many of the fruits of affluence. Yet his mood last week was black as a moonless night.

"Every day," he said, "I rise at the same time, have the same cup of coffee, take the same route to the office, see the same business associates, and do pretty much the same thing I always do. My life may as well be on autopilot. Each month—each year—blends into the next. I feel like I'm just marking time."

Some would argue that John should thank his lucky stars for all the problems he doesn't have. After all, there's nothing terribly wrong with his life, except that he feels like he isn't really living it.

Countless others feel the same way. Caught up in boredom, tedium, or existential angst, they lack a feeling of transcendence. They might benefit from listening to the Transcendentalists, a group of reformists, writers, and intellectuals active in New England in the 1830s.

Leading the movement was the renegade minister, essayist, and poet-philosopher Ralph Waldo Emerson. Another dominant figure was Henry David Thoreau, an avid naturalist, essayist, reform advocate, and civil disobedient. Both men wrote eloquently about society, culture, and the human condition.

Thoreau believed that as we get older we fall into a routine, gradually and mindlessly beating a track for ourselves. Bogged down with daily trifles, we lose our gusto for living. The great mass of men, he wrote, live lives of quiet desperation. More than 150 years ago, Thoreau blamed this on the rat race and materialism:

- *Most men would feel insulted if it were proposed to employ them in throwing stones over a wall, and then in throwing them back, merely that they might earn their wages. But many are no more worthily employed now.*
- *Men labor under a mistake. The better part of the man is soon ploughed into the soil for compost. By a seeming fate, commonly called necessity, they are employed, as it says in an old book, laying up treasure, which moth and rust will corrupt and thieves break through and steal. It is a fool's life, as they will find when they get to the end of it, if not before.*

Thoreau wanted to avoid this trap. So he escaped to Walden Pond for two years "to live deep and suck out all the marrow of life."

"I went to the woods because I wished to live deliberately," he wrote, "to front only the essential facts of life, and see if I could not learn what it had to teach, and not, when I came to die, to discover that I had not lived."

Of course, vanishing into the woods isn't a realistic option for most of us. Some might even say it smacks of running from your problems rather than confronting them. But Thoreau believed that personal peace and serenity are found only in communion with nature. It is where great harmony and existential truth are discovered.

For Transcendentalists, nature is the key to spiritual attainment. It offers the solitude to think about how we spend our time. It provides the silence where Thoreau's "different drummer" can be heard. Do not live foolishly like other men, he warned, but according to universal laws. That meant studying the ancients, revering wisdom, and living according to its dictates.

A successful life, Thoreau argues, is built on simplicity, independence, magnanimity, and meaningful work. Reading him today awakens something inside us that modern society suppresses. Thoreau asks us to make a new estimate of ourselves, to think bravely about our lives, and boldly ask, "How shall I live?"

My friend John—and others suffering from similar ennui—might benefit from answering his call for personal renewal. Thoreau reminds us that human life is a great privilege. We have the whole world to devour and explore, if we will only awaken to it.

Some may call the Transcendentalists dreamers. And there is certainly an element of idealism here. But they were also chroniclers of the human spirit. And their advice to scorn appearances, conduct your life with wisdom and integrity, and transcend the often-deadening effects of modern culture is timeless.

We're only here for a visit, they remind us. Life should be an ecstasy. Or as Thoreau famously said, "To affect the quality of the day, that is the highest of arts."

EMERSON: THE QUINTESSENTIAL AMERICAN

My last essay on Henry David Thoreau and the Transcendentalists generated quite a bit of interest from readers wanting to know more.

Transcendentalism, of course, reached its ascendancy more than 150 years ago. Yet it casts a long shadow and still speaks to us today, especially during tough political and economic times. So let's take a closer look at the movement and its inspiring founder and leader, Ralph Waldo Emerson.

A theologian, essayist, orator, and poet, Emerson is variously described as America's own philosopher, our first literary giant, the father of the environmental movement, and the founder of what literary critic Harold Bloom calls "the American religion," a distinctive blend of individualism and self-reliance.

Emerson's philosophy, Transcendentalism, began as a ferment in the Unitarian church. It was not a religious movement, however, but a spiritual one. There were no doctrines, houses of worship, or ritualized devotions. Emerson emphasized not belief in a particular creed but rather independent thinking, good works, and the development of character.

His interest was in the principles that unite us, not the doctrines that divide us. Following Jesus' insistence that the kingdom of

Heaven is within you, Emerson sought moral universals, what he called "interior truth." He insisted, for example, that if the Confucians in China, the stoics of Athens, the noblest Buddhists, and the wisest Christians all met and conversed, they would find themselves of one mind.

Like Thoreau, he also believed that solitude in nature leads to true enlargement of the mind and spirit. His books, he said, "should smell of pine and resound with the hum of insects."

His words had a powerful effect on his contemporaries, bringing Walt Whitman "to a boil," as the poet himself put it. (In turn, Whitman's universal voice, descriptive style, and free verse form became the nation's single most distinctive contribution to world poetry.)

Emerson was not just a contemplative theologian, however. He was also a man of action. A passionate abolitionist, he spoke out forcefully against slavery, calling it not just an institution but "a destitution."

How does this nineteenth-century philosopher speak to us today? Like William James, the great psychologist who followed in his footsteps, Emerson recognized that most of our difficulties start right between our ears. The first key to resolving your problems is to upgrade your thinking. "This time, like all times, is a very good one," said Emerson, "if we but know what to do with it."

We also fail to recognize how our problems benefit us by strengthening us, advancing our interests. When a man "is pushed, tormented, defeated," he wrote, "he has a chance to learn something; he has been put on his wits; on his manhood; he has gained facts; learns his ignorance; is cured of the insanity of conceit; has got moderation and real skill."

If it doesn't seem that way now, recognize that it may in the future. It's often just a matter of perspective. "The years teach much," Emerson said, "which the days never know."

Like his fellow Transcendentalists, Emerson lived a simple life and warned of the trap of materialism. Financial success, he said, lies never in the amount of money we have, but in the relation of income to outgo. "It is a cold, lifeless business," he wrote, "when you go to the shops to buy something which does not represent your life and talent, but a goldsmith's."

Of course, much of the pressure to seek and display affluence comes not from within but from society itself. The world wants you to live according to its opinion, not your own. "Every brave heart must treat society as a child," he said, "and never allow it to dictate."

Emerson is hard to categorize and impossible to sum up. He described himself as an endless seeker, devoting his life to understanding the human mind and the mysteries of existence.

American literature, philosophy, religion, and social policy have all been strongly affected by his words and deeds. Historians say he may have had more influence in the shaping of American thought than any other individual—and is second only to Lincoln as a spokesman for the country's highest ideals.

Yet Emerson modestly claimed that he taught just one principle, the infinitude of the private man. "Nothing is at last sacred," he said, "but the integrity of your own mind."

■ THE LIFE YOU CAN SAVE

Philosopher Peter Singer has a question for you.

As you are walking to work, you pass a small pond and see a toddler splashing along the shoreline. As you get closer, you notice that the child isn't playing. She is struggling frantically to keep from drowning. There are no other adults around. Would you jump in to save her, even if it meant you'd have to change your clothes and be late for work?

"Of course," you reply. "The life of a child is far more important than arriving at work on time."

But let's say you were wearing a pair of expensive shoes. Would you still jump in to save her, even if it meant ruining your shoes?

"What kind of question is that?" you ask. "Who wouldn't sacrifice a pair of expensive shoes to save the life of a child?"

Hang on to that sense of outrage for a minute. You're going to need it.

According to the United Nations International Children's Emergency Fund (UNICEF), every year 9.7 million children under five die easily preventable deaths. That's over 1,100 every hour of every day.

Some of these children die because they don't have enough to eat, others from easily treatable conditions like malaria, measles, or diarrhea. This is not only an immense tragedy but a moral stain on a world as rich as ours.

The World Bank reports that 1.4 billion men and women around the world currently live on less than $1.25 a day. A survey of over 60,000 of them in 73 countries found that extreme poverty like this means:

- You probably live in an unstable house, made of mud or thatch, that is liable to collapse in severe weather.
- You lack adequate food, education, clothing, sanitation, and health care.
- You often eat one meal a day, sometimes having to choose between stilling your child's hunger or your own.
- You have no safe drinking water. (Or you may need to carry it a long way and, even then, it may not be safe until you boil it.)
- If a family member becomes ill and you need money to see a doctor, you may have to borrow from a moneylender who charges usurious rates—and you may never be free of the debt.
- You have a pervading sense of powerlessness, misery, and shame because you cannot provide adequately for your family.

In the West, we tend to think we're living a morally good life if we aren't doing anything to hurt anyone else. But what are we doing to alleviate the suffering of others?

It's not just a matter of ethics. It's a matter of conscience.

Giving to the poor is a tenet of every major faith. The Hebrew word for "charity," *tzedakah,* means "justice," suggesting that giving to the poor is not optional but an essential part of living a just life.

The Bible contains over 3,000 references to alleviating poverty, making this a central moral issue for Christians. Jesus said it is how we act toward "the least of these brothers of mine" that will determine whether we inherit the kingdom of God.

Pastor Rick Warren, author of *The Purpose Driven Life* (Zondervan, 2002), visited South Africa a few years ago and came across a tiny church operating from a dilapidated tent and sheltering 25 children orphaned by AIDS. He said it was "like a knife through the heart: I realized they were doing more for the poor than my entire megachurch."

He later added, "I couldn't care less about politics, the culture wars. My only interest is to get people to care about Darfurs and Rwandas."

Americans are charitable people. Studies show that we give around 2.2 percent of our gross national income. That's significantly more than any other country, and about double the level of charitable giving in most other rich nations. Seventy percent of U.S. households make some form of gift to charity each year.

Most of us tend to give to our local communities—and that's good. But poverty is a different animal here. Ninety-seven percent of those classified as poor by the U.S. Census Bureau own a color TV. Three quarters own a car. Three quarters own a VCR or DVD player. Three quarters live in an air-conditioned home. Obesity is epidemic.

This is not the kind of poverty that kills 18 million people annually. Every day, over a billion men, women, and children around the world do not have their most basic human needs met. Singer estimates that the cost of raising someone from extreme poverty to a self-sustaining existence is less than $200.

We all know the common objections to international aid. Some are concerned about what happens when our generally inept government gives money to a thoroughly corrupt one overseas. (No one wants his or her money to wind up in some kleptocrat's bank account.) In the past, a lot of official aid has been misconceived and misdirected. And I don't argue with those who claim that the long-term solution is trade, not aid.

But it is possible to reduce misery and suffering without involving a government agency—and without having to worry that your donation breeds dependency.

The nonprofit Grameen Foundation, for example, is fighting world poverty with microcredit. It makes millions of tiny loans to the world's poorest people (especially women), with a 97 percent repayment rate. The money allows them to buy seeds, start a business, pay a doctor, or cope with a family emergency. It helps lift them out of poverty and lead lives of respect, dignity, and opportunity. For more information, visit www.grameenfoundation.org.

Occasionally, I write about the International Rescue Committee (IRC) and its mission. Founded by Albert Einstein, the IRC serves refugees and communities victimized by oppression or violent conflict. When thousands run from natural disasters, war, or repression, the IRC is there, providing food and water, shelter, health care, and education.

Both Grameen and the IRC are highly efficient, top-rated charities. Donations are fully tax deductible.

A couple of years ago, I wrote a column about the IRC and provided a link to its website. I have no idea how many readers chose to donate, but I was gratified that so many wrote to tell me they did.

A few weeks later, I received a letter from a wealthy gentleman who was in the middle of updating his estate plan. After investigating the IRC and its fine work, he arranged to make the organization the beneficiary of nearly half his estate. That letter made my day.

Of course, I couldn't have told him about the IRC if my cousin Judith hadn't encouraged me to become a donor years ago. And she wouldn't have told me if her friend Mach hadn't gotten her involved. You never know the far-reaching effect your words may have, especially if they stir someone's conscience.

We all spend money every day on things that we would hardly miss if they were gone. In *The Life You Can Save* (Random House, 2009), Peter Singer writes:

> Do you have a bottle of water or a can of soda beside you? If you are paying for something to drink when safe drinking water comes out of the tap, you have money to spend on things you don't really need. Around the world, a billion people struggle to live each day on less than you paid for that drink. You can help them.

Does it make sense to care about the drowning child in front of you but not about the dying child in a distant country? If you visited these people and saw their plight with your own eyes—as you may have—I know your heart would break and your wallet would open.

So this may be a good time to ask yourself: What ought I be doing to help?

If you feel impelled to give generously, I salute you. At the very least, you probably felt a bit of outrage at the idea that you wouldn't sacrifice a pair of expensive shoes to save someone's life.

Here's an opportunity: www.theirc.org.

■ Coming of Age in the Milky Way

Isaac Asimov once noted that the phrase that generally heralds new discoveries in science is not "Eureka!" but rather "That's funny . . ."

This was certainly the case in 1967. Two radio engineers, Arno Penzias and Robert Wilson, were working on satellite communications for Bell Laboratories when they were troubled by a persistent background noise—an unfocused, unrelenting hiss that made their experimental work impossible. No matter what they did, they couldn't get rid of it. Worse, it was coming from every point in the sky, day and night, through every season.

It was some time before the two men realized they had stumbled on the edge of the visible universe, 90 billion trillion miles away. They were "seeing" the first photons—the most ancient light in the universe—though time and distance had converted them to microwaves, just as astrophysicist George Gamow had predicted two decades earlier.

Penzias and Wilson had made one of the greatest scientific discoveries of all time.

Since time immemorial, human beings have gazed up at the night sky and wondered about our cosmic origins. We puzzled. We theorized. We created myths and stories. But we couldn't know because we didn't have the tools.

Now we do.

Today, cosmological theories are tested—and either accepted or rejected—based on 'observations from powerful ground-based telescopes containing vast mirrors, housed in observatories the size of giant warehouses, and planted on remote mountaintops. Scientists also use spectroscopes, satellites, radio telescopes, supercomputers, particle accelerators, and one rather spectacular space telescope named after the pioneering astronomer who got the ball rolling.

In 1929, Edwin Hubble discovered that the distant fuzzy patches in his telescope at the Mount Wilson Observatory were actually other galaxies, each composed of billions of stars. Even more astonishing, these galaxies are rapidly moving away from us—and each other.

This eventually led to Hubble's Law: If the galaxies are receding then:

1. Tomorrow they will be farther from us.
2. But yesterday they were closer to us.
3. And last year they were closer still.
4. At some point in the past, everything was piled together and squeezed into a tiny volume.

Seven decades of observation and experimentation reveal that the universe kicked off with a titanic explosion approximately 13.7 billion years ago.

That's an awfully tough thing to conceptualize, and cosmologists have struggled to find ways to describe it in simple language. Three popular attempts are:

- The Big Bang was the explosion of space, not an explosion in space.
- The Big Bang happened everywhere, not at one point in space.
- Space is in the universe rather than the universe being in space.

Because the time since the Big Bang is hard to wrap your mind around, so astronomer Carl Sagan devised an ingenious illustration.

He called it his "Cosmic Calendar." And it provides a lesson in humility. Here's how it works:

Imagine that the 13.7-billion-year history of the universe is compressed into one calendar year. The Big Bang occurred in the very first second of January 1, and the current moment is the last second of the last minute of December 31. Using this compressed time scale, each month equals a little over 1.1 billion years. Each day represents 40 million years. Each second covers 500 years of history.

The Milky Way coalesces in March. The sun and planets form in August. The first life—single celled—shows up in September, the first multicellular organisms in November. The first vertebrates appear on December 17. Dinosaurs show up on Christmas Eve (and become extinct on December 29). Modern humans finally appear at 11:54 PM on December 31. And all of recorded history occupies the last 10 seconds of the last minute of the last day of the year. The pyramids were built nine seconds ago. The Roman Empire fell three seconds ago. Columbus discovered America one second ago.

Talk about putting things in perspective. . . .

As someone who has invited dozens of friends and colleagues to peer through his Meade telescope, I know that many people are skeptical of Big Bang cosmology. And that's a good thing in one sense. Our knowledge grows only through continual, methodical doubting. Few of us doubt our own conclusions, however, so science rewards and honors those men and women who correct their colleagues' inaccurate conclusions. Only theories supported by evidence and experimentation—and able to withstand the most rigorous attacks by opponents—ultimately survive.

The Big Bang model has lasted more than 70 years, and the evidence keeps mounting. (For an excellent overview, I recommend *Big Bang: The Origin of the Universe* [Harper Perennial, 2005] by particle physicist Simon Singh, a highly readable book on the subject.)

Yet some reject the theory on religious grounds. Most Western faiths have made their peace with it, however. The scientific account of our origins has already been accepted by Reform Judaism, the Roman Catholic Church, and most mainstream Protestant denominations.

And there is still plenty here for the theologically inclined to chew on. What caused the Big Bang? Why are the physical constants just right to allow galaxies, planets, and, ultimately, conscious life? Where do the physical laws come from? If they aren't of divine providence, how can they be explained? Why is nature shadowed by a mathematical reality? In short, why do theoretical physics work?

Even the most radically materialist scientists have to have faith in the rational intelligibility of the universe. Otherwise, what's the point of the scientific enterprise?

As Carl Sagan wrote in *The Demon-Haunted World* (Ballantine Books, 1997):

> Science is not only compatible with spirituality; it is a profound source of spirituality. When we recognize our place in an immensity of light-years and in the passage of ages, when we grasp the intricacy, beauty, and subtlety of life, then that soaring feeling, that sense of elation and humility combined, is surely spiritual.

After many thousands of years, we are privileged to be part of the first generation to have a rational, coherent, and elegant explanation of the origin of everything we see in the night sky. Surely, this is one of the grandest achievements of the human intellect and spirit.

Explanations of our origins strike a deep chord in most of us.

We've always had an intense need to feel connected to something larger than ourselves. Now we know that we are—and in the most profound way.

Our cosmic history also generates a deep sense of reverence while deflating our conceits. We live on a beautiful planet, bountiful with life. But it is also a cosmic speck, orbiting a humdrum star in the far suburbs of a common galaxy, afloat in a vast ocean of nearly empty space, in a universe in which there are far more galaxies than people.

Yet we should feel some pride and astonishment, too. It took less than an hour to make the atoms, a few hundred million years to make the stars and planets, but more than 10 billion years to make human beings.

As physicist Paul Davies writes in *The Goldilocks Enigma* (Allen Lane, 2006):

> Somehow the universe has engineered, not just its own awareness, but also its own comprehension. Mindless, blundering atoms have conspired to make not just life, but understanding. The evolving cosmos has spawned beings who are able not merely to watch the show, but to unravel the plot.

In short, we are living relics of ancient history, intimately tied to the cosmos, composed of wandering stardust. We are the way the universe thinks about itself.

Astronomers, physicists, and cosmologists often rhapsodize about the scale, the majesty, the harmony, and elegance of the universe. Yet, in truth, they are only discovering what the poets have known all along:

> We shall not cease from exploration
> And the end of all our exploring
> Will be to arrive where we started
> And know the place for the first time . . .
> —T. S. Eliot, 1942

THE LITERATURE
OF TRUTH

According to Dr. Jon D. Miller, director of the Center for Biomedical Communications at Northwestern Medical School, the number of scientifically literate adults in the United States has doubled over the past 20 years.

The bad news? That only gets us up to 20 percent.

Polls show that only 48 percent of Americans know that humans didn't live at the same time as dinosaurs. Less than half know that electrons are smaller than atoms. Only small minorities know what DNA is or can define a molecule. (Citizens of other nations don't fare much better, incidentally. Members of the European Union, for example, actually score worse.)

Science has been called the literature of truth, the systematic classification of experience, the antidote to superstition.

We live in a world highly dependent on the fruits of science. Yet polls show that most of us have little scientific knowledge and lack even a superficial understanding of the enterprise itself. Does this matter?

Yes. Without some minimal scientific understanding, we can't possibly have informed opinions on important issues. We surrender our ability to participate as responsible citizens in society.

Uncle Sam, for instance, spends more than $100 billion annually on science agencies, university laboratories, and grants for independent research. Most of us—including our elected representatives—know very little about where this money is going or why.

Yet there is an even more compelling reason we should remedy our ignorance in this area: Scientific illiteracy diminishes the quality of our lives.

For most of human history, our ancestors looked up at the sky at night and never realized the twinkling lights were other suns unimaginably far away.

We created myths to explain the phases of the moon and the appearance of comets, meteor showers, and solar eclipses. Floods, hurricanes, earthquakes, plagues, and volcanic eruptions were attributed to angry gods.

Our ancestors hadn't the slightest inkling that the universe is nearly 14 billion years old or that our sun is one of more than 200 billion stars in the Milky Way, itself one of hundreds of billions of galaxies.

Of course, few scientific truths are self-evident. Many are counter-intuitive. It is by no means obvious, for example, that empty space has structure or that everything is made of the same basic elements.

Science writer Isaac Asimov once noted that we are among the tiny fraction of 1 percent of human beings fortunate enough to live in the era where science finally got the big questions right.

Until Einstein worked them out between 1905 and 1916, we didn't know the basic rules that govern the universe. We didn't realize the universe itself is expanding before Edwin Hubble discovered it in 1923. We couldn't fathom the mind-bending rules that govern subatomic particles until the advent of quantum theory around the same time.

Of course, science makes no claim to truth with a capital T. All scientific knowledge is provisional, subject to revision.

But science is successful, in part, because it acknowledges human failings. It knows that pride, ignorance, and prejudice can send us off the rails.

Yet the scientific method, with its error-correcting mechanisms, advances knowledge through reason and evidence, rejecting authority, overturning misconceptions, and revealing successive approximations of the truth.

Today, the basic picture is complete. No future scientist, we can safely say, will disprove the principles of chemistry, the germ theory of disease, or the interrelatedness of all life on earth.

Yet despite all that science tells us—knowledge that would astonish our ancestors just a few generations removed—many smart, talented people can't be bothered to learn.

We appreciate the countless medical and technological benefits that extend and improve our lives. But most of us know very little about the history of the cosmos or life on earth. And that can't help but diminish our awareness and understanding.

Fortunately, it isn't hard to change that. Here are just a few suggestions:

1. Subscribe to *Scientific American*. I took this magazine years ago and, quite frankly, found it tough sledding. But today the magazine is much improved. It is written primarily for nonspecialists. Jargon is minimal or concisely explained. Most articles begin with a short summary of the key concepts and findings. And the terrific monthly columns by science historian Michael Shermer and physicist Lawrence Krauss alone justify a subscription.

2. Rent or collect the fabulous BBC documentaries with naturalist David Attenborough, especially *Planet Earth, The Trials of Life, Blue Planet, Life on Earth,* and *The Living Planet.* (Astronomer Carl Sagan's *Cosmos* series is still a classic, too, nearly 30 years on.)

3. For a crash course, read *The Canon: A Whirligig Tour of the Beautiful Basics of Science* (Houghton Mifflin Harcourt, 2007) by Natalie Angier or, if you prefer your science served with hilarity, *A Short History of Nearly Everything* (Broadway, 2010) by the master himself, Bill Bryson.

Science, in essence, is just a tool, a window on the truth. There are, of course, other forms of human intellectual endeavor—religion, art, philosophy, and literature—whose expressions of human truth can be neither confirmed nor denied by scientific methods.

But without critical thinking, without the skeptical evaluation of claims, we become susceptible to pseudoscience, quack medical advice, nonsense, and mumbo jumbo. Carl Sagan often referred to science as our "baloney-detection kit."

And there are other benefits. Science teaches us wonder, community, oneness, and humility. Paleontologist Stephen Jay Gould once remarked that the one common feature of all scientific revolutions is the dethronement of human arrogance.

Without natural science, we may also miss great beauty and understanding. In *Unweaving the Rainbow* (Houghton Mifflin Harcourt, 1998), Oxford biologist Richard Dawkins writes:

> After sleeping through a hundred million centuries we have finally opened our eyes on a sumptuous planet, sparkling with color, bountiful with life. Within decades we must close our eyes again. Isn't it a noble, an enlightened way of spending our brief time in the sun, to work at understanding the universe and how we have come to wake up in it? . . . Who, with such a thought, would not spring from bed, eager to resume discovering the world and rejoicing to be a part of it?

YOUR CONNECTION TO EVERYTHING

I didn't mean to set off a firestorm. But my last piece on scientific illiteracy generated more mail than any column I've written.

Most respondents sent me a verbal high-five, agreeing that a basic understanding of science enriches our lives and broadens our perspective. Yet a vocal minority insist that the natural history of the world as revealed by science is unsettling, terrifying, or just plain preposterous.

These folks imagine themselves at war with biology, comparative anatomy, physiology, genetics, geology, paleontology, archaeology, biochemistry, ecology, physics, biochemistry, astronomy, spectroscopy, and cosmology. And the spitballs were flying. . . .

The angriest letters came from readers who claimed that science leads to materialism—the notion that physical matter is all there is—and materialism invariably leads to atheism. This, no doubt, comes as a surprise to the tens of thousands of practicing scientists who call themselves believers.

And it seems like a lot of the hostility results from a basic confusion of science with metaphysics. Metaphysics, which transcends disciplines, investigates the fundamental nature of being. Science is more pedestrian, collecting data through observation and experiments, developing theories to explain the evidence, and subjecting claims to scrutiny through peer review.

The core principal behind this approach is called "methodological naturalism." It stipulates that all scientific hypotheses are tested and explained solely by natural causes and events. Geneticist J. B. S. Haldane noted 75 years ago that when he set up an experiment he had to assume, as a practical matter, that no god, angel or devil affected its course.

It's not that science rules out the possibility of entities or causes outside of nature. They just aren't considered during scientific investigations. (Or, as Michigan State University science philosopher Robert Pennock quips, "Science is godless in the same way that plumbing is godless.")

Do science and religion really need to square off like the Hatfields and the McCoys? Perhaps not. As the late Stephen Jay Gould wrote in *Rocks of Ages* (Trafalgar Square, 2001):

> Science tries to document the factual character of the natural world, and to develop theories that coordinate and explain these facts. Religion, on the other hand, operates in the equally important, but utterly different realm of human purposes, meanings, and values—subjects that the factual domain of science might illuminate, but can never resolve. . . . Science gets the age of rocks, and religion the rock of ages; science studies how the heavens go, religion how to go to heaven.

Most of us accept this. We seek enlightenment from a variety of sources. It's just that science and religion approach the world in very different ways. Science, in particular, advances only as authority and conventional knowledge are overturned.

Yet both can offer us wisdom and consolation. In *The Sense of Wonder* (Harper & Row, 1965), naturalist Rachel Carson said:

> Those who dwell, as scientists or laymen, among the beauties and mysteries of the earth are never alone or weary of life. . . . There is symbolic as well as actual beauty in the migration of the birds, the ebb and flow of the tides, the folded bud ready for the spring. There is something infinitely healing in the repeated refrains of

nature—the assurance that dawn comes after night, and spring after the winter.

Astronomer Carl Sagan took this view of nature to a higher level. His *Cosmos* miniseries, watched by more than 600 million people worldwide, is the proud story of how through the searching of 40,000 generations of our ancestors we have finally come to discover our coordinates in space and in time. And how through the methods of science we have been able to reconstruct the sweep of cosmic history and to find our own part in its great story.

Sagan viewed the study of the cosmos as a genuine source of spirituality, inspiring both discovery and devotion. In *Pale Blue Dot* (Ballantine Books, 1997), he wrote, "A religion, old or new, that stressed the magnificence of the universe as revealed by modern science might be able to draw forth reserves of reverence and awe hardly tapped by conventional faiths."

Sagan called science a kind of "informed worship," a reminder of our connection with the rest of the universe. We are all starstuff, he reminded us, made of atoms—the heavy elements—forged in the fiery hearts of distant stars.

Sagan was a polymath. (Isaac Asimov, the science writer and long-time leader of Mensa International, once said that Carl Sagan and physicist Marvin Minsky were the only two people he'd ever met whose intelligence was greater than his own.) And Sagan studied the world's religions with the same hunger for learning he brought to scientific subjects.

He saw irrationality and dogmatism as enemies of both science and religion. And he found amazement and humility in our investigation of the heavens, as well as a profound sense of the sacred.

Sagan died of a rare blood disorder in 1996. Yet his mission to promote scientific and human understanding lives on.

THE DIFFERENCE BETWEEN KNOWING AND BELIEVING

A Rabbi, a Christian, a Muslim, a Sikh, and a Mormon are sitting at a table. An atheist is questioning them.

It sounds like the start of a bad joke, I know. But I'm actually describing "The Sacred Text Project" at a conference in Las Vegas last week. Five religious leaders and scholars were there to advance and defend their sacred scriptures. Moderating the discussion was Michael Shermer, founder and publisher of *Skeptic* magazine and author of *How We Believe.*

Shermer announced up front that he would brook no political correctness. He didn't want these scholars to talk about their common goals or general spiritual principles. He wanted them to defend their differences. And he didn't mince words. He began by asking the panelists to explain how they knew their sectarian beliefs were right and their fellow panelists were wrong.

Each responded eloquently, in some cases poetically, about their particular faith. But they couldn't—or wouldn't—answer Shermer's question directly. That demonstrated wisdom and discretion. After all, the question was designed to put them one move away from checkmate. No panelist could offer definitive evidence. None would accept any other's answer as "the right one." And if the sectarian tenets of any religion could be proven beyond the shadow of a doubt, why call it faith?

Historians of science like Shermer and the theologians on the panel seek "the truth" from different angles. Science begins with the null hypothesis, the assumption that whatever claim is under investigation is not true until proven otherwise.

Next come the laboratory experiments and statistical tests. The burden of proof, which must be repeatable, falsifiable, statistically significant, and published (along with the data) in peer-reviewed journals, is necessarily high.

Fundamentalists often claim that scientists are arrogant, full of hubris. And no doubt some scientists are. Yet this hardly describes the scientific enterprise itself. Even when the results of controlled experiments appear conclusive, no scientific claim is beyond doubt. Science views all knowledge as provisional.

Every finding falls on a graduated scale somewhere between absolute truth and absolute falsity, but never at either end. It's okay to say, "I don't know," "I'm not sure," or "Let's wait and see."

This is particularly true when physicists, astronomers, cosmologists, and other scientists grapple with the Great Unknown.

In *The Pleasure of Finding Things Out* (Perseus Books, 1999), physicist Richard Feynman writes:

> The size of the universe is very impressive, with us on a tiny particle whirling around the sun, among a hundred thousand million suns in this galaxy, itself among a billion galaxies. . . . There are atoms of which all appears to be constructed, following immutable laws. Nothing can escape it; the stars are made of the same stuff, and the animals are made of the same stuff, but in such complexity as to mysteriously appear alive—like man himself. . . . To see life as part of the universal mystery of greatest depth, is to sense an experience which is rarely described. It usually ends in laughter, delight in the futility of trying to understand. These scientific views end in awe and mystery, lost at the edge in uncertainty. . . .

Science acknowledges—and makes arrangements to overcome—human limitations and fallibility. It begins with the proposition that we are examining things that are unknown or poorly understood.

To gain knowledge, we must remain modest, conceding what we don't know.

Science, on the one hand, is a tool for understanding the natural world and advancing technology. It helps us distinguish what we might like to be true from what is probably true.

Religion, on the other hand, addresses moral questions beyond the purview of science, important questions like "Should I do this?" and "What will happen if I do?" It underscores the primacy of love, the brotherhood of men, the value of the individual.

Yet at their best, both emphasize an important principle—one scientists and theologians can equally embrace: a deep sense of humility.

■ THE LESSONS OF HAITI*

What can be said about Haiti that hasn't already been said this week?

Already the poorest nation in the Western hemisphere, Tuesday's earthquake has left hundreds of thousands dead and injured and made a million or more homeless. This catastrophe will surely go down as one of the worst natural disasters of all time. Yet events like these tend to occur with depressing regularity.

It seems like only yesterday—in fact it is astonishing to realize it was nearly seven years ago—an undersea earthquake off Sumatra caused a tsunami with waves up to 100 feet high, killing nearly 230,000 people in 14 countries. As in Haiti, the people in the vicinity were simply going about their business and had virtually no warning.

Earthquakes aren't the only culprits, of course. In 2005, Hurricane Katrina slammed the Gulf Coast, leaving more than 2,000 dead. In 1985, Nevado Del Ruiz claimed more than 25,000 lives in Colombia, mostly from the mudflow that resulted from the volcanic eruption.

Historian David McCullough has written movingly about one of the great disasters in American history, the Johnstown Flood. After especially heavy rains one year, the South Fork Dam broke,

---

*Editor's note: This essay was written the week a catastrophic magnitude 7.0 earthquake hit 16 miles west of Port-au-Prince on January 12, 2010.

sending 20 million tons of water at 40 mph toward the city of 30,000 below. According to Victor Heiser, a survivor who rode a section of his barn roof to safety, "I could see a huge wall advancing with incredible rapidity down the diagonal street. It was not recognizable as water, it was a dark mass seething with houses, freight cars, trees and animals."

Thousands died. Yet even this disaster pales in comparison to the massive Yellow River Flood of 1931. Historians estimate it killed between one and four million rural Chinese.

Even if you're fortunate enough to live in an area where the ground doesn't shake, hurricanes don't blow, and tornadoes are unlikely to lift your roof in the middle of the night, there are other potential threats, including The Big One.

On March 23, 1989, an asteroid bigger than an aircraft carrier— more than a half-mile wide—traveling at 46,000 miles per hour, passed through Earth's orbit less than 400,000 miles away. A few hundred thousand miles may not sound like a close shave, but in astronomical terms this was a near miss. Earth had been at that point just six hours earlier. Had the asteroid struck our planet, scientists estimate the energy released would have been equivalent to 1,000 to 2,500 megatons of TNT (or 1,000 to 2,500 one-megaton hydrogen bombs). It could have been what one astrophysicist called "a civilization-ending event."

There was no time to panic. No one saw the asteroid until it had passed by. (And to think you lived to tell your grandkids about it.)

Throughout history, tens of millions of our relatives and ancestors have succumbed to earthquakes, floods, hurricanes, tornados, cyclones, tsunamis, droughts, famines, and pandemics. That these are "acts of God"—if you're not a Pat Robertson follower—is a tough concept to swallow.

Yet if there is anything good to be said about the events in Haiti this week, it is how millions around the world are now putting their troubles and self-interests aside, at least for a moment, to lend a hand. The situation is dire. Yet money, food, clothing, medicine, and other essentials are pouring in.

The crisis in Haiti also helps put our own lives in perspective. The security of your job, the performance of your 401(k), and the size of your bank account are pretty small potatoes compared to the trauma of having a child or grandchild trapped inside a collapsed schoolhouse.

So consider the suffering in Haiti. And be thankful. Except for the sheerest accidents of birth and circumstance, it could be you and your family in the rubble.

■ YOUR TRIP TO "THE UNDISCOVERED COUNTRY"

On the way to a conference last week, I caught a connecting flight in Charlotte.

As I approached my gate, I looked up and noticed a sign: Terminal Destinations. It was an airport health spa, but it reminded me of the debate I was on my way to hear between Dinesh D'Souza, a Christian apologist and author of *Life after Death,* and Michael Shermer, a historian of science, columnist for *Scientific American,* and author of *Why People Believe Weird Things.*

The two men have polar views on the subject of life after death, something we all consider from time to time, however vaguely.

Shakespeare called death "the undiscovered country, from whose bourn no traveler returns." No one knows what lies beyond the veil. Yet the idea of an afterlife is an old and enduring one.

Ancient Egyptians believed the soul leaves the body and travels to the Kingdom of the Dead. Royal tombs were filled with food, clothing, jewelry, even slaves, for enjoyment in the next life.

In *The Odyssey,* Homer refers to an afterlife of eternal bliss in Elysium. In *The Myth of Er,* Plato describes souls being sent to the heavens for a reward or underground for punishment. The Vikings envisioned Valhalla, where after death they would do battle by day and enjoy victory feasts and revels at night. American Indians dreamed of Happy Hunting Grounds full of deer and bison.

The afterlife is a key component of every major religion. Buddhists and Hindus have traditionally believed in reincarnation. Muslims imagine heaven as an oasis with palm trees and dates. For Christians, Jesus' resurrection and promise of eternal life is foundational. Many take comfort in the words of Saint Paul: "We will not all die, but we will all be changed, in a moment, in the twinkling of an eye, at the last trumpet."

Of course, the opposing view, the notion that "when we die, we die, and that's it" doesn't exactly generate a warm, fuzzy feeling. As Woody Allen said, "I don't want to achieve immortality through my work. I want to achieve immortality through not dying. I don't want to live on in the hearts of my countrymen. I want to live on in my apartment."

Polls show that more than 80 percent of Americans believe in some form of afterlife. In non-Western cultures, the percentage approaches 100 percent.

Even those with an entirely secular viewpoint prefer to believe that some part of them lives on after death, that they will ultimately be reunited with family and friends. ("And pets!" a neighbor chimes in.)

Many find consolation in the afterlife for another reason. It's tough to watch how often the wicked triumph and the good suffer in this world. There's something reassuring about cosmic justice, the idea that someday we will each be held to account. I remember how as a child when some poseur or busybody in my hometown would pass away, my father would often remark—with just the right touch of irony—that he had "gone to his reward."

Of course, skeptics and rationalists like Shermer reject this whole line of thinking. He argues that we are material creatures and when our bodies disintegrate there is simply nothing left to support our consciousness. Anything else is wishful thinking.

D'Souza dismisses this materialist view, although he concedes it is natural to have doubts. He tells the story of the English vicar who was asked whether he expected to go to heaven and what he thought he would find there. "Well, I suppose I believe in eternal bliss if it comes to that," he replied, "but I wish you wouldn't bring up such depressing subjects."

Shermer understands these migivings. If we were certain of an afterlife, he argues, we would not fear death as we do, mourn quite so agonizingly the death of loved ones, or hold debates on the subject. As one of the nation's preeminent skeptics, he has studied near-death experiences, past-lives research, and psychic mediumship, and found them all wanting.

How about all those patients who reportedly died, were enveloped in peace and white light, and then returned to tell us about it?

Their accounts often conflict and are unreliable, he says. Most had experienced serious trauma or were heavily sedated. On close inspection, research into postlife experiences is generally weak, anecdotal, or terminally flawed. He adds that, "All those patients who supposedly died and came back have one thing in common. They weren't actually dead."

There are dissenters in the scientific community, however. One of them is respected physicist Paul Davies, who writes in *The Fifth Miracle* (Simon & Schuster, 1999) that the laws of nature are rigged not only in favor of life, but in favor of mind, that mind is written into the laws of nature in a fundamental way.

Philosophers add that just because we aren't able to detect another realm with our five senses, it doesn't necessarily follow that the numinous doesn't exist.

In sum, we don't have scientific proof of the afterlife. (And if such a thing were possible, what would be the role of faith?) Nor can skeptics persuade the majority that death is the end.

So, rather than engaging in metaphysical speculations, perhaps we should concentrate on life before death.

A friend once asked me the old question about what I would do if I knew I had only six weeks to live. I know he was only trying to find out whether I'd play Augusta National or take a trip to Bora Bora or whatever. But I answered that I'd probably be so depressed by the news I wouldn't find much joy in anything.

So he amended his question. "Okay, let's say you just got hit by a bus. You're dead. What do you most regret not having done?"

Now that's a provocative question.

Death reminds us that our time here is limited, vanishing, and exceedingly precious. It puts things in perspective and suggests we get moving. What is your plan for living the best possible life? What are your grandest dreams and aspirations? Are you pursuing them or putting them off for "someday"?

Death is a reminder that our purpose is not just to survive but to flourish. The great challenge of life is to use your time and freedom to do and become what you want.

That isn't always easy. It takes courage. As Shakespeare said, "Cowards die many times before their deaths / The valiant never taste of death but once."

Yet many of us live in denial of death. (Teenagers especially.) When I was an investment manager, I routinely dealt with individuals who were too spooked by the prospect of their own demise to set up an estate plan or even write a simple will. This feeling is widespread, apparently. Studies show that 7 in 10 Americans die intestate.

What are they hiding from? It is only when you accept your own impermanence that you recognize what is most important in life. Death prioritizes things, especially as you get older, and forces you to confront the shallowness of material pursuits. Your focus inevitably moves from the ephemeral to the transcendental.

Accepting rather than ignoring death can cause a radical shift in perspective. You realize how important it is to live fully rather than face the pain of not having lived. You appreciate the meaning that can be found in work, in family, in faith, in friends, and in community.

Meditating on your own death helps you develop an attitude of equanimity, an acceptance of your ultimate fate. A stoic outlook is the mark of a mature, reflective person. As Mark Twain said, "I do not fear death. I had been dead for billions and billions of years before I was born, and had not suffered the slightest inconvenience from it."

Preparing for death is not just a matter of deciding what to leave to whom. The thought of our passing motivates us to talk to others, give advice, say things we have been meaning to say, and give thanks for being alive. It is only when we take full account of death that we are able to say yes to life.

Sometimes, of course, we are forced to confront the passing of those near us, often when we least expect it. While only time salves this wound, in retrospect mourning and saying goodbye are some of our most poignant moments.

And it raises again the fundamental questions. Am I a good father? Son? Brother? Friend? Mate? Community member? Am I acting ethically? Am I making good use of my talents and abilities? Am I living fully?

I don't think you can answer these questions honestly until you've fully accepted your own mortality. And when you have, you can thank death.

Why? For making your choices perfectly clear.

THE BEGINNING OF WISDOM

I watched in horror last week as my 11-year-old daughter, Hannah, plunged 180 feet down Cheakamus Canyon toward the river raging below. My wife, Karen, and I had both tried to talk her out of it. But she wouldn't be dissuaded.

She wanted to jump.

Of course, she was attached to a bungee cord, one that "exceeded Australian specifications" (whatever that means). And Whistler Bungee—an hour north of Vancouver and just below Whistler's 2010 Olympic Village—has been in business for seven years with a perfect safety record.

Still, I got the willies just looking down through the 300-foot span we crossed. This was a murderous height. It would take at least three burly men to get me out on that platform.

"You don't have any problem with this?" I asked a member of Canada's Olympic ski team who was suiting up for a jump as we arrived.

"Not at all," she laughed. "What could go wrong?"

"That's the difference between you and me," I said. "I have more imagination than that."

Of course, I knew my fear was emotional not rational; otherwise, I would never have let my daughter jump. That she really wanted to jump still astonishes me. After all, this is the same girl who insists on cracking her bedroom door at night so she can see the light in the hallway.

We hate to admit it but most of our fears are irrational. Everyday life just isn't that dangerous anymore. Technology, engineering, and modern medicine have eliminated most of the sharp edges.

Yet we can't escape our past. Our fears evolved as a basic survival mechanism. They arise in response to perceived threats, triggering a "fight or flight" response.

For most of us, it's flight (or avoidance). And studies show our fears are fairly universal: spiders, snakes, heights, public speaking, and death.

As Jerry Seinfeld once quipped, "According to most studies, people's number one fear is public speaking. Number two is death. Does that sound right? This means at a funeral most people would rather be in the casket than doing the eulogy."

Our greatest inhibitor, of course, is fear of failure. Consciously or not, it can paralyze us, keeping us from applying for the promotion, taking the risk, meeting the girl, asking for the order, experiencing the unknown. It's always easier to stick with the safe, the comfortable, the familiar.

Yet every time we choose safety, we reinforce fear. We nurture it. Only when we overcome this debilitating emotion do we really begin to live. "He who is not every day conquering some fear has not learned the secret of life," said Ralph Waldo Emerson.

How is fear conquered? By doing what we think we can't do, again and again. When I was young, for example, public speaking made me nervous. Today, I relish the opportunity to address a large group.

After a wildly turbulent flight 30 years ago, I became a white-knuckle flier for a while. But now I'm awash in frequent flier miles.

Fear is the great barrier to success. It gives small things big shadows. It is the inverse of faith, trapping us between regret for the past and anxiety about the future.

Yet few things warrant the fear we grant them. We run not from genuine threats but imaginary bogeymen. As Bertrand Russell observed, "To conquer fear is the beginning of wisdom."

And the rewards are many. Waiting for you on the other side of fear is freedom: Freedom from anxiety. Freedom from regret. Freedom from a life unlived. Fortune really does favor the brave.

Marianne Williamson writes:

> Our deepest fear is not that we are inadequate. Our deepest fear is that we are powerful beyond measure. It is our light, not our darkness, that most frightens us. We ask ourselves, who am I to be brilliant, gorgeous, talented and fabulous? Actually, who are you not to be? . . . We are all meant to shine, as children do. And as we let our own light shine, we unconsciously give other people permission to do the same. As we are liberated from our own fear, our presence automatically liberates others.

Does this mean—like Hannah—that I'm willing to embrace "Whistler's Ultimate Adrenaline Rush" and plummet toward the Cheakamus River?

That depends. How many burly guys have you got?

OF LOST SOULS AND LUCKY STIFFS

I was saddened to read my parents' obituaries this week. Those who know them have often described them as dear friends, "good people," and pillars of the community.

In our small hometown, for instance, my dad was—at one time or another—president of just about everything: the chamber of commerce, the YMCA, the Rotary Club, the perpetually strapped local golf club, and so on.

Yet their obituaries don't begin to capture them as individuals. Maybe that's why they had me read them over. After all, they're not dead yet. In fact, I don't know anyone more alive. . . .

Though in their 80s, my parents are active, healthy and—as always—having the time of their lives, even playing a particularly vicious game of doubles ping-pong and regularly beating the pants off my wife Karen and me.

So why am I reading their obituaries?

Some people can't deal with the thought of their eventual demise. My parents don't have that problem. The living trust is done. The will is updated. The funeral plans are made. The kids have all been told which knickknacks around the house will be whose.

Now I learn their obituaries are written, too. But not particularly well. The information they've jotted down is skeletal, bare facts that don't begin to do the job. There's a long list of relatives and descriptions of who predeceased whom, for instance. But where's the beef?

Where's the story about the time my mother awoke in the middle of the night when she heard someone poking around under the bed and—assuming it was me—chased a burglar down the stairs and out of the house?

Or the time the family station wagon broke down on the way back from a ski trip and we decided to hitchhike the last 40 miles home? Since there were five of us (my Dad, my three brothers, and me), we split into two groups so it would be easier to catch a ride. It's an odd memory: riding in a stranger's car on a freezing winter day, passing my dad and younger brother on the side of the road with their thumbs in the air . . . and not stopping.

Obituaries don't always cover important milestones like these. And that's unfortunate. After all, an obituary is not just a notice of a death. It's the story of a life, perhaps even an inspiration for the eulogy or the start of a memorial.

In the best cases, an obituary can rise to the level of literature. In 1988, an unsigned obit of jazz great Chet Baker in *The Times* of London said:

> There were certainly off-nights, but even when his trumpet tone was practically transparent, his singing voice a whisper, and the music seemingly in imminent danger of coming to an absolute halt, his innate musicianship could still achieve small miracles of wounded grace.

Other obits, like this one by Hugh Massingberd of the *Daily Telegraph,* are less poetic:

> The 3rd Lord Moynihan, who has died in Manila, aged 55, provided, through his character and career, ample ammunition for critics of the hereditary principle. His chief occupations were bongo-drummer, confidence trickster, brothel-keeper, drug-smuggler and police informer. . . .

Most of us, of course, will never be famous (or infamous) enough to merit an obituary in *The New York Times* or some other national paper. The first and only time a hometown paper will write a word about the vast majority of local citizens is when they've passed away. As obit writer Richard Pearson likes to say, "God is my assignment editor."

It's a tough job. Working in the hurricane of emotion that swirls around the newly dead, the obituary writer routinely deals with unknown subjects and distraught survivors while doing his or her best—on a tight deadline—to write something accurate, lively, and memorable.

Even under the best circumstances, summing up a life is an awesome responsibility. The goal is to honor the deceased, to inform the community, to help families learn more about one of their own members—and perhaps about themselves.

Obituaries weigh someone's life and accomplishments, communicating the significance of a person, a place, an era. The best are not simply portraits of grief. They inspire the living, reminding us what matters most.

Obituaries rarely mention the board meeting, the pay raise, the financial statement, or the Rolex Presidential. Rather, they remind us of the importance of family, friendship, and community, perhaps inspiring us to emulate the best qualities of the deceased.

That will be a tall order when my parents' day comes. Their attitude, humor, and irrepressible zest for living have set a near-impossible standard for the rest of the family. Still, it's a star to steer by.

As Marilyn Johnson, author of *The Dead Beat* (HarperCollins, 2006), says, "I wish I'd known him" is the response every good obit writer tries to elicit. And words those of us still living might endeavor to deserve.

How to Pull the
Universe Out of a Hat

For thousands of years, our ancestors believed we live at the center of a caring universe, that we are made in the image of the Creator, and—if we are good and just—that we are headed for an afterlife of eternal bliss.

It's a beautiful picture, embraced by millions of the world's faithful today. Yet modern science provides little support. Now world-renowned physicist Stephen Hawking has gone a step further, promoting one of the most controversial ideas yet: that the universe created itself out of nothing.

His new book *The Grand Design* (Bantam, 2010), a *New York Times* best seller, is an attempt to answer humanity's oldest and most persistent question: How did the universe begin?

As a kid, I often lay awake at night puzzling over this. What bothered me wasn't that I didn't know the answer. It was that I couldn't imagine there was an answer. My Sunday school teacher said I was overthinking the matter. God created the universe.

"Well, who created God?" I asked.

"God doesn't need a creator," he answered, smiling. "He's God."

"Well, if God can exist without a creator," I asked, "why not the universe?"

"Everything has to have a creator," he explained, "otherwise, it couldn't exist."

"Then how does God exist?" I persisted.

The smile disappeared. His patience had ended. It was time to move on to the fishes and the loaves. . . .

However, Hawking, the Lucasian professor of mathematics at the University of Cambridge for 30 years and the recipient of numerous awards and honors in science, has never stopped thinking about this most basic of questions and has sallied on where my Sunday school teacher left off.

Hawking is famous for his groundbreaking work in cosmology and quantum gravity, especially with black holes. He has done key scientific work regarding gravitation and general relativity. And more than 20 years ago, he had a runaway hit with *A Brief History of Time* (Bantam, 1998), a physics book for the general public that was a best seller for a record-breaking 237 weeks.

Of course, if you investigate the history of time, the obvious question is "Where do you begin?" Physicists answer that time is actually the fourth dimension of space, so you start with the Big Bang 13.7 billion years ago. Hawking wrote that asking what happened before the Big Bang is like asking what lies north of the North Pole.

Yet he kept pursuing the question anyway, his work on the subject intensifying since the book's publication in 1988. And to say his latest thinking on the subject is provocative is an understatement.

Hawking now claims we live in a multiverse—that ours is just one of many universes that appeared spontaneously out of nothing, each with different laws of nature. Furthermore, the cosmos does not have a single existence or history, but rather every possible history of the universe exists simultaneously. (Wait . . . it gets better.) He further suggests that we don't create history, but rather history creates us when we observe it.

These notions sound counterintuitive, implausible, and completely absurd (not to mention unscientific). Hawking expects and invites those reactions. Once we move beyond the Newtonian physics that govern the three-dimensional objects in our everyday world—and wander into the atomic or subatomic realm ruled by quantum physics—experience and intuition go out the window.

For instance, it is by no means obvious that everything—from the moon to asparagus to human beings—are all made of the same stuff. Yet all you see around you, both organic and inorganic, is made of the same short list of elements on the periodic table.

Likewise, we aren't generally aware that the table in front of us is not solid but rather a constantly vibrating illusion. Everything is made of atoms—and atoms are mostly empty space.

A friend once remarked about how ignorant the ancients were to believe the earth was flat and the sun, the stars, and the planets revolved around it. But why the disdain? After all, that's exactly how it looks.

There is much we couldn't have known before the advent of specialized tools and the scientific method. Science has a long history of upending our notions about the nature of reality. Only in recent times, for instance, have we known that time is relative, the universe is expanding, and all living things share a common ancestry.

We accept these things because there are mountains of evidence to support them. But the universe arising spontaneously out of nothing—what kind of science is that?

Hawking says his conclusions are consistent with quantum physics, a deeply mysterious field not well understood even by physicists themselves. Yet it works. Quantum experiments have led to fantastic advances in precision measurement and revealed much about the nature of the universe. Quantum physics agrees with observation, has never failed a test, and has been tested more than any other theory in science.

Yet, at the end of *The Grand Design,* Hawking writes, "the true miracle is that abstract considerations of logic lead to a unique theory that predicts and describes a vast universe full of the amazing variety that we see."

Hold on. Abstract considerations of logic? Science is supposed to be based on observation, evidence, and experimental confirmation.

I thought maybe I was missing something. So I checked in with my favorite science expert, Michael Shermer.

Michael said he loved the book, but seconded my reservations. This is not science. At least, not yet. Until Hawking's conclusions can be tested—and at least potentially disproved—they fall into the category of philosophical musings, metaphysical speculation, or protoscience.

There is room for faith to coexist with reason when it comes to questions about the beginning of the universe. And humility is always a virtue. So any discussion of our ultimate origins ought to begin with a basic acknowledgment: We simply don't know.

It Makes Everything Meaningful

One night a few weeks ago, my six-year-old son, David, came down from bed and put his head on my shoulder. In a mournful voice and with a tear in this eye, he said, "Dad, I just can't believe it's all going to end."

At school earlier that day, a buddy had told him—with apparent relish—that one day in the future our sun would explode and incinerate the planet and everyone on it.

I told David this was not true. What his friend described was a supernova, an explosion that marks the dramatic end for some stars, but not our sun. The single factor that decides whether a star will explode at the end of its life is mass. And our sun would need to be at least four times heavier to die in that kind of cataclysmic explosion.

"So the sun is not going to destroy the earth?" he asked, looking into my face for reassurance.

Here I was tempted to fudge a bit. (After all, it was bedtime.) But I've always believed it's better to teach kids to face unpleasant realities rather than ignore or deny them.

I told him that scientists believe that in four or five billion years, the sun will exhaust its fuel—its supply of hydrogen—and bloat into a red giant. As the sun expands, its heat will boil away the oceans and the earth will become molten again.

He looked a bit downcast at this information.

"But the good part," I added, "is that this won't happen for billions of years, long after you and everyone you know are gone. By then, it is possible that human beings will have developed the technology to venture out to other planets orbiting different stars. Our descendants may actually flourish in some other part of the galaxy."

He shrugged off my optimistic tone. When you're in second grade, the idea that you and everyone you know will some day be dead doesn't exactly rouse your spirits, even if its billions of years from now. (David still grapples with the concept of "next week.")

This led us to a second and more important discussion. I told David that he is young and strong and likely to live a long, long time, longer than he can imagine. But I also reminded him that everything that lives eventually dies. That's just the way things are.

It's sad to contemplate leaving this world or losing someone we love. But at some point—if we are fortunate enough to live that long—we become old and frail. Life loses its quality. Death becomes a blessing.

It doesn't always feel that way for us, the survivors, who grieve our losses deeply. But death is part of the tapestry of life. We couldn't exist without it. I often tell David, for instance, that everything on his plate was once alive: the fruit, the vegetables, the meat, even the pasta (in a roundabout way). He should be thankful. If they didn't die, he couldn't live.

Without the death of plants and animals—and our ancestors—there wouldn't be room for us. The earth can't support limitless populations. We all struggle to survive. But, eventually, the old leave to make room for the new.

Science writer Connie Barlow and her husband, Reverend Michael Dowd, help kids deal with death and dying as a natural process. She sometimes asks a group of children, "Do any of you have a grandparent who has already become an ancestor?" Instead of hesitating, the kids eagerly raise their hands. At one church, a boy proudly proclaimed, "My grandma became an ancestor on January 26, 2004!"

Without death, we couldn't honor those who came before us. We couldn't set important goals. We couldn't prioritize our lives. Time would not be precious.

Death separates the meaningful from the trivial. (Just ask someone with a cancer diagnosis how important next week's big budget meeting is.) It's shocking how often it takes the death of someone we know to knock us out of our complacency and make us take stock of what really matters.

In the end, death makes everything possible. Without the death of mountains, there would be no sand or soil. Without the death of ancient forests and glaciers, there would be no northern lakes. Without the death of dinosaurs, there would be no humans. Without the death of stars—the event that forges the heavy elements that make up you and everything around you—there would be no planets and no life.

As tragic as death can be, especially when it comes unexpectedly, it orders our lives and gives them meaning. Death reminds us that life is to be fully and exuberantly lived, and then graciously and gratefully given up.

I think David is getting it. When his sister, Hannah, came home from school one day and found Misty, her pet hamster, dead, David put his arm around her and said, "I'm sorry, Hannah." Then turning philosophical, he added, "But, you know Hannah, dying is just part of living."

And, indeed, it is.

■ The Truth about Myths

While talking movies with a buddy the other day, I mentioned that I thought *Braveheart*, a historical drama about Scottish revolutionary William Wallace, is a particularly inspiring film.

"But the retelling is so romanticized, it isn't true," my friend insisted. "How can a story be inspiring if it isn't real?"

Many readers would agree, I'm sure. In our literal-minded world, a heroic story—in print or in film—is only meaningful to the extent that it is factual. A myth is mere entertainment or, worse, a lie.

But this isn't necessarily so. A myth can also be a metaphor, one ripe with meaning. It can take the particular and turn it into a universal. Even when a story isn't factual, it can point to something beyond the facts. Myths are not about knowledge but wisdom.

Since the Enlightenment, our view of history has been primarily concerned with what actually happened. But in the premodern world, people knew accounts were often unreliable. They were more concerned with what an event *meant*.

They saw a myth as an event that happened once (or not at all) but that, in some sense, also happens all the time. Mythology deals with timeless events and emotions: birth, sickness, anguish, loss, fortune, fear, celebration, death.

Myths have existed across all times and cultures. From the beginning, human beings invented tales that placed our lives in a larger setting and gave them meaning and direction. The hero myth, in particular, is designed not just to provide us with an icon but to allow us to tap into a vein of heroism within ourselves.

A hero, by definition, is someone who has devoted his life to something larger than himself. When a person becomes a model for other people's lives, he or she can become mythologized. We see this often in athletics. Sports provide us with vivid examples of excellence, triumph over adversity, and the attainment of greatness.

Historically, however, myths served another role. They explained our world and our place in it. The source of mythology is often a profound anxiety about problems that cannot be alleviated by practical thought.

For example, early societies recognized that we must kill and eat to live. Myths were created to explain this mystery. As Laurence G. Boldt writes, "If you spend the better part of a day tracking and hunting an animal and then watch it suffering as it dies from your arrow or spear, you are going to have a different feeling for that food than if you go to a crowded supermarket, pick up a cellophane-wrapped meat, and throw it into the shopping cart." Myths were needed to soothe the human conscience, to justify and sanctify the killing. But those myths no longer resonate with us today.

The most enduring traditions emerged between 800 and 200 BC, a period German philosopher Karl Jaspers called the "Axial Age." During this time, humanity experienced a flowering of spiritual development with Confucianism and Taoism is China, Buddhism and Hinduism in India, monotheism in the Middle East and Greek rationalism in Europe. It was then that people began to see both their limitations and their possibilities with unprecedented clarity. Axial sages taught that justice, integrity, and compassion benefit both the individual and society. More than two millennia later, these traditions still endure.

In his PBS special *The Power of Myth* with Joseph Campbell, Bill Moyers said:

> What human beings have in common is revealed in myths. Myths are stories of our search through the ages for truth, for meaning,

for significance. We all need to tell our story and to understand our story. We all need to understand death, and we all need help in our passages from birth to life and then to death. We need for life to signify, to touch the eternal, to understand the mysterious, to find out who we are.

Campbell, an expert in comparative mythology, devoted his life to researching and studying the world's wisdom traditions. He concluded that traditional mythologies serve four essential functions:

The first is to awaken human consciousness to the *mysterium tremendum*, the mystery and glory of the universe *as it is*.

The second is to present an image of the cosmos that underpins the order of our lives.

Third is to validate and support a specific moral order.

The fourth is to help carry the individual through the various stages and crises of life.

Today, of course, we generally turn to science for the first two, a sense of awe at the grandeur of the universe and a better understanding of nature. But has the scientific method really, in the words of novelist Saul Bellow, "made a housecleaning of belief"?

Clearly not. A scientific understanding of the world is not compatible with a literal interpretation of Genesis. But ancient myths have value. They give us insights into the deeper meaning of life. They make us more fully conscious of what really matters. If something changes our hearts and minds, is it not somehow valid?

Mythology expresses our innate sense that there is more to the world than meets the eye, something that goes beyond mathematics, language, and art.

Ancient traditions guide us toward right action. They keep us from living inauthentic lives. They wake us from the sin of inadvertence, the state of not being truly awake. They tell us, in effect, *change your life*.

Metaphors are not just old, discredited tales, once mistaken for truth. They carry the human spirit forward. They can be a form of spiritual instruction, a method of transforming consciousness, of achieving a sense of transcendence. The aim of all mythology is psychological transformation.

Today, we can see beyond the symbols to the riches they represent. There you encounter a consciousness of the world that was missing in the world you formerly inhabited.

Campbell insisted that myths convey universal truths. They are about self-discovery and self-transcendence, one's role in society, and the relation between the two:

> It's important to live life with the experience, and therefore the knowledge, of its mystery and of your own mystery. This gives life a new radiance, a new harmony, a new splendor. Thinking in mythological terms helps to put you in accord with the inevitables of this vale of tears. You learn to recognize the positive values in what appear to be the negative moments and aspects of your life. The big question is whether you are going to be able to say a hearty yes to your adventure. The adventure of a hero.

Your Place In
"The Great Story"

Over dinner a few months ago, my friend Marcy told me she was struggling with what she calls "the great questions."

Who am I? Where am I going? What's it all about?

She was visiting a new church and had picked up a few books on philosophy, religion, and science, but felt a bit overwhelmed.

"There's an awful lot to cover here," she said. "Where do you suggest I start?"

I told her it depended on where her interests lay and that she would probably end up following her own path. But I did recommend a good trailhead: Big History.

You can't know where you're going if you don't know where you've been. Big History provides some context, using not just the knowledge and insights of historians, but of archaeologists, cosmologists, geologist, and biologists, too. The result is a grand synthesis—based on the latest discoveries—that explains our place in creation.

Why is this important?

As Dr. Joel Primack, a distinguished professor of physics at the University of California, explains, "Without a meaningful, believable story that explains the world we actually live in, people have no idea how to think about the big picture. And without a big picture, we are very small people."

Yet this portrait is anything but easy to find. Professors Bob Bain and Lauren McArthur Harris of the University of Michigan recently asked over 75 world history teachers at a workshop to quickly compile a five-minute history of the United States.

Most had no problem, using a thread that included Native Americans, European settlement and colonization, the American Revolution, the Civil War and Reconstruction, expansion and industrialization, two World Wars, the Depression and New Deal, the Cold War, civil rights, and so on.

Next, they asked them to craft a five-minute history of Western Civilization. Again, the teachers had little difficulty finding common markers: the River Valley civilizations, classical Mediterranean civilization, the Middle Ages, the Renaissance, the Reformation, the Enlightenment, the rise of nation-states, exploration, democratic revolutions, and so forth.

But when they asked the same group to create a five-minute account of world history, they were stymied. They couldn't decide what to include, got bogged down with details and lacked sufficient knowledge to form a coherent narrative. And these were world history teachers!

Their experience underscores the trouble most of us have gaining a genuine sense of the past. The subject is so broad and diverse that it is easy to get overwhelmed by a blizzard of facts that lacks any meaningful interpretation.

Big History provides one. It is a story that weaves the past, including both human history and prehistory, into a single tapestry. Unlike traditional history, which focuses on political movements and key personalities, Big History deals with evolutionary changes and patterns that link us to a common background.

You already know that you share a national history with millions of others and a personal history with a much smaller subset. But consider the history you share with the rest of humanity, the natural world, and even the stars and planets. At this grand scale, it is not possible to cover the actions and accomplishments of great individuals, men and women we should know and strive to emulate. The goal here is to understand our interconnections and, ultimately, our place in the world.

For example, paleontologists estimate that *Homo sapiens* emerged from East Africa roughly 200,000 years ago. Since then, we've climbed from savages to scientists. A few notable developments along the way include:

1. *Speech.* The development of articulate expression took us from warning cries and mating calls to philosophy and lyric poetry. Without language, reason would never have gotten off the ground.

2. *Fire.* This discovery made us less dependent on climate, less fearful of the night, and offered a thousand things for dinner that were inedible before. (For an interesting take on this era, I recommend *Quest for Fire,* perhaps the funniest movie without dialogue ever made.)

3. *The conquest of the animals.* Today, most of us think of animals as either pets or food. But before we took dominion of the earth, leaving a cave or your hut was a potentially life-threatening risk.

4. *Agriculture.* Without the development of crops and livestock, our ancestors could not have made the transition from hunting and gathering to civilization. Yet 98 percent of human history is preagricultural.

5. *Social organization.* There was no security and prosperity until we learned that disputes could be settled without picking up a rock or a club. Cooperation and compromise led to progress, knowledge, and wealth.

6. *Morality.* There can be no lasting peace without justice or conscience. More than 2,000 years ago, Buddha said, "Hurt not others with that which pains yourself." Confucius said, "What you do not yourself desire, do not put before others." Hindu scripture counseled, "Treat others as you would be treated." Jesus of Nazareth said, "Do unto others as you would have them do unto you."

Societies that adopted this ethos survived. The others did not. It's that simple.

7. *Tools*. Without machines—like the wheel, the hammer, and the knife—there was little we could build or achieve. New and ever-improving tools eased our burdens and vastly improved the quality of life.

8. *Education*. Each generation passes along its discoveries and accumulated wisdom to the next. We are born savages. Education makes us human.

9. *Writing and print*. Writing made permanent the achievements of the mind. Printing carried them to the corners of the earth.

10. *Mathematics and science*. Society could not have advanced without the enlightenment of the mind. From the electron microscope to the Hubble space telescope, science has revealed a universe vastly larger and more splendid than the ancients could possibly have imagined.

Yet 5,000 years of recorded history relates only a millionth of the lifetime of the earth. We seldom think of it, but the planet has a history, too. So does the solar system. And so does the universe as a whole. Yet, thanks to the discoveries of science, it is only relatively recently that we have pieced our earliest chapters together.

We now know, for instance, that the present universe sprang into existence 13.7 billion years ago. The solar system formed 4.5 billion years ago. The first signs of microscopic life arrived 3.7 billion years ago. And the largest-ever mass extinction occurred 252 million years ago. How we know these things are true is one of the most fascinating aspects of studying Big History.

If you are interested in learning more, there are a number of excellent books available. A few favorites are *What on Earth Happened* by Christopher Lloyd (Bloomsbury USA, 2008), *Big History* by Cynthia Stokes Brown (New Press, 2007), and *This Fleeting World* by David Christian (Berkshire, 2004).

Christian, an Oxford-educated scholar and professor of history at San Diego State University, is one of the founding figures of the

Big History movement. He has taught the subject since 1989 and even coined the term, whimsically, in a 1991 article.

Christian realized that the story of our beginnings crosses various branches of knowledge and is generally scattered across academic disciplines. Worse, it is almost never presented chronologically. That makes it tough to grasp the big picture. Students and seekers, like Marcy, often find themselves lost, confused, or tied up in knots.

One solution is "Big History: The Big Bang, Life on Earth, and the Rise of Humanity," a 48-lecture course taught by David Christian and available through the Teaching Company on DVD, audio CD, or audio download. (Just visit www.teach12.com.)

The course is in easy-to-digest 30-minute lectures that are short on glossy production but long on distilled wisdom. Christian doesn't just relate the big picture. He puts in into context and makes it accessible to the layman.

In an early episode, for instance, he tries to convey the immensity of our solar system and points out that a modern passenger jet flying at roughly 550 miles per hour takes about five hours to cross the continental United States. Traveling at the same speed, you would need 18 days to reach the moon, 20 years to reach the sun, 82 years to reach Jupiter, and 750 years to reach Pluto, my favorite ex-planet.

How long would it take to reach the next nearest star, Alpha Centauri, 25 trillion miles away? The answer is five million years. Yet, cosmologically, this is right next door.

There are roughly 100 billion stars in the Milky Way, most (except for double stars) separated by a plane flight of five million years or more. The Hubble has revealed more than 100 billion other galaxies out there, each stuffed with billions of stars. The science journal *Nature* recently noted that there are approximately 300 sextillion stars in the universe, about three time more than earlier estimates (300 sextillion is 3 followed by 23 zeroes). What does this mean? That there are more stars in the known universe than grains of sand on all the beaches and deserts on earth.

The universe isn't just bigger than you imagine. It's bigger than you *can* imagine.

The only way Big History won't make your head swim is if you aren't paying attention (which may explain why we missed most of this in college). However, it's only within the past few decades that scientists have had the specialized instruments and dating techniques to know where we came from and how we got here.

Big History is a crash course in your connection to everything: other people, the natural world, the rest of the cosmos. What is the benefit of this larger perspective?

Our world has never been more interconnected. Yet we define ourselves in the ways that divide us: national boundaries, culture, language, religion. The truth is we are all united in the most profound ways, not just as a global community but as a cosmic one. (This may sound a little Kumbaya, but that doesn't make it any less true.) Understanding the past allows us to think more clearly about the future.

Your story transcends the history of particular nations, ethnic groups, individual species, even organic matter. It reveals your deep spiritual connection to the rest of humanity . . . and to everything else.

As cell biologist and essayist Lewis Thomas observed:

> I go back, and so do you, like it or not, to a single Ur-ancestor, whose remains are on display in rocks dated approximately 3.5 thousand million years ago, born a billion or so years after the earth itself took shape and began cooling down. . . . I cannot get that out of my head. It has become the most important thing I know, the obligatory beginning of any memoir, the long-buried source of language. We derive from a lineage of bacteria, and a very long line at that. Never mind our embarrassed indignation when we were first told that we came from a family of apes and had chimps as near-cousins. That was relatively easy to accommodate, having at least the distant look of a set of relatives. But this new connection, already fixed by recent science beyond any hope of disowning the parentage, is something else again. . . . We are all in the same family—grasses, seagulls, fishes, fleas and voting citizens of the republic. . . . Humble origins indeed.

The journey is a fantastic one because it is grounded in what geologists call deep time, eons going back beyond our ability to comprehend.

Yet there is grandeur here. Reverend Michael Dowd, an author and educator, calls our modern understanding "The Great Story," the sacred history of everyone and everything, from our cosmic genesis, to the formation of galaxies and the origin of life, to the development of consciousness and culture, to the emergence of ever-widening circles of care and concern. He defines Big History as a glorious revelation—a public one, available to anyone with an open heart and an inquiring mind.

Like my friend Marcy, you may be uncertain where you're going or what it's all about. After all, men and women have pondered these questions for thousands of years.

Big History can help. It offers a vital perspective, a map of your place in space and time. And while we should never stop asking who we are or where we're headed . . . it's pretty mind-blowing to discover where we've been.

SEVEN PRINCIPLES
OF SPIRITUALITY

When I first began writing *Spiritual Wealth*, I tried to avoid any misunderstanding by explaining to readers what I meant by the phrase.

Everything you own that you can put a dollar figure on—your house, your car, your bank account, your stock portfolio, your over-sized Callaway all-titanium driver—these I refer to as *material wealth*. And the things you appreciate that are, in fact, priceless—your health, your family, your hobbies, a sunset at the beach, autumn leaves—these are *spiritual wealth*.

Despite my use of the word *spiritual*, I never intended to write for or against any religious point of view. My only two objectives were (a) to ruminate on ideas about the good life and (b) to keep the discussion as inclusive and uplifting as possible. I used the term *spiritual* in its most general sense, to denote "a raising of the spirit."

The overwhelming majority of feedback I've received over the past three years was positive. I heard from tens of thousands of readers around the world, including people of all religious faiths (and no faith). Most thanked me for my thoughts and told me I had stimulated their own.

But I quickly learned that you cannot write a column about spiritual things without stepping on some people's toes. To my surprise, and almost without exception, the angriest, bitterest letters I received were from self-described Christians.

One wrote, "Spirituality has nothing to do with compassion, tolerance, forgiveness, humility, charity, or self-transcendence. It is about accepting Jesus Christ as your personal Lord and Savior. End of story."

This puzzled me. Shouldn't it at least be "beginning of story"?

We all know people who describe themselves as "spiritual but not religious." Apparently, there are others out there who are "religious but not spiritual."

Another reader, "Al," responded to my pluralistic essay about Jerusalem with this abrupt note, "You stand for everything . . . and nothing."

I routinely shrug off remarks like this, but for some reason that day I felt provoked. "Not so, Al," I shot back. "I stand against those who have it all figured out."

Within seconds of hitting the send button, I felt a bit sheepish. Why didn't I just let it go? Al's views on religion are no threat to me—and neither are anyone else's (provided, of course, they don't have a knife to my throat).

I feel strongly that it's possible to have a productive exchange of views on religion. It isn't always easy because it requires open-mindedness and restraint, qualities that don't generally come to the fore in religious discussions. But historian and scholar Karen Armstrong described an excellent approach in a recent interview:

> A Socratic dialogue never ends with somebody defeating somebody else and forcing them into another frame of mind. A Socratic dialogue is actually a spiritual exercise, and Socrates said it would not work unless it was conducted at every single point with gentleness. You offer your opinion to your conversation partner as a gift, expressing it beautifully. And he would listen and allow

it into his heart and would give you something back, too. And you would not enter into one of these conversations unless you expected to be changed by the encounter. Otherwise, you end up with a diatribe, not a dialogue.

There is more than a little wisdom here.

In order to stay above the fray, I generally avoided controversial questions about religion and spirituality. And when asked if I could explain what I meant when I used the term *spiritual*, I was happy to respond promptly: probably not.

Spirituality is such a broad term, covering everything from the severest fundamentalism to the wackiest New Age ideas. An unabridged dictionary offers more than a dozen definitions. And I can't encapsulate the word either.

But after giving the matter more than a little thought—and provoking more than a few others to do the same—I've decided to take a stab at defining spirituality as I see it. These are just a few personal convictions. I make no claim that the list is exhaustive. But here are seven areas where I believe most thinking people can agree:

1. *You recognize the eternal mystery.* There is a great puzzle at the center of our existence. When did time begin? Where does space end? Why is there something instead of nothing? Theologians answer these questions by referring to God, an all-loving, all-powerful being that exists in a realm beyond time and space. Materialists find this explanation unsatisfactory, but can offer no better explanation of their own.

   Maybe this is a good place to establish some common ground. At the moment of unknowing, we realize the profundity of our ignorance. This is the start of the spiritual quest. We pursue understanding because we know we do not have it. Is it not absurd to insist one minute that God is beyond understanding, beyond imagining, and then argue the next that someone else's conception is wrong? Spirituality begins with the realization that conceptions of the divine are largely differences of imagination.

2. *You have a genuine sense of awe.* The Milky Way is bigger than our brains can imagine. Light, traveling 186,000 miles per second, takes 100,000 years to cross our galaxy. Yet a recent Hubble Deep Field image indicates there are over 240 billion galaxies in the visible universe. And a recent German supercomputer simulation put that number even higher: 500 billion. Looking up on a starry night and being awestruck by the beauty and grandeur of the universe is a deeply spiritual feeling.

   Einstein said:

   > The finest emotion of which we are capable is the mystic emotion. Herein lies the germ of all art and all true science. Anyone to whom this feeling is alien, who is no longer capable of wonderment and lives in a state of fear, is a dead man. To know that what is impenetrable for us really exists and manifests itself as the highest wisdom and the most radiant beauty, whose gross forms alone are intelligible to our poor faculties—this knowledge, this feeling . . . that is the core of the true religious sentiment.

3. *You appreciate the sacredness of life.* No one knows how life began or how widespread it may be in the universe. Scientists are working on it, but the answer eludes us. Many holy texts insist our origins are supernatural. Science, of course, searches for a naturalistic explanation. But whatever metaphysical road you travel, the reality is that inorganic matter became organic. Is that not miraculous in the truest sense of the word? We are not outside of nature but intimately connected with it at the deepest levels. Conscious human beings are nothing less than the universe reflecting on itself. It took almost three centuries for this remarkable insight to become the common opinion of scientists, but mystics have been saying it for millennia.

4. *You are profoundly grateful for your life.* It is easy to take our lives for granted. After all, life is all we have ever known. How easily we forget that we are only here for a visit. What

wouldn't rich men like Rockefeller, Carnegie, or Howard Hughes give to be alive again, even if only to spend a few hours sitting by a pool at a roadside motel? Money is nothing compared to the blessing of being alive.

And what a slim chance you had of getting here. In *A Short History of Nearly Everything* (Broadway, 2003), Bill Bryson writes:

> You have been extremely—make that miraculously— fortunate in your personal ancestry. Consider the fact that for 3.8 billion years, a period of time older than the Earth's mountains and rivers and oceans, every one of your forebears on both sides has been attractive enough to find a mate, healthy enough to reproduce, and sufficiently blessed by fate and circumstances to live long enough to do so. Not one of your pertinent ancestors was squashed, devoured, drowned, starved, stranded, stuck fast, untimely wounded, or otherwise deflected from its life's quest of delivering a tiny charge of genetic material to the right partner at the right moment in order to perpetuate the only possible sequence of hereditary combinations that could result—eventually, astoundingly, and all too briefly—in you.

5. *You have a well-developed ethical sense.* When it comes to morality, there are two primary rules. The first is to treat others as you would be treated. (That one is pretty golden.) The second is when you say you're going to do something, do it.

    I do think we have a responsibility to do more than just keep our word and not injure others, however. The consideration of others through action or charity must be some part of an ethical life. Philosopher Daniel Dennett writes:

    > There are many people who quite innocently and sincerely believe that if they are earnest in attending to their own personal "spiritual" needs, this amounts to living a

morally good life. I know many activists, both religious and secular, who agree with me: These people are deluding themselves.

Millions of men, women and children will not have a good meal today. Tens of millions more live lives more affected than our own. We should not forget them—or disregard the old, the weak, the poor, the oppressed, or the imprisoned.

6. *You strive for higher consciousness and wisdom.* This is where spirituality can get a little fuzzy. But higher consciousness can be described in practical terms. It means striving to live the best life while also recognizing the limits of your understanding. It means adopting an attitude of acceptance toward life and our fellow human beings. Higher consciousness is about grace and civility. It's about recognizing what is sacred, what is worth protecting.

Wisdom is about knowing what to do and when. It's also about understanding when to leave things alone. I'm fond of psychologist Williams James's definition: Wisdom is knowing what to overlook.

7. *You seek a life of meaning.* What is the purpose of life? You can look at the natural world and see that all living things struggle to survive and pass their genes on to the next generation. From a biological standpoint, this is our purpose. But where do we find meaning?

For most of human history, men and women were too busy trying to survive to ponder the question. In the modern era, theologians have wrestled with the question. Philosophers and their students have tied themselves in knots over it. You can spend the rest of your days reading and soul searching and never find the answer. Why? Because the meaning of life is invented, not discovered. We each have a responsibility to determine what we are living for and invest our lives with meaning that we find significant.

Australian author Matthew Kelly has the right idea. He says the essential goal in life is to become "the-best-version-of-yourself." You begin the process of transformation and self-realization when you ask what it would take to become the best version of yourself physically, intellectually, emotionally and spiritually. As Robert Louis Stevenson said, "To be what we are, and to become what we are capable of becoming, is the only end in life."

If you follow these seven principles, will that make you a "spiritual person"? Perhaps. But I'm skeptical even of this.

True religion is not about what you believe but how you behave. For example, I have a hard-driving, trash-talking, largely unreflective friend who spends most of his time getting and spending. He doesn't go to church. He doesn't meditate. And I can't imagine him thinking about the splendor of the natural world or his place in it. Yet he recently registered with the National Bone Marrow Donor Program in the sincere hope that he might help some total stranger survive. That makes him one of the more spiritual people I know.

Perhaps genuine spirituality is not unlike Justice Potter Stewart's famous litmus test for pornography: We may not be able to define it. But we know it when we see it.

AFTERWORD

Having written nearly 150 of these *Spiritual Wealth* essays over the past three years, this is probably a good time for some summing up.

I want to, first of all, thank my good friend and colleague Julia Guth for publishing a column completely outside our core area of competence—investment advice—especially since there was never a prospect of any financial gain. The mountain of feedback we received, however, indicates we did create a lot of goodwill. When you are in business, what flows from that can't be calculated. But it shouldn't be underestimated either.

I also want to thank my regular readers, who provided a valuable service by critiquing my work each week, letting me know when they thought I hit the mark or missed it wide. They offered new information, caught occasional errors and chided me when I lapsed into the passive tense. (Sorry, I have never had a real editor.)

It was especially rewarding to hear back from men and women around the world with detailed knowledge about the subjects under discussion. This was especially helpful since an essayist, almost by definition, is a generalist, not a specialist.

I am also grateful for the eloquent letters from readers around the world who have thought deeply about—and still wrestle with—many of the ideas discussed here. The depth of their understanding surprised me, although perhaps it shouldn't have. Spiritual issues, even more than political ones, are generally considered too heavy or too sensitive for social conversation. You can know someone for years—even a lifetime—and never have an inkling of his or her innermost thoughts and beliefs. Usually, we are left to extrapolate them from their behavior.

While I am on the subject of behavior, some readers have asked whether I live up to the many ideals discussed in these pages. I would love to tell you that I have found the perfect balance between work and play, that I spend the majority of my waking hours exercising regularly, eating properly, tending to the poor, reading Shakespeare and listening to Mozart, and emulating the lives of Gandhi and Marcus Aurelius, but—alas—my friends and family members wouldn't stand for it. (And there are too many cream pies lying around to even try.) So, while the subjects of these essays are close to my heart, many of the ideals remain aspirational, even for the author—perhaps especially for the author, a deeply flawed work-in-progress.

Why do I keep writing these essays? I don't know. Some people have to write the way cows have to give milk. I'm in the perfect line of work for a daydreamer. And while my writing has a long way to go, there couldn't be a better way for me to while away the hours than reading, researching, and scribbling. To me, it's not work. It's pleasure. As livelihoods go, it's tough to beat.

I mentioned in my most recent book, *The Secret of Shelter Island* (John Wiley & Sons, 2009), that I really intended these words for the benefit of Hannah and David. That remains the case here. They are too young to get most of this now, but my hope is that someday they will pick up this book and learn a little something about their world . . . and, perhaps, their dad.

APPENDIX

RECIPE FOR MOM'S INSANELY GREAT VEGETABLE SOUP

Ingredients:

1 gallon water
1 beef soup bone
1 lb. stew beef cut into small cubes
1–2 chopped onions
1 large can of crushed tomatoes
3–4 cups shredded cabbage (or 1 package of coleslaw mix)
1–2 turnips cut in chunks
1½ cups elbow macaroni
12 oz. frozen corn
12 oz. frozen lima beans
12 oz. cut okra

Here's where it gets tricky: salt, seasoning, Tabasco, Worcestershire, V8, beef broth, and chili powder "to taste." (Don't ask me how she always gets these just right.)

Boil the beef bone and meat in water (covered) for 90 minutes. Add onions, cabbage (coleslaw), and tomatoes, and boil 30–40 minutes.

Remove bone and add 2 tablespoons of salt.
Add frozen vegetables and cook 30 minutes, seasoning (again)
   to taste.
Add macaroni and continue to simmer.
Add seasonings to make mildly spicy.
Keep seasoning to taste.
Voila!

Either this is the greatest vegetable soup recipe ever or my mother
has a preternatural sense of "seasoning to taste." Good luck. I personally have not been able to duplicate her perfection, but she
swears it's all here.

FURTHER READING

Alison, Jay, and Dan Gediman. *This I Believe: The Personal Philosophies of Remarkable Men and Women.* New York: Holt Paperbacks, 2007.

Allen, James. *The Wisdom of James Allen: Including As a Man Thinketh, The Path to Prosperity, The Mastery of Destiny, The Way of Peace, and Entering the Kingdom.* San Diego, CA: Laurel Creek Press, 1997.

Anderson, Walter Truett. *The Truth about Truth.* New York: Tarcher, 1995.

Ariely, Dan. *Predictably Irrational, Revised and Expanded Edition: The Hidden Forces that Shape Our Decisions.* New York: Harper Perennial, 2009.

Armstrong, Karen. *A Short History of Myth.* New York: Canongate, 2006.

Armstrong, Karen. *The Case for God.* New York: Anchor, 2010.

Beckett, Sister Wendy. *Joy Lasts: On the Spiritual in Art.* Los Angeles: J. Paul Getty Museum, 2006.

Bloom, Harold. *Shakespeare: The Invention of the Human.* New York: Riverhead Trade, 1999.

Bowman, James. *Honor: A History.* New York: Encounter Books, 2006.

Branden, Nathaniel. *Self-Esteem Every Day: Reflections on Self-Esteem and Spirituality.* New York: Fireside, 1998.

Branden, Nathaniel. *The Art of Living Consciously: The Power of Awareness to Transform Everyday Life.* New York: Fireside, 1999.

Buell, Lawrence. *The American Transcendentalists: Essential Writings.* New York: Modern Library, 2006.

Campbell, Joseph, with Bill Moyers. *The Power of Myth.* New York: Anchor, 1991.

Campbell, Joseph. *The Hero's Journey: Joseph Campbell on His Life and Work,* 3rd ed. Novato, CA: New World Library, 2003.

Carr, Nicholas. *The Shallows: What the Internet Is Doing to Our Brains.* New York: W. W. Norton, 2010.

Christian, David. *This Fleeting World: A Short History of Humanity.* Great Barrington, MA: Berkshire Publishing Group, 2007.

Covey, Stephen R. *The Speed of Trust: Live from L.A.* New York: Covey, 2009.

Cox, Gary. *How to Be an Existentialist: or How to Get Real, Get a Grip and Stop Making Excuses.* New York: Continuum, 2009.

de Botton, Alain. *The Pleasure and Sorrows of Work.* Hamish Hamilton, 2009.

D'Agnese, Joseph, and Denise Kiernan. *Signing Their Lives Away: The Fame and Misfortune of the Men Who Signed the Declaration of Independence.* San Francisco: Quirk Books, 2009.

D'Souza, Dinesh. *Life After Death: The Evidence.* Washington, DC: Regnery Publishing, 2009.

Davies, Paul. *The Goldilocks Enigma: Why Is the Universe Just Right for Life?* New York: Mariner Books, 2008.

Dowd, Michael. *Thank God for Evolution: How the Marriage of Science and Religion Will Transform Your Life and Our World.* New York: Penguin Group, 2009.

Durant, Will. *The Greatest Minds and Ideas of All Time.* New York: Simon & Schuster, 2002.

Dutton, Denis. *The Art Instinct: Beauty, Pleasure, and Human Evolution.* New York: Bloomsbury Press, 2010.

Earnshaw, Steven. *Existentialism: A Guide for the Perplexed.* New York: Continuum, 2007.

Flynn, Thomas R. *Existentialism: A Very Short Introduction.* New York: Oxford University Press, 2006.

Ford, S. Dennis. *Sins of Omission.* Minneapolis, MN: Fortress Press, 1990.

Frankenberry, Nancy K. *The Faith of Scientists: In Their Own Words.* Princeton, NJ: Princeton University Press, 2008.

Gabler, James M. *Passions: The Wines and Travels of Thomas Jefferson.* Baltimore: Bacchus Press, 1995.

Gandhi, Mahatma, Louis Fischer, M. K. Gandhi. *The Essential Gandhi: An Anthology of His Writings on His Life, Work, and Ideas,* 2nd ed. New York: Vintage, 2002.

Gates, Bill, Sr., and Mary Ann Mackin. *Showing Up for Life: Thoughts on the Gifts of a Lifetime.* New York: Crown Business, 2010.

Geldard, Richard C. *The Essential Transcendentalists.* New York: Tarcher, 2005.

Gilbert, Roger et al. *The Quotable Walker.* Guilford, CT: Lyons Press, 2000.

Gombrich, E. H. *The Story of Art.* London: Phaidon Press, 2006.

Gosling, Sam. *Snoop: What Your Stuff Says about You.* New York: Basic Books, 2009.

Grayling, A. C. *Meditations for the Humanist.* New York: Oxford University Press, 2003.

Hahn, Thich Nhat. *Savor: Mindful Eating, Mindful Life.* New York: HarperOne, 2011.

Hailman, John. *Thomas Jefferson on Wine.* Jackson, MS: University Press of Mississippi, 2009.

Hawking, Stephen, and Leonard Mlodinow. *The Grand Design.* New York: Bantam, 2010.

Hawking, Stephen. *Illustrated Theory of Everything: The Origin and Fate of the Universe.* Beverly Hills, CA: Phoenix Books, 2009.

Hodgkinson, Tom. *How to Be Idle: A Loafer's Manifesto.* New York: Harper Perennial, 2007.

Huxley, Aldous. *The Perennial Philosophy: An Interpretation of the Great Mystics, East and West.* New York: Harper Perennial, 2009.

Johnson, Marilyn. *The Dead Beat: Lost Souls, Lucky Stiffs, and the Perverse Pleasures of Obituaries.* New York: Harper Perennial, 2007.

Kashdan, Todd. *Curious?: Discover the Missing Ingredient to a Fulfilling Life.* New York: William Morrow, 2009.

Kaufman, Stephen E. *Living Tao Meditations/Tao Te Ching.* North Clarendon, VT: Tuttle Publishing, 1998.

Kirshenbaum, Sheril, and Chris Mooney. *Unscientific America: How Scientific Illiteracy Threatens our Future.* New York: Basic Books, 2009.

Leach, Robert J., and Peter Gow. *Quaker Nantucket: The Religious Community Behind the Whaling Empire.* Nantucket, MA: Mill Hill Press, 1996.

Lipsky, David. *Although Of Course You End Up Becoming Yourself: A Road Trip with David Foster Wallace.* New York: Broadway, 2010.

Magee, Bryan. *Confessions of a Philosopher: A Personal Journey through Western Philosophy from Plato to Popper.* New York: Modern Library, 1999.

Maher, John M., and Dennie Briggis. *An Open Life: Joseph Campbell in Conversation with Michael Toms.* New York: Harper Perennial, 1990.

Manchester, William. *A World Lit Only by Fire: The Medieval Mind and the Renaissance: Portrait of an Age.* New York: Little, Brown, 1993.

Manjoo, Farhad. *True Enough: Learning to Live in a Post-Fact Society.* Hoboken, NJ: John Wiley & Sons, 2008.

Marino, Gordon. *Basic Writings of Existentialism.* New York: Modern Library, 2004.

Marsalis, Wynton. *Moving to Higher Ground: How Jazz Can Change Your Life.* New York: Random House, 2009.

Mitchell, Stephen. *Tao Te Ching: A New English Version.* New York: Harper Perennial, 2006.

Mitchell, Stephen. *The Essence of Wisdom.* New York: Broadway, 1999.

Moses, Jeffrey. *Oneness: Great Principles Shared by All Religions, Revised and Expanded Edition.* New York: Ballantine Books, 2002.

Murray, Charles. *Human Accomplishment: The Pursuit of Excellence in the Arts and Sciences, 800 B.C. to 1950.* New York: Harper Perennial, 2004.

Needleman, Jacob. *The Spiritual Emerson: Essential Works by Ralph Waldo Emerson.* New York: Tarcher, 2008.

Osbon, Diane K. *Reflections on the Art of Living: A Joseph Campbell Companion.* New York: Harper Perennial, 1995.

Postman, Neil. *Amusing Ourselves to Death: Public Discourse in the Age of Show Business.* New York: Penguin, 2005.

Raymo, Chet. *When God Is Gone, Everything Is Holy: The Making of a Religious Naturalist.* Notre Dame, IN: Sorin Books, 2008.

Red Pine, trans. *Lao-tzu's Taoteching, 3rd Revised Edition.* Phoenix: Copper Canyon Press, 2009.

Robins, Stephen. *The Importance of Being Idle: A Little Book of Lazy Inspiration.* London: Prion, 2001.

Rosenblum, Mort. *Chocolate: A Bittersweet Saga of Dark and Light.* New York: North Point Press, 2006.

Sagan, Carl. *The Varieties of Scientific Experience: A Personal View of the Search for God.* New York: Penguin, 2007.

Singer, Peter. *The Life You Can Save: Acting Now to End World Poverty.* New York: Random House, 2009.

Singh, Simon. *Big Bang: The Origin of the Universe (P.S.).* New York: Harper Perennial, 2005.

Spiegelman, Willard. *Seven Pleasures: Essays on Ordinary Happiness.* New York: Farrar, Straus and Giroux, 2009.

Stanley, Thomas J. *Stop Acting Rich: . . . And Start Living Like a Real Millionaire.* Hoboken, NJ: John Wiley & Sons, 2009.

Towler, Solala. *Tales from the Tao: The Wisdom of the Taoist Masters.* London: Duncan Baird, 2007.

Tyson, Neil de Grasse, and Donald Goldsmith. *Origins: Fourteen Billion Years of Cosmic Evolution.* New York: W. W. Norton, 2005.

Wallace, David Foster. *This Is Water: Some Thoughts, Delivered on a Significant Occasion, about Living a Compassionate Life.* New York: Little, Brown, 2009.

Walsh, Peter. *It's All Too Much: An Easy Plan for Living a Richer Life with Less Stuff.* New York: Free Press, 2007.

Warren, Frank. *PostSecret: Confessions on Life, Death, and God.* New York: William Morrow, 2009.

Winget, Larry. *Your Kids Are Your Own Fault: A Guide For Raising Responsible, Productive Adults.* New York: Gotham, 2009.

Wright, Robert. *The Evolution of God.* Boston: Back Bay Books, 2010.

Zinsser, William. *Writing to Learn.* New York: Harper Paperbacks, 1993.

ACKNOWLEDGMENTS

This is my third book, and each one turned out to be a bigger project than I originally imagined. Thanks to everyone at John Wiley & Sons who helped pull this one together, especially Debra Englander, Kelly O'Connor, and Stacey Fischkelta.

I wish I had a big staff—or even a single editor—to thank for helping me research and write these essays. But this was almost entirely a solo project. Not that I'm complaining. I would rather spend an afternoon writing an essay than going to the beach or playing a round of golf. (If you saw my backswing, you'd understand why.) I learned a lot researching and writing this book and am always grateful for an opportunity to remedy my ignorance.

There are, of course, many people who deserve special appreciation, beginning with the great thinkers and writers I quote in these pages. Particular thanks go to those writers whose work was instrumental in helping form my own views, especially John Templeton, Karen Armstrong, Bryan Magee, and Joseph Campbell.

I want to thank my publisher and good friend Julia Guth for endorsing the *Spiritual Wealth* project from the beginning and for writing the overly-kind Foreword here. My Web team—Martin Denholm, Erick Shutz, and Karen Schildt—deserve special commendation for enduring all my late-Friday-afternoon submissions and many last-minute edits.

Special thanks also to my wife, Karen. It's not easy living with someone who spends most of his waking hours reading, writing, or gazing off into the distance—and not terribly exciting to watch either, I imagine. Thanks, Karen, for putting up with me.

I do want to clear up a misunderstanding about the acknowledgments in my most recent book, *The Secret of Shelter Island*. I'm referring specifically to the part where I said, "I hate Bill Bryson. All writers should. If you don't know why, read everything he's written."

This was intended—I thought it was obvious—as a compliment. Bryson is not just my favorite contemporary author. He is the kind of writer who makes the rest of us feel like amateurs, frauds, and poseurs, that our true calling is not writing, but perhaps driving nails, running a day care center, or working at the local Waffle House. I have never met Bill Bryson. But I have read him—and I sit at his feet.

So imagine my embarrassment when I began receiving letters from readers around the world asking the same pointed question: Why would I dismiss a fine, talented writer like Bill Bryson?

Let me take this opportunity to set the record straight: I hate Bill Bryson. All writers should. If you don't know why, read everything he's written. *Twice.*

ABOUT THE AUTHOR

Alexander Green is the Investment Director of The Oxford Club, the world's largest investment club. He is also Chief Investment Strategist of Investment U, the editor of *Spiritual Wealth*, and the author of two national bestsellers: *The Gone Fishin' Portfolio* and *The Secret of Shelter Island: Money and What Matters.*

He has been featured on *Oprah & Friends*, CNBC, National Public Radio (NPR), Fox News, and *The O'Reilly Factor* and has been profiled by *The Wall Street Journal, BusinessWeek, Forbes,* and many others.

He currently lives in Charlottesville, Virginia, and Winter Springs, Florida, with his wife, Karen, and their children, Hannah and David.

Websites:
www.spiritualwealth.com
www.oxfordclub.com
E-mail: feedbacksw@gmail.com

INDEX

Abbott, John S. C., 51
Achievement and enjoyment, 120
Adams, Abigail, 196
Adams, James, 66, 96
Adaptation to Life (Vaillant), 23
Addison, Joseph, 88
Afterlife, 247–248
Agassi, Andre, 177
Agassi, Mike, 177
Aging prediction, 23
"Alabama" (music), 32
Alexander the Great, 164, 203
Allen, James, 42–45
Allen, Woody, 248
American Visionary Art Museum, 129, 132
Amusing Ourselves to Death (Postman),
    135–136
Angier, Natalie, 236
Anna Karenina (Tolstoy), 151
Aristotle, 138
Armstrong, Karen, 167, 206
Arnold, Matthew, 142
Art, 77–80
The Art Instinct (Dutton), 80
The Art of Living Consciously (Branden), 185
As a Man Thinketh (Allen), 42, 44–45
Asimov, Isaac, 229, 235, 240
Aspirationals, 6

Asteroids, 245
Attenborough, David, 236
Authority, 181
Authors, 199
Axial Age, 266

Bain, Bob, 270
Ballou, Sullivan, 111–112
Barker, Chet, 256
Barlow, Connie, 263
Beckett, Wendy, 70
Beethoven, Ludwig van, 33
Bellow, Saul, 267
Big Bang, 230
Big Bang: The Origin of the Universe (Singh),
    231
Big History, 269–275
Big History (Brown), 272
"Big History: The Big Bang, Life on Earth,
    and the Rise of Humanity" (Christian),
    273
Bill and Melinda Gates Foundation, 16–17
Bin Laden, Osama, 67
Bismarck, Otto von, 66
Bloom, Harold, 221
Blue Planet (Attenborough), 236
Boldt, Laurence, 12, 266
Books, 20, 198–201

Boss, Alan, 214
Bowman, James, 65
Branden, Nathaniel, 67–68, 183–187
Brave New World (Huxley), 136
Braveheart, 265
Braxton, Carter, 62–64
A Brief History of Time (Hawking), 259
Brown, Cynthia Stokes, 272
Brown Jim, 176–177
Bryson, Bill, 236
Buckley, Lori, 121
Buddha, 150, 159, 271
Buddhism, 158–161
Buffett, Warren, 10, 17, 118
Burnet, Dana, 64

A Calendar of Wisdom (Tolstoy), 151–153
Campbell, Joseph, 266, 267, 268
*The Canon: a Whirlygig Tour of the Beautiful
    Basics Of Science* (Angier), 236
Carlson, Rachel, 239–240
Carnegie, Andrew, 14
The Case for God (Armstrong), 206
Challenges in history, 195–197
Channing, William Henry, 122
Charity, 224–228
Chocolate, 89–91
Christian, David, 272–273
Churchill, Winston, 139, 155, 179, 196
Clarke, Oz, 98
Classical music, 85–86
Classics, 140–142
Clean Sweep (TV program), 58
ClimateGate scandal, 182
Clutter, 58–61
Collins, Billy, 52
Coltrane, John, 32
Compassion and successful living,
    167–168
Confucius, 271
Consumerism vs. accomplishments, 9
Conversation, 110–112
Core principles, 26
Core values, 48–49
Cosmic Calendar, 231
Cosmos, 229–233, 272–273
Cosmos (Sagan), 236, 240
Covey, Stephen M. R., 28
Creation, 258–261
Curiosity, 71–73

Da Vinci, Leonardo, 80
D'Agnese, Joseph, 62
Davies, Paul, 233, 249
Davis, Miles, 125
Dawkins, Richard, 181, 237
The Dead Beat (M. Johnson), 257
Death, 247–251, 262–264
Deep time, 273
The Demon-Haunted World (Sagan), 232
DeVries Peter, 52
*Dialogue Concerning the Two Chief World
    Systems* (Galileo), 215
Dickinson, Emily, 142
Diogenes, 164
Disasters, 244–246
Dowd, Michael, 263, 275
D'Souza, Dinesh, 247, 248
Durant, Will, 51, 155, 169
Dutton, Denis, 80

Early, Gerald, 126
Earthquakes, 244
Eco-revelation, 146–148
Education and income, 5
The Education of a Speculator (Niederhoffer),
    177
Einstein, Albert, 61, 194, 216, 227, 235
Electronic media, 110
Electronic media addiction, 19–20
Eliot, T. S., 233
Emerson, Ralph Waldo, 27, 184, 213, 218,
    221–223, 253
Endicott, John, 189
"Essay Concerning Human Understanding"
    (Locke), 82
Essential Spirituality (Walsh), 167
The Evolution of God (Wright), 167
Exercise, 74–75

Faith, 213
Faith and reason, 261
Family, 49–50
Fear, 12, 252–254
Federal income tax, 8
Feynmann, Richard, 242
The Fifth Miracle (Davies), 249
Financial crisis impact, 1
Fleischmann, Martin, 182
Floods, 244–245
Ford, Dennis, 117

Ford, Henry, 15
Forecasting mistakes, 178
Foreman, George, 125
Forgan, Duncan, 214
Fox, George, 191
Franklin, Barry, 74
Franklin, Benjamin, 63, 96
Freedom, 35–36, 203
Freeman, John, 120–121
Freud, Sigmund, 89–91

Gabler, James, 95
Galileo, 98, 215, 216
Gamow, George, 229
Gates, Bill, 10, 15, 17
Getz, Stan, 114
Ghandi, Mohandas, 67, 192–194
Gide, Andre, 80
Global poverty, 225
Goals, 162–165
The Goldilocks Enigma (Davies), 233
Goodall, Jane, 78
Gould, Stephen Jay, 237, 239
Grameen Foundation, 226
The Grand Design (Hawking), 258
Grant, W. T., 22
Grant study, 22–24
Gratitude, 34
The Great Conversation, 167
The Great Transformation (Armstrong), 167
The Greatest Minds and Ideas of All Time (Durant), 155, 169
Greeks and civilization, 202–204
Greenewalt, Crawford, 93
Guth, Julia, 77–80, 170

Haiku, 105–106
Haiti, 244–246
Haldane, J. B. S., 239
Hamilton, Alexander, 66
Handel, George Frideric, 32
Happiness, 31–34
Happiness and money, 33
Hardships, 195–197
Harris, Lauren McArthur, 270
Hawking, Stephen, 258–260
Hayroudinoff, Rustem, 85
Hazlitt, William, 103
Heiser, Victor, 245
Heroes, 154–157, 266

Herrick, Robert, 32
Homer, 247
Honor, 65–68
Honoring the Self (Branden), 183
How to live, 151–153
Hubble, Edwin, 230, 235
Hubble's Law, 230
Human Accomplishment (Murray), 79, 156
Human development, 271–272
Humility, 176–178, 243
Hummingbirds, 92–94
Hurricane Katrina, 244
Huxley, Aldous, 136
Hyperspending, 6

Idleness, 137–139
Infinite Jest (Wallace), 135
International Rescue Committee (IRC), 227
Internet, changes driven by, 18–19
Investment portfolio, 1
Inward development, 43–45
Irvine, William B., 162
It's All Too Much (Walsh), 58

James, William, 222
Jaspers, Karl, 266
Jazz, 123–127
Jazz & Heritage Festival, 107
The Jazz Channel Presents Kenny Rankin, 115
Jefferson, Thomas, 63, 64, 95–97, 145
Jesus of Nazareth, 75, 138, 271
John Paul II, Pope, 216
Johnson, Marilyn, 257
Johnson, Paul, 139
Johnson, Samuel, 103
Johnstown Flood, 244–245
Journeys of a Lifetime: 500 of the World's Greatest Trips (National Geographic), 84
Judaism, 205–207
Justice, 225
Juvenal, 65

Kant, Immanuel, 119
Kashdan, Todd, 72
Kepler, Johannes, 214
Kepler Space Telescope, 214, 217
Khayyam, Omar, 98
Kiernan, Denise, 62, 64
Kind of Blue (Davis), 125

Kindle, 199
King, Martin Luther, 67, 99
King, Steven, 109
The Kiss (Klimt), 77, 80
Klimt, Gustav, 77
Knowing and believing, 149–150

Lao Tzu, 172–174
Lawrence, Robert, 190
Leibnitz, Gottfried, 166
The Leopard (Collins), 52–53
Life After Death (D'Souza), 247
Life satisfaction, 23
The Life You Can Save (Singer), 227
Lincoln, Abraham, 64
Lipsky, David, 135
Literacy, 110–112
Living consciously, 183–187
The Living Planet (Attenborough), 236
Lloyd, Christopher, 272
Locke, John, 82–83
Love, Norman, 91
"Lying on a Hammock at William Duffy's
    Farm in Pine Island Minnesota"
    (Wright), 104

Mackey, John, 166
Madoff, Bernie, 66
Manchester, William, 39
Marcus Aurelius, 208–210
Marine Corps (Puryear), 200
Marsalis, Winton, 123–124, 126
Marx, Karl, 14, 154, 157
Massingberd, Hugh, 256
Materialism, 219, 238
Maugham, William Somerset, 105
McCartney, Paul, 114
McCullough, David, 196, 244–245
Meaningful work, 11
Meditations (Aurelius), 208–210
Melancholy, 32
"Messiah" (music), 32
Metaphysics, 238
Methodological naturalism, 239
Microcredit, 226
Middle Ages, life during, 39–40
Miller, Henry, 78
Miller, Jon D., 234
The Millionaire Mind (Stanley), 6
The Millionaire Next Door (Stanley), 6

Millionaires
    lifestyle, 6
    numbers of, 9
    popular activities of, 8
Mindful living, 99–100
Minsky, Marvin, 240
Money as freedom, 14
Monroe, James, 96
Moore, Gordon, 15
Morris, William, 58–59
Mothers, 51–54
Moving to Higher Ground (Marsalis), 126
Moyers, Bill, 266–267
Mozart, Wolfgang, 140, 141
Multiverse, 259
Murray, Charles, 67–69, 79–80, 156
Music, 85–88
Myths, 265–268

Nantucket, MA, 188–189
Nature, 273
Negative visualization, 55–57
Neruda, Pablo, 94
Nevado Del Ruiz, 244
The New Lifetime Reading Plan, 142
New Orleans, LA, 107–109
Newness, 140–142
Newton, Isaac, 216
Nhat Hanh, Thich, 99–100
Niederhoffer, Victor, 177
1984 (Orwell), 136
Noble Truths, 159–160
Nozick, Robert, 33

Obituaries, 255–258
"Ode to the Hummingbird" (Neruda), 94
The Odyessy (Homer), 247
On Desire: Why We Want What We Want
    (Irvine), 36–37
1,000 Places to See Before You Die (Schultz), 84
Orwell, George, 136
Oviedo y Valdes, Gonzalo Fernández de, 90
"Ozymandia" (Shelly), 104–105

Pacifism, 190
Packard, David, 15
Pale Blue Dot (Sagan), 240
Parenting, 46–50
Pater, Walter, 86
Peale, Norman Vincent, 55, 57

Pearson, Richard, 257
Penzias, Arno, 229
Perennial Philosophy, 166
Perennialism, 166–169
Pericles, 203
Personal freedom, 158–161
Perspective, 38–41
Peters, Tom, 29
Phelps, William Lyon, 200
Photons, 229
Planet Earth (Attenborough), 236
Plato, 78, 127, 247
The Pleasure of Finding Things Out
    (Feynmann), 242
Poetry, 103–106
Pons, Stanley, 182
Pope, Alexander, 66
Popular music, 87
Positive visualization, 57
Postman, Neil, 135
Postsecret submissions, 129–132
Poverty, 225, 226
The Power of Myth (Campbell), 266
The Power of Positive Thinking (Peale), 55
Precious (movie), 118
Primack, Joel, 269
Principles, 25–27
Professional golfers, 158
Proust, Marcel, 78
Publilius Syrus, 65
The Purpose Driven Life (R. Warren), 225
Puryear, Bo, 199–200

A Quaker Book of Wisdom (Lawrence), 190
Quaker wisdom, 188–191
Quest for Fire, 271

Radical generosity, 14–17
Rand, Ayn, 117, 155–156
Rankin, Kenny, 113–115
Reading, 20
Reagan, Ronald, 138
Reason and evidence, 181
Reason and faith, 261
Reed, James, 101
Religion vs. science, 241–243
Religions, 211–213
Republic (Plato), 78
Retirees, 12
River Out of Eden (Dawkins), 181

Roberts, Marcus, 124
Rockefeller, John, 15
Romantic love, 11
Romantic Manifesto (Rand), 156
Roosevelt, Teddy, 14
Russell, Bertrand, 253
Ryan, Kay, 104

Sagan, Carl, 72, 230–231, 232,
    237, 240
Sandburg, Carl, 103
Schopenhauer, Arthur, 86, 141
Schultz, Patricia, 84
Science vs. religion, 241–243
Scientific American, 236
Scientific discoveries, 214–217
Scientific illiteracy, 234–237
The Secret of Shelter Island (Green), 128
Secrets, 128–132
Seinfeld, Jerry, 253
Selective exposure, 180
"Self Reliance" (Emerson), 27
Self-esteem, 183–187
Self-Esteem Every Day (Branden), 187
Self-fulfillment, 11
Seneca, 56
The Sense of Wonder (Carlson),
    239–240
Seven Practices of a Mindful Eater
    (Nhat Hanh), 99
Shakespeare, William, 32, 140, 250
Shealy, Craig, 117, 119
Shelly, Percy Bysshe, 104–105, 204
Shermer, Michael, 241, 247, 248, 249,
    260–261
A Short History of Nearly Everything
    (Bryson), 236
Signing Their Lives Away (Kiernan and
    D'Agnese), 62
Simon, Herbert, 118
Singer, Peter, 224, 226, 227
Singh, Simon, 231
Sins of Omission (D. Ford), 117
The Six Pillars of Self-Esteem (Branden), 183
Skousen, Mark, 208
Sloth, 116–119
Slowing down, 120–123
Solnit, Rebecca, 76
Soul Gestures in Southern Blue
    (Marsalis), 124

Spiritual development, 266
Spirituality, 211–213
Stanley, Thomas J., 6, 7
Status anxiety, 37
Stevens, Wallace, 106
Stevenson, Robert Louis, 98
Stoics and stoicism, 31, 56, 163–164,
    208–210
*Stop Acting Rich and Start Living Like a Real
    Millionaire* (Stanley), 6, 7
Success, 22–24
Systematic withdrawal calculation, 2

Taleb, Nassim, 167–168
Tao Te Ching, 171
Taoism, 170–175
Taylor, Maura, 109
Television, 19, 110
    watching133–136
This Fleeting World (Christian), 272
Thomas, Lewis, 273
Thoreau, Henry David, 218–219
Thornton, Bruce, 190
Times of London, 256
Tolstoy, Leo, 151–153
Tradition, 181
Transcendentalism, 218–220, 221–223
Travel, 81–84
Trust, 28–30
Truth, 179–182
Tutu, Desmond, 194
Twain, Mark, 138, 250
The Tyranny of E-mail (Freeman), 120

Unweaving The Rainbow (Dawkins), 237
U.S Job Retention Survey, 10

Vaillant, George, 22, 23–24
Van Gogh, Vincent, 32
Voltaire, 11
Volunteer work, 12

W. S. Kellogg Foundation, 15
Walking, 75–76
Wallace, David Foster, 26, 135
Wallace, William, 265
Walsh, Peter, 58–59
Walsh, Roger, 167
Wanderlust: A History of Walking (Solnit), 76
War and Peace (Tolstoy), 151
Ward, James Allen, 154
Warren, Frank, 128–129, 132
Warren, Rick, 225
Washington, George, 63, 96, 143–145
Wealth
    American attitude towards, 14
    vs. earnings, 5–6
Wealth of interests, 69–70
West, Mae, 121
What on Earth Happened (Lloyd), 272
White, Paul Dudley, 76
Whitman, Walt, 222
Whitney, John, 28–29
Why People Believe Weird Things (Shermer),
    247
Wilder, Thornton, 109
Will, George, 66
William B. Irvine, 36–37
Williams, Tennessee, 32
Williamson, Marianne, 254
Wilson, Robert, 229
Wine, 95–98
Woods, Tiger, 158
Work, self definition from, 10
A World Lit Only by Fire (Manchester), 39
Wright, James, 104
Wright, Robert, 167

Yellow River Flood, 245

Zeitlin, Denny, 71–72
Zen and the Art of Making a Living (Boldt),
    12–13